DIMINISHED DEMOCRACY

D0596456

THE JULIAN J. ROTHBAUM DISTINGUISHED LECTURE SERIES

DIMINISHED DEMOCRACY

*From Membership to Management
in American Civic Life*

THEDA SKOCPOL

UNIVERSITY OF OKLAHOMA PRESS : NORMAN

Also by Theda Skocpol

States and Social Revolutions: A Comparative Analysis of France, Russia, and China (New York and Cambridge, 1979)

Vision and Method in Historical Sociology (New York and Cambridge, 1984)

(with Peter Evans and Dietrich Rueschemeyer) *Bringing the State Back In* (New York and Cambridge, 1985)

Protecting Soldiers and Mothers: The Political Origins of Social Policy in the United States (Cambridge, 1992)

Social Revolutions in the Modern World (Cambridge and New York, 1994)

Social Policy in the United States: Future Possibilities in Historical Perspective (Princeton, 1995)

(with Dietrich Rueschemeyer) *States, Social Knowledge, and the Origins of Modern Social Policies* (New York and Princeton, 1996)

Boomerang: Clinton's Health Security Effort and the Turn Against Government in U.S. Politics (New York, 1996)

(with Morris P. Fiorina) *Civic Engagement in American Democracy* (Washington, D.C., 1999)

The Missing Middle: Working Families and the Future of American Social Policy (New York, 2000)

Library of Congress Cataloging-in-Publication Data

Skocpol, Theda.
    Diminished democracy : from membership to management in American civic life / Theda Skocpol.
        p.   cm. — (The Julian J. Rothbaum distinguished lecture series ; vol. 8)
    Includes index.
    ISBN 978-0-8061-3627-1 (hc : alk. paper)
        1. Political participation—United States.   2. Civil society—United States.
    3. Democracy—United States.   I. Title.   II. Series.

JK1764 .S544 2003
306.2'0973—dc21

2002029138

This book is published with the generous assistance of the Kerr Foundation, Inc.

Diminished Democracy: From Membership to Management in American Civic Life is volume 8 in The Julian J. Rothbaum Distinguished Lecture Series.

The paper in the book meets the guidelines for permanence and durability of the Committee on Production Guidelines for Book Longevity of the Council on Library Resources, Inc. ∞

4   5   6   7   8   9   10

For Bill and Michael

In democratic countries knowledge of how to combine is the mother of all other forms of knowledge; on its progress depends that of all the others.

Democracy does not provide a people with the most skillful of governments, but it does provide that which the most skillful government often cannot do: it spreads throughout the body social a restless activity . . . and energy never found elsewhere.

Politics not only brings many associations into being, it also creates extensive ones. The common interests of civil life seldom naturally induce great numbers to act together. . . . But in politics . . . it is only large associations which make the general value of this method plain. . . . A political association draws a lot of people at the same time out of their own circle; however much differences in age, intelligence, or wealth may naturally keep them apart. . . . Once they have met, they always know how to meet again. . . .

So one may think of political associations as great free schools to which all citizens come to be taught the general theory of association.

—Alexis de Tocqueville, *Democracy in America*

CONTENTS

FOREWORD

AMONG THE MANY GOOD THINGS that have happened to me in my life, there is none in which I take more pride than the establishment of the Carl Albert Congressional Research and Studies Center at the University of Oklahoma, and none in which I take more satisfaction than the Center's presentation of the Julian J. Rothbaum Distinguished Lecture Series. The series is a perpetually endowed program of the University of Oklahoma, created in honor of Julian J. Rothbaum by his wife Irene, and son, Joel Jankowsky.

Julian J. Rothbaum, my close friend since our childhood days in southeastern Oklahoma, has long been a leader in

Oklahoma civic affairs. He has served as a Regent of the University of Oklahoma for two terms and as a State Regent for Higher Education. In 1974 he was awarded the University's highest honor, the Distinguished Service Citation, and in 1986 he was inducted into the Oklahoma Hall of Fame.

The Rothbaum Lecture Series is devoted to the themes of representative government, democracy and education, and citizen participation in public affairs, values to which Julian J. Rothbaum has been committed throughout his life. His lifelong dedication to the University of Oklahoma, the state, and his country is a tribute to the ideals to which the Rothbaum Lecture Series is dedicated. The books in the series make an enduring contribution to an understanding of American democracy.

CARL B. ALBERT

Forty-sixth Speaker
of the
United States House of Representatives

PREFACE AND
ACKNOWLEDGMENTS

IT ALL STARTED IN THE MIDDLE of the 1990s, when I assembled a small team of students to work with me on tracking down a hunch—that there had been more large, translocal voluntary membership associations active in America's past than scholars and pundits presume. Debates about America's civic health today struck me as being based on mistaken assumptions about the past, but I was not sure. With little funding at first, a small group of us set out to develop a valid list and documented details about the largest voluntary associations in U.S. history, imagining that this task would take only a couple of years (how many could there have been?). Years later, the Civic Engagement Project at Harvard arrived at an estimate of nearly five dozen very large membership associations that had surpassed one percent of the U.S. adult population at some point in the nation's history. By then, my fellow researchers and I were hooked into an ongoing set of investigations, tracking the emergence and growth of many kinds of voluntary associations, large and small. Understanding the changing shape of civic voluntarism in America—viewed through the lens of the rise and fall of different types of organizations—had become our obsession.

As this suggests, for many years I have been privileged to collaborate with a shifting set of wonderful colleagues and graduate and undergraduate students on myriad investigations of U.S. voluntary associations. This book is one of many products to emerge from these collaborations, a number of which are still ongoing. My associates and I in the Civic Engagement Project at Harvard University have not only learned an amazing amount, we have had a lot of fun as historical detectives tracking down heretofore lost or downplayed pieces of America's rich civic past. Our work has taken us far beyond the confines of Widener Library. With the assistance of often-elderly officials of many of the voluntary associations we are documenting, we have dug up the records and learned about the fascinating histories of great American voluntary associations, ranging from the Odd Fellows and the Independent Order of Good Templars to the Grange and the General Federation of Women's Clubs to the Order of the Eastern Star and the Loyal Order of Moose—groups whose names are rarely heard these days in centers of higher learning. Once highly educated Americans would have been members and leaders of such cross-class voluntary federations. Now many barely know about them—and that is part of the story we learned from our investigations of the changing shape of American civic voluntarism.

I am especially indebted to Marshall Ganz, Ziad Munson, Jennifer Oser, Bayliss Camp, Jocelyn Crowley, Rachael Cobb, and Casey Klofstad as some of my closest partners in these endeavors. Many others have also made important contributions to the Civic Engagement Project, some as participants in research teams and others by obtaining research materials or analyzing data from afar. For such assistance, I am happy to acknowledge Ruth Aguilera, David Earl Anderson, Glen Bessmer, Christian Brunelli, Sandy Chung, Susan Crawford, Jillian Dickert, Anne Marie Flores, Kristin Goss, Julia Green, Janna Hansen, Andrew Karch, Orit Kent, Meyer Kestnbaum, Ariane Liazos, Sean McKee, Regina Mercado, Robert Mickey, Gigi Parris, Anita Renton, Julia Rubin, Elizabeth Rybicki, Cameron Sheldon, Andrea Sheppard, Brian Shillinglaw, David Siu, Michele Swers, Julianne Unsel, Kalaivani Sankarapandian, Miranda Worthen, and Christine Woyshner. I ask forgiveness from others whose names I may have inadvertently omitted from this list.

Thanks to David Beito, David Fahey, Gerald Gamm, and Robert D. Putnam for sharing data from their own research on the history of U.S. voluntary associations. And a special thanks to many archivists, in-house historians, and officers of voluntary associations, and to independent scholars studying particular associations, all of whom went out of their way to help my research collaborators and me learn about membership trends and associational histories. For example, Albert Saltzman, Supreme Secretary of the Knights of Pythias, who works out of a small office in Quincy, Massachusetts, cheerfully put up with many visits from me and my collaborators, giving us virtually free rein to dig out documentary gems from the old boxes in his office. And after I visited Betty Briggs, General Grand Secretary at the Washington, D.C., headquarters of the Order of the Eastern Star, she was kind enough to donate to the Civic Engagement Project and the Harvard University libraries an entire set of triennial reports dating back to 1876. Beyond these special people, a fuller list of individuals and their organizations include Bill and Ginnie Beattie (Woman's

Christian Temperance Union), Joanne Benson (March of Dimes), Susan Brosnan (Knights of Columbus), Chris Coble (studying Christian Endeavor), John Concannon (Ancient Order of Hibernians), Robert Cox (American Legion), Julie Crudele (Greenpeace), Douglas Fraser (United Auto Workers), Edna Glass (Improved Order of Red Men and Daughters of Pocahontas), Abraham Holtzman (studying the Townsend movement), Charles Johnson (studying the German National Alliance), Mike Kelley (Benevolent and Protective Order of Elks), Jane Kinsman (American Red Cross), Janice Krahn (Aid Association for Lutherans), Raymond Lodato (studying environmental groups), Janet Mahon (Shriners), Steven Morrow (Independent Order of Odd Fellows, Massachusetts), William Moore (studying the Masons), Greg Nagle (Boy Scouts), Vern Paul (Veterans of Foreign Wars), Robert Proudly (Masonic Service Organization), Joe Reilly (Christian Coalition of Massachusetts), Bob Reynolds (AFL-CIO), Anthony Snyder (National Fraternal Congress of America), Cynthia Swanson (General Federation of Women's Clubs), Mark Tabbert (Museum of Our National Heritage), Roger J. Talbert (National Grange), Barbara Weitzer (Women's International Bowling Congress and American Bowling Congress), Brian Williams (American Red Cross), Joyce Wright (Pythian Sisters), and Robert Zieger (studying the Congress of Industrial Organizations). Again, I apologize for inadvertent omissions, as I am sure to have missed some of the many people who helped my research teams.

This book also benefitted from new contacts I made in the worlds of antique collectors and Ebay bidders. Special thanks to Jim Berkel of Florida and New York, who sold me rare and unusual membership badges; to Jim Davenport of

Colorado, who provided pictures and facts about Woodmen fraternal groups; and John Karnes of Missouri, who
provided copies of rare fraternal rituals.

Books are never written just by authors sitting alone at
a computer. They also grow out of repeated intellectual
encounters—at professional meetings, in research work-
shops, during visiting lectures. This book originated as a
series of Rothbaum Lectures sponsored during fall 1999 by
the Carl Albert Center at the University of Oklahoma. At
that time, the Center was directed by Ron Peters, and I am
grateful to him and his colleagues for warm hospitality during my fascinating week in Oklahoma, during which I was
privileged to meet Julian Rothbaum and Joel Jankowsky as
well as David Boren, President of the University of Oklahoma. Traveling around the state after my lectures, I found
some of the old documents I used to write this book.

Before and after lectures in Oklahoma, I presented aspects
of the arguments and evidence for this book in many venues, too many to list individually here. From Europe to California to the U.S. heartlands, thanks to all the audiences
whose questions and pointed comments helped me along
the way. A special thanks to the American Politics Research
Workshop at Harvard, whose participants have repeatedly
helped to hone the ideas embodied here. A number of close
friends and colleagues have provided personal support and
intellectual stimulation in this work, especially Ellen Fitz-
patrick, Morris P. Fiorina, Elinor Ostrom, Paul Pierson, and
Sidney Verba. Robert D. Putnam has been a constant source
of helpful data and provocative arguments. Although the
two of us disagree on some crucial issues, where else, in any
major university, would two senior colleagues be so happy
to chat and swap data about the PTA and the Elks?

The research on which this book is based has been funded over the years by many institutions, including the Bertelsmann Foundation, the Russell Sage Foundation, the Pew Charitable Trusts, the John D. and Catherine T. MacArthur Foundation, and the Weatherhead Center for International Affairs and the Children's Studies program at Harvard University. The Ford Foundation deserves special thanks for supporting several major aspects of my research into American civic life—and I am profoundly grateful for the friendship and intellectual support of Constance Buchanan, the Ford Foundation officer with whom I have worked most closely through many phases of this endeavor.

With other colleagues at the University of Oklahoma Press, Jean Hurtado, Marian J. Stewart, and Sheila Berg deserve special thanks for shepherding my manuscript to publication. My assistants at Harvard, Abby Peck in Sociology and Lilia Halpern-Smith at the Center for American Political Studies in the Government Department, also contributed to this book in many crucial ways, keeping me going on all my other projects at the same time.

Diminished Democracy is dedicated to my husband, Bill Skocpol, and to our beloved son, Michael Allan Skocpol, whose middle name comes from my father, Allan Barron, a lifelong Civil War buff. My dad would, I trust, be pleased with this book, in which the Civil War plays a starring role. Bill Skocpol shares my love for Americana, and he is the one who discovered William Durgin's grave and immediately understood its significance. Michael is our link to America's future—hopefully, a flourishing democratic future.

Theda Skocpol

Cambridge, Massachusetts

DIMINISHED DEMOCRACY

CHAPTER 1

WARREN DURGIN'S GRAVESTONE— UNDERSTANDING AMERICAN CIVIC DEMOCRACY

MORE THAN A MILE DOWN A narrow winding road, the earthly remains of William Warren Durgin of North Lovell, Maine, lie in a small out-of-the-way cemetery peppered with tiny headstones nestled amid trees along a brook. The unpretentiousness of Durgin's resting place is appropriate for a backwoods farmer, lumberman, and spoolmaker who lived most of his long life—just over ninety years stretching from December 18, 1839, through January 27, 1929—in this rural region of woodlands, rocky fields, and small hamlets at the western edge of Maine, bordering Kezar Lake and facing the foothills of the White Mountains in neighboring New Hampshire.[1]

But the headstone for "William W. Durgin" is a surprise. On a large granite slab towering above the others, an inscription tells of the life-defining moment when Durgin served as "One of Abraham Lincoln's bearers and escort to Springfield Ill. Helped to place Remains in tomb." After four years of service in the Union army during the Civil War, 1st Sergeant Durgin was chosen one of eight pallbearers, including illustrious officers and four "first Sergeants . . . selected with reference to their Age, length of Service and good soldierly conduct for escort duty to the remains of President Lincoln to Springfield, Illinois."[2] He helped to carry the presidential casket to the hearse, escorted it to the Capitol where Lincoln lay in state, and rode the famous funeral train as it made its lugubrious way from Washington, D.C., to Springfield, passing through such cities as "Baltimore, Harrisburg, Philadelphia, New York, Albany, Buffalo, Cleveland, Columbus, Chicago, [and] Indianapolis," all of which Durgin still recalled many decades later, just a year before his death, when he was interviewed by a newsman.[3]

As if serving as Lincoln's pallbearer were not enough, Durgin's gravestone tells us much more about the doings of the man known in life by his middle name, Warren. Under the dates bracketing his birth and death, a boldly engraved line says that Warren Durgin was a "G.A.R. Commander"— that is, the elected head of his local post of the Grand Army of the Republic, the post–Civil War association of Union veterans. The next line of the stone indicates Durgin's affiliation with the "P. of H.," the Patrons of Husbandry, or Grange; Durgin was probably a member of Kezar Lake Grange No. 440 of North Lovell. Finally, in an oblong rectangle at the very top of the gravestone appear three intertwined loops— a sure signal to those in the know that Warren Durgin was affiliated with a leading U.S. fraternal association, the Independent Order of Odd Fellows, no doubt as a member of Crescent Lodge No. 25 of North Lovell.[4]

Warren Durgin's gravestone first came to my attention after my husband, Bill Skocpol, learned about it while driving the back roads of western Maine.[5] Out of curiosity about the man whose life and death the gravestone marked, we obtained more information and leads from the Lovell Historical Society. When I later went to see the gravestone first-hand, I was stuck by how many strands of America's civic history Durgin's story illuminates.

The sight brought home to me, for one thing, how much the meaning of associational affiliation has changed. Gazing through the dappled forest sunlight from the vantage point of many decades later, I could readily understand why Durgin would want to proclaim for all eternity his service as Abraham Lincoln's pallbearer. But given such momentous wartime service, why add the ties to the Grand Army of the Republic (GAR), the Grange, and the Odd Fellows? Much as I value my own memberships in the American Political Science Association and the Social Science History Association, two fine scholarly organizations in which I have had the privilege to hold high office, I could not quite imagine asking for "APSA" and "SSHA" to be chiseled into my gravestone. Warren Durgin was part of a civic world no longer intuitive for me, in which associational membership was, in and of itself, honorable and intensely significant.

Other reflections came to mind. By the time I saw Durgin's resting place, I had already done enough research into the history of U.S. voluntary associations to realize that this humble man, a poor farmer and laborer, had been a member, indeed an officer, in exactly the same voluntary associations joined by many of the most privileged and powerful Americans of his day. The GAR, the Grange, and the Odd Fellows not only appear on Durgin's gravestone. During the decades surrounding 1900, these same associations were proudly listed in the biographical profiles of the businessmen, well-to-do farmers, and educated professionals who served as Maine's U.S. senators and representatives and as its elected state officials.[6] What is more, the same associations were frequently cited by the more urbane and

cosmopolitan officials of Massachusetts. Indeed, membership in them was proclaimed by elites in and out of government all over the United States.[7]

As we will soon learn, the Odd Fellows, the GAR, and
the Grange were three of the largest and most encompassing voluntary membership associations in U.S. history. These
and dozens of other major voluntary membership associations were launched by civic organizers who took inspiration from America's federally organized republican polity—
so much so that they modeled their organizations after U.S.
governmental institutions, creating vast, nation-spanning
federations consisting of local chapters linked together into
representatively governed state and national bodies. Union
victory in the massive Civil War of the 1860s was a key
watershed in this story, for it gave renewed impetus to the
creation and spread of cross-class voluntary federations,
like those Warren Durgin joined and had later emblazoned
on his gravestone.

Durgin's joint proclamation of Civil War service and
membership in great voluntary associations thus made
symbolic as well as biographical sense. As U.S. leaders did
when they saved the Union by mobilizing volunteer armies
and relief networks, the organizers of America's greatest
voluntary associations practiced cross-class fellowship.
They aimed to gather good men or women (and occasionally,
as in the case of the Grange, men and women together)
into vast, encompassing associations that mirrored—and
had the power to influence—the democratic republic of
which they were a part. Not only Warren Durgin, therefore, but millions of other Americans of modest means could
readily become members, even officers, of the same voluntary associations that enrolled the most privileged and

powerful citizens. Although particular associations rose and fell, memberships shared across class lines were characteristic of much of American civic life from the mid-nineteenth through the mid-twentieth century—that is, for all the decades of Durgin's earthly span, plus a few more.

A TRANSFORMED CIVIC WORLD

But how greatly American civic life has changed by now! In the early-twenty-first-century United States, it is almost impossible to imagine a humble man like Warren Durgin belonging to the same nationwide voluntary associations as the high and mighty. To the extent that nationally influential membership associations still flourish, they are likely to be *professional* groups (such as the APSA and the SSHA in which I am an active participant). Otherwise, U.S. civic life has been extraordinarily transformed. Where once cross-class voluntary federations held sway, national public life is now dominated by professionally managed advocacy groups without chapters or members. And at the state and local levels "voluntary groups" are, more often than not, nonprofit institutions through which paid employees deliver services and coordinate occasional volunteer projects. In our contemporary civic world, it is much easier to imagine Warren Durgin as the client of a nonprofit agency, or as a recipient of charitable assistance, than it is to envisage him as an active member of any voluntary association that includes people from a broad range of social backgrounds— apart, perhaps, from a church.

Another shift seems to have happened as well. No longer are supreme acts of national citizenship—such as Warren Durgin's Civil War service—understood as going hand in hand with active participation in voluntary associations. And no longer do we highlight the achievements of politically active, cross-class voluntary associations, like the GAR and the Grange to which Durgin belonged. (Durgin was a Civil War pensioner, and the GAR agitated politically for generous benefits to all Union veterans.) For some years now, America's most visible and loquacious politicians, academics, and pundits have proclaimed that voluntary groups flourish best *apart* from active national government—and disconnected from politics. The downplaying of the governmental and political wellsprings of civic engagement is subtle among academics and middle-of-the-road commentators but quite blatant among conservative pundits. As Christopher Beem shows in a wide-ranging review, contemporary writers of all stripes focus on local community and consider "governmental actions, and the actions of large political organizations . . . at best irrelevant to, and, at worst, inimical" to a healthy civil society.[8]

Through his well-known books, *Making Democracy Work* and *Bowling Alone*, political scientist Robert D. Putnam has done more than any other contemporary scholar to shape understandings of civic engagement.[9] In Putnam's view, family picnics, local choral societies, and neighborhood bowling leagues are fonts of civic engagement. His key concept "social capital" encompasses feelings of social and political trust, plus all sorts of interpersonal social connections—from informal ties of family members, friends, and neighbors to recurrent participation in organized groups—as long as those connections entail repeated face-to-face interchanges. Well-networked local communities have pride of place in his assessments of social capital, because recurrent interactions have often been centered in them. Putnam privileges primary interpersonal ties above all other forms of social and political activity, because he believes such interactions uniquely foster trust and cooperation. The more face-to-face group interaction a nation has, the healthier its people and the more efficient its government and economy will be.[10]

Although their theories of civil society differ from Putnam's, liberal and moderate communitarians such as Michael Sandel, Jean Bethke Elshtain, and William Galston similarly privilege local community and interactions among family members, friends, and neighbors. In Sandel's major work, *Democracy's Discontent*, healthy civic life is portrayed in Jeffersonian terms as an aspect of local community, with national government at best irrelevant and at worst inimical to republican virtue.[11] Similarly, the final report of the Council on Civil Society, a national commission cochaired by Elshtain, decries weakened family life, local fragmentation, and declining standards of personal responsibility as the chief sources of civic decline in the United States.[12] Government and politics barely figure in this report—and they are equally marginal to the portrayals of healthy civic life and indices of decline to be found in the report of another recent national commission coordinated by Galston.[13]

The delinking of civic engagement from politics and national government takes on an even harder edge among contemporary U.S. conservatives—for many of them adhere to a zero-sum conception, in which the more the national state "intervenes" in society, the less the citizenry engages. With a few exceptions (such as the intellectuals clustered around the *Weekly Standard*), contemporary American conservatives routinely portray active national government as inimical to a healthy civil society. In an influential statement, political theorists Michael S. Joyce and William A. Schambra finger the liberal-progressive "vision of national community" and the concomitant growth of "a massive, centralized federal government" as the chief enemies of "natural" civic community, which they believe is rooted in autonomous families, neighborhoods, and local ethnic and voluntary groups able to solve social problems on their own, without involving extralocal government.[14] Similarly, Peter Drucker contrasts America's tradition of "voluntary group action from below" to "the collectivism of organized governmental action from above," while in his inimitably colorful way, George Will speaks of voluntary groups as neighborly "little platoons" doing battle with "the federal government's big battalions."[15]

Misleading beliefs such as these jarred against sea changes in American perceptions and hopes in the aftermath of the terrorist attacks of September 11, 2001—which, like the outbreak of wars in the past, spurred an upsurge of patriotism and national fellow feeling. Suddenly, Americans regained faith in national government and became eager to contribute to shared public endeavors.[16] After September 11, moreover, some leaders called for new domestic social security programs to aid the unemployed and spread the sacrifices caused by the coincidence of terrorism and national economic recession. Strong voices also urged the administration of President George W. Bush to seize the opportunity to promote national civic revitalization, perhaps by calling for a new, compulsory national service program for *all* of the nation's youth.[17] Federal initiatives of this sort could translate patriotic feelings into action, proponents argued, by giving millions of Americans a new sense of active, participatory citizenship.

But in the immediate aftermath of the crisis as well as before, President Bush remained leery of bold new domestic social initiatives. And U.S. leaders in general were much more reluctant to expand civilian efforts at home and engage in mass civic mobilization than their counterparts had been at the start of earlier U.S. wars. Although the president did eventually call for a modest expansion of AmeriCorps, the nationally managed U.S. public service program, in the crucial months immediately after September 11, 2001, his most audible messages stressed the need for people to buy more in the private marketplace in order to stimulate the economy.[18] In his calls for heightened civic involvement, President Bush highlighted local efforts and called on Americans to give money to private charities.[19] His administration's chief priority for strengthening civil society consists of a "Faith-based Initiative" designed to encourage churches and local community groups, rather than government, to tend to the needs of the poor and the vulnerable.[20]

Were he to revisit the United States today, Alexis de Tocqueville would be puzzled at so much emphasis on nonpolitical civic localism, for he believed that vigorous democratic government and politics nourish and complement a participatory civil society. Warren Durgin clearly lived in a full-fledged version of Tocqueville's civic America, where "democracy" spread "throughout the body social a restless activity . . . and energy never found elsewhere" and "political associations" were "great free schools to which all citizens come to be taught the general theory of association."[21] By contrast, early-twenty-first-century Americans live in a diminished democracy, in a much less participatory and more oligarchicly managed civic world.

Even more worrisome, many thinkers misdiagnose the civic challenges America faces today, for they have forgotten that national community, active government, and democratic mobilization are all vital to creating and sustaining a vibrant civil society. The true lessons of America's civic past are fading from view.

EXPLAINING THE RISE AND TRANSFORMATION OF U.S. CIVIC DEMOCRACY

This book tells a big story about the interplay of democratic politics and civic voluntarism in the United States, offering a bird's-eye view of association building and patterns of civic leadership from the birth of the nation to the present. The evidence and arguments I present should provoke debate, for they challenge accepted wisdom on both ends of the political spectrum.

Contrary to conservative presumptions, I document that American civic voluntarism was never predominantly local and never flourished apart from national government and politics. Large-scale, translocal membership groups took shape from early in the history of the U.S. Republic and then spread into every part of the country and every sector of the population during the decades between the 1820s and the 1960s. Americans joined and led voluntary associations not merely to interact with friends and neighbors and solve local problems but also so as to reach out to fellow citizens of a vast republic and build the organizational capacity to shape national culture and politics. Through times of war and peace, U.S. representative institutions and public policies encouraged the growth of voluntary federations—which, in turn, often got involved in politics to influence the course of public policy. In the United States, democratic governance and civic voluntarism developed together, whatever today's conservatives may want to believe.

Yet I will also challenge the liberal article of faith that American civil society has become steadily more democratic since the 1960s. Liberals tend to attribute virtually all healthy developments in contemporary U.S. democracy to the Civil Rights struggles of the 1960s, which were followed by feminist agitations and a variety of other movements for minority rights and public interest causes. Of course, such movements expressed important democratic aspirations, broke down old barriers to full participation, and put new issues on the public agenda. But the social movements of the 1960s and 1970s also inadvertently helped to trigger a reorganization of national civic life, in which professionally managed associations and institutions proliferated while cross-class membership associations lost ground. In our time, civicly engaged Americans are organizing more but joining less. Solidarity across class lines has dwindled, even as racial and gender integration has increased. The professionally managed organizations that dominate American civic life today are, in important respects, less democratic and participatory than the pre-1960s membership federations they displaced.

How do I know? The reader has every right to wonder about the evidence for arguments advanced in this book. Telling a vivid story accessible to a broad readership has been an important goal for me; yet this is also a serious work of empirically rigorous scholarship, based on years of original research. This book uses new bodies of evidence to develop fresh explanations of historical and contemporary trends in American civic life. So let me conclude this opening chapter by spelling out my approach and suggesting the kinds of data I have amassed.

My basic explanatory approach is historical, both in the sense of taking long-term developments seriously and in the sense of paying careful attention to coincident events that may help to explain abrupt shifts in associational life. Today, many scholars and pundits are debating the health of American civil society. Some analysts (like Robert Putnam and the communitarians mentioned above), worry about the contemporary decline of local groups and face-to-face social connections. Other analysts (including political scientist Jeffrey Berry and sociologist Debra Minkoff) view current trends more optimistically, stressing the new social movements of the 1960s and 1970s and subsequent proliferation of new advocacy groups.[22] But both the "worriers" and the "optimists," as I label them, tend to rely on snapshots of evidence about the very recent past.[23] Most of America's long civic history serves as mere foil and backdrop, as the worriers use survey data to show that Americans since the 1950s are joining and participating less, while the optimists document the increase in organizational foundings since the 1960s.

This book, by contrast, goes back much farther in U.S. history, tracing long-term processes to make sense of the societal and political conditions that originally allowed the United States to become a nation of organizers and joiners of membership-based associations. Then the book dissects the developments of the past half century, to pinpoint the confluence of social, political, and technological shifts that spurred the rise of professionally managed civic organizations. History matters in my analysis, not just because it is intrinsically interesting—though it certainly is—but also because the enlarged perspective of history brings into clearer view the overall societal and institutional contexts in which civic changes have emerged and played out. How can we understand the recent shift from membership to management if we do not first grasp how and why the United States originally became a civic nation, a country of avid organizers and joiners of membership-based associations?

In addition to taking historical processes and conjunctures seriously, I focus on civic *organizations*—in a departure from the nowadays typical scholarly reliance on individual-level attitude data collected in national sample surveys. Back in 1963 Gabriel Almond and Sidney Verba published *The Civic Culture,* a highly innovative and influential study that used representative national surveys to measure the civic attitudes and self-reported behaviors of citizens of the United States, Great Britain, Germany, Italy, and Mexico.[24] This study demonstrated with fresh empirical data what classical observers had long argued, that Americans were (at least as of the 1960s) especially likely to join and play active roles in voluntary associations. So great was the impact of this pioneering book that sociologists and political scientists, in effect, subsequently redefined the questions they asked about civic life to fit the statistical and survey-research tools most in vogue in behavioralist social science.

This was a big change. From the travel commentaries written by Alexis de Tocqueville in the 1830s and by Lord James Bryce in the 1890s through historian Arthur Schlesinger Sr.'s "Biography of a Nation of Joiners" published in the 1940s, leading analysts of U.S. civic life had always examined the rise and fall of voluntary *organizations* considered in broad societal context. They did not just look at masses of individual citizens as potential joiners. They examined the kinds of organizations leaders were creating and considered what sorts of groups were available for citizens to join. But following the publication of *The Civic Culture* and with the increasing use of computers, national sample surveys, and sophisticated statistical modeling, the focus narrowed to a preoccupation with individuals' attitudes and choices about voting or affiliating with voluntary groups.

In the hands of maestros such as Verba and his associates, contemporary behavioralist research using survey data has given us nuanced national snapshots of mass behavior and statistically sophisticated tests of models designed to explain variations in degrees of individual civic participation by educational status, gender, race, and so forth.[25] But there have also been downsides to survey-based research, because it has averted attention from leaders and the organizations that actually encourage and channel civic activity, making it very difficult to sort out the causes and consequences of changing patterns of mass activity. Even when ongoing surveys—such as the General Social Survey and the National Election Study—have posed the same questions repeatedly to comparable national samples, the stretch of time covered, from the mid-1970s to the mid-1990s, has been both too short and too recent to illuminate the roots of late-twentieth-century transformations.

Even more worrisome, the questions survey researchers ask are very general. We learn, for example, how many voluntary groups individuals join but very little about the specific organizational structures, purposes, or social constituencies of those groups. In an era when civic leaders are organizing and running very different kinds of voluntary organizations from those that held sway before the 1960s—and at a time when Americans mean very different things by civic involvement than they once did—it is simply not sufficient to count affiliations with vague types of groups or to ask people how many "community meetings" they have attended in the past year. Behaviorialist models have had little choice but to rely on such general sample survey questions, yet as a result their explanatory value is less than often claimed. Behavioralist models reveal little about who is organizing what kinds of associations at particular times; they ignore questions about the interaction of associations with government; and they neither describe nor explain changes in the entire universe of U.S. voluntary associations.

Working from what scholars call a "historical-institutionalist" perspective, my focus throughout this book is on voluntary organizations, as well as on the changing social and political conditions that have influenced—and been influenced by—the strategies of leaders who launch and direct various kinds of voluntary groups.[26] If, as Tocqueville wrote, Americans have excelled at the "knowledge of how to combine" that is so critical to achieving democratic solidarity and leverage, then organized efforts are the best place to look for civic trends and transformations. We must not simply count group memberships, but look into the various kinds of associations that have flourished in various times and circumstances. We must aim to explain how U.S. voluntary associations have changed over time and consider what difference the changes have made for our democracy.

To trace such developments, I have been able to draw on previous studies by historians and social scientists, who have written much of value about religious institutions, social movements, and electoral dynamics. Yet I also rely on unique, newly assembled data about voluntary associations and civic leadership. In recent years, my research collaborators and I—working together in the Harvard Civic Engagement Project—have documented the characteristics and development of various types of voluntary associations throughout U.S. history. For each era of history, we have situated very large membership associations in relation to smaller membership groups and other kinds of civic entities. We have also developed new data about the changing civic affiliations of elites and investigated the strategies and models used by civic organizers, the men and women who have launched and led various types of voluntary associations in different historical periods. More will be said about specific data sets and sources of evidence at appropriate points throughout this book. For now, suffice it to say that by looking at particular types of organizations, tracing processes of associational change over long stretches of time, and examining the behavior of elites as well as of ordinary citizens, my fellow researchers and I have learned startling and fascinating things that cast recent U.S. civic transformations in fresh light.

LOOKING AHEAD

Let us plunge in to the story and the analysis. In chapter 2, I explain how the United States developed into a flourishing civic democracy—how America originally became a nation of organizers and joiners of membership-based voluntary associations that operated in close symbiosis with representative government and democratic politics. Chapter 3, drawing on unusual sources of evidence, looks more intimately at the past, considering what participation in voluntary membership associations meant for members, organizers, and American citizens in general. Chapters 4 and 5 then shift the focus to the contemporary era. I describe and analyze the extraordinary reorganization of U.S. civic life after the 1960s, seeking to make sense of the abrupt shift from membership-based voluntary associations to managerially directed advocacy groups and civic institutions.

Finally, once we have grasped the paradoxes of recent civic reorganizations—changes that have made America both more and less democratic—we can explore the larger implications in chapter 6 and contribute in chapter 7 to the ongoing debate about what should done to revitalize U.S. civic life. From the perspective of history, I will argue, currently fashionable nostrums lose much of their luster—and we can envisage more promising reforms that might help to reinvent for our time the best features of the classic American civic democracy in which Warren Durgin lived and died. History will not, and should not, repeat itself; but we can, perhaps, forge a future that more effectively rhymes with the civic symphonies of the American past.

CHAPTER 2

HOW THE UNITED STATES
BECAME A CIVIC NATION

THE CIVIC CREATIVITY OF AMERICANS "of all ages, all stations in life, and all types of disposition" has long been admired.[1] "Voluntary organization," writes Arthur Schlesinger, affords Americans "their greatest school of self-government. . . . In mastering the associative way they have mastered the democratic way."[2] Yet despite long-standing agreement that voluntarism is central to American democracy—and notwithstanding its frequent invocation in theoretical and policy pronouncements—surprisingly little is known about how the United States actually became a nation of civic organizers and joiners. Stereotypes prevail in the absence of systematic knowledge.

TODAY'S ACCEPTED WISDOM: SMALL WAS BEAUTIFUL

Even scholars and pundits who disagree about contemporary America's civic health share a mythical image of the past. Imagining that U.S. civil society was local and intimate, they envision voluntary groups as originally bottom-up and scattered creations, fashioned here and there in relatively bounded communities by immediate neighbors and personal friends. According to accepted wisdom, voluntary groups once had room to flourish in the absence of supra-local governance. "Our reliance upon voluntary associations to achieve social goals stems from the widespread division and dispersal of authority in the United States" and from our dependence "on private religious associations to guide our public moral philosophy," declares a recent report by the Council on Civil Society, which offers nary a footnote in support, so self-evident does this statement seem to commission members.[3] "Before the modern age," declare Michael Joyce and William Schambra in a crisp formulation of today's conventional wisdom, American "civic life was characterized by both its self-containment and its cohesiveness. Individuals were closely bound one to another by strong families, tightly knit neighborhoods, and active voluntary and fraternal groups. Through these small, local, 'human-scale' associations, Americans not only achieved a sense of belonging and connectedness but also tackled the full range of social and human problems that today have largely become the province of government."[4]

VOLUNTARISM AND DEMOCRATIC NATION BUILDING

Small-was-beautiful understandings of America's civic past may be taken for granted today, but it wasn't always that way. Analysts of earlier eras believed that much of U.S. voluntarism was translocal in scope and intimately tied to the building of national democracy. Alexis de Tocqueville is cited today as an exponent of apolitical localism, but in the famous chapter in *Democracy in America* titled "On the Use Which Americans Make of Associations in Civil Life," he offered just one specific example, the massive temperance movement of the 1830s, in which "one hundred thousand men . . . publicly promised never to drink alcoholic liquor" because they wanted to "support sobriety" by their collective "patronage" instead of making "individual representations to the government."[5] Similar accounts of nineteenth-century U.S. voluntary associations appear in the 1890s classic, *The American Commonwealth*, where Lord Bryce portrayed them as ramified networks spanning the continent, "a species of political organization which figures in State and even in presidential contests." "Such associations have great importance in the development of opinion, for they rouse attention, excite discussion, formulate principles, submit plans, embolden and stimulate their members, and produce that impression of a spreading movement which goes so far towards success with a sympathetic and sensitive people."[6]

Building on such insights in his "Biography of a Nation of Joiners," a presidential address to the American Historical Association published in 1944, Arthur Schlesinger provides the most complete overview of U.S. civic voluntarism in the context of democratic nation building. Focusing on "voluntary bodies of sizable membership, reasonably long duration, and fairly large territorial extent," Schlesinger portrays the development of a "vast and intricate mosaic" of associations "reaching out with interlocking memberships to all parts of the country."[7] In colonial America, he asserts, voluntarily established associations were few and far between and typically tied to local church congregations. But the struggles of the colonists for independence from Britain taught "men from different sections valuable lessons in practical cooperation," and "the adoption of the Constitution stimulated still further application of the collective principle."[8]

A new associational model crystallized in the early 1800s, a time of flux and experimentation in the democratizing U.S. Republic. Ambitious civil organizers converged on a standard approach: They chose an "imposing" name, "sent forth . . . agents on the wide public," and "multiplied" "subsidiary societies . . . over the length and breadth of the land." Associations began to organize along the lines of "the Federal political system, with local units loosely linked together in state branches and these in turn sending representatives to a national body."[9] Then the Civil War intervened. Union victory brought a "heightened sense of nationality" and "Northern endeavors to plan far-flung undertakings," thus giving "magnified force" to association building in the late 1800s.[10] Highlighting the role of ambitious national organizers who took inspiration from struggles to create and sustain representative national government, Schlesinger's 1944 interpretation is very much at odds with the localist notions of America's civic past that hold sway today.

NEW EVIDENCE FOR THE OLD VIEW

The older view turns out to be right. In this chapter and the next, I present systematic evidence that classic American civic associations were large and translocal networks, not self-enclosed bodies restricted to particular places. And I show the many ways in which civic voluntarism was thoroughly intertwined with government activities and popular politics. Mass-mobilizing U.S. wars and inclusive public social programs have involved and fostered civic voluntarism on a national as well as local scale. For most of our nation's history, civic voluntarism and bold public undertakings went hand in hand. Classic voluntary associations

(as I will label the popularly rooted membership groups that flourished from the mid-nineteenth through the mid-twentieth century) were usually federations that brought citizens together across class lines while linking thousands of local groups to one another and to representatively governed centers of state and national activity.

It is one thing to aspire to map the history of U.S. voluntarism, quite another to approach this goal in a reliable way. There is no handy reference book—or computer disk—to which one can turn to map the rise and fall, the purposes and forms, of voluntary associations throughout U.S. history. Much can be learned from in-depth monographs about particular regions or communities, and there are impressive histories of major associations and particular categories of groups.[11] But the partial insights of such studies are hard to add up; and only a few scholars have documented the long-term spread of various types of groups across many places.[12] To fill the gap, my colleagues and I have investigated the origins and development of voluntary membership associations in America, from 1790 to the present.[13] Our research triangulates among various sources of data and looks for overlaps between national and local voluntary groups.

We first set out on what we supposed would be a modest effort to map all very large associations in American history. Other scholars have studied political parties and religious denominations, so we would supplement their work by identifying and documenting all other voluntary associations that had ever enrolled 1 percent or more of U.S. adults as "members" (according to whatever definition of individual membership each group used). If groups formally restrict membership to men or women, then 1 percent of the

U.S. adult male or adult female population serves as the benchmark; if both genders are accepted into the group, then 1 percent of the entire adult population is the benchmark. No other relaxations of the demanding size criterion are made, because we seek a window into American civil society and democracy over time. Tracing very large voluntary membership associations seems promising for this purpose, because these groups have by definition been very popular and widespread.

Originally we expected to find perhaps one or two dozen very large membership associations; but many years later, we have identified fifty-eight very large groups, listed in table 2.1 in chronological order of their foundings in the United States.[14] For each group on our master list, we are developing a complete quantitative and qualitative profile, gathering information on the intentions of each organization's founders and data about membership trends, associational structure, group activities, and group relationships to government, political parties, and religious institutions. In this chapter, I concentrate on the vast majority of associations that were founded and grew very large before World War II.

How much can we learn by looking at very large membership associations? Even if there are more of them than one might expect, they might have been just the icing on the cake of classic American voluntarism. As today's conventional wisdom posits, the vast majority of membership groups might have been particular, local creations (or else very small translocal associations confined to particular states). To situate the very largest associations in relation to others, my research colleagues and I have analyzed several additional kinds of evidence. Historical as well as current

TABLE 2.1
Large Membership Associations in U.S. History

Organization	Founding		Ending	National, State, and Local Units?	Directly Involved in Politics?	Decades above 1% of Men, Women, or Adults
Ancient and Accepted Free Masons	1733	Boston				1810s to present
Independent Order of Odd Fellows	1819	Baltimore		yes		1840s–1950s
American Temperance Society	1826	Boston	1865	yes	yes	1830s–1840s
Gen. Union for Promoting Observance of the Christian Sabbath	1828	New York	1832	yes	yes	1830s
American Anti-Slavery Society	1833	Boston	1870	yes	yes	1830s
Improved Order of Red Men	1834	Baltimore		yes		1900s–1920s
Washington Temperance Societies	1840	Baltimore	ca. 1848		yes	1840s
Order of the Sons of Temperance	1842	New York	ca. 1970	yes	yes	1840s–1850s
Independent Order of Good Templars	1851	Utica, NY		yes	yes	1860s–1870s
Young Men's Christian Association	1851	Boston		yes	war partner	1890s to present
Junior Order of United American Mechanics	1853	Philadelphia	ca. 1970	yes	yes	1920s–1930s
National Education Association	1857	Philadelphia		yes	yes	1970s to present
Knights of Pythias	1864	Washington, D.C.		yes		1870s–1930s
Grand Army of the Republic	1866	Decatur, IL	1956	yes	yes	1860s–1900s
Benevolent and Protective Order of Elks	1867	New York				1900s to present
Patrons of Husbandry (National Grange)	1867	Washington, D.C.		yes	yes	1870s, 1910s–1920s
Order of the Eastern Star	1868	New York		yes		1910s to present
Ancient Order of United Workmen	1868	Meadville, PA		yes		1880s–1900s
Knights of Labor	1869	Philadelphia	1917		yes	1880s
National Rifle Association	1871	New York		yes	yes	1980s to present

Organization	Founded	City	Disbanded			Active period
Nobles of the Mystic Shrine	1872	New York		yes	yes	1910s–1980s
Woman's Christian Temperance Union	1874	Cleveland		yes		1910s–1930s
Royal Arcanum	1877	Boston		yes	yes	1900s
Farmers' Alliance	1877	Lampasas, TX	1900	yes		1880s–1890s
Maccabees	1878	Port Huron, MI		yes		1900s–1910s
Christian Endeavor	1881	Portland, ME		yes		1880s–about 1920s
American Red Cross	1881	Washington, D.C.			war partner	1910s to present
Knights of Columbus	1882	New Haven, CT			war partner	1910s to present
Modern Woodmen of America	1883	Lyons, IA		yes		1890s–1930s
Colored Farmers' Alliance	1886	Houston, TX	1892	yes	yes	1880s–1890s
American Federation of Labor (AFL-CIO after 1955)	1886	Columbus, OH		yes	yes	1880s to present
American Protective Association	1887	Clinton, IA	ca. 1911	yes	yes	1890s
Woman's Missionary Union	1888	Richmond, VA		yes	yes	1920s to present
Loyal Order of Moose	1888	Louisville, KY		yes		1910s to present
National American Woman Suffrage Association	1890	Washington, D.C.	1920	yes	yes	1910s
Woodmen of the World	1890	Omaha, NE		yes		1900–1930s
General Federation of Women's Clubs	1890	New York		yes		1900s–1970s
American Bowling Congress	1895	New York		yes	yes	1930s to present
National Congress of Mothers (PTA)	1897	Washington, D.C.		yes	yes	1920s to present
Fraternal Order of Eagles	1898	Seattle, WA		yes	yes	1900s–1980s
German American National Alliance	1901	Philadelphia	1918	yes	yes	1910s
Aid Association for Lutherans	1902	Appleton, WI		yes		1970s
American Automobile Association	1902	Chicago		yes		1920s to present
Boy Scouts of America	1910	Washington, D.C.		yes	war partner	1930s to present
Veterans of Foreign Wars	1913	Denver, CO		yes	yes	1940s to present
Ku Klux Klan (Second)	1915	Atlanta	1944	yes	yes	1920s

TABLE 2.1 (cont.)
Large Membership Associations in U.S. History

Organization	Founding		Ending	National, State, and Local Units?	Directly Involved in Politics?	Decades above 1% of Men, Women, or Adults
Women's International Bowling Congress	1916	St. Louis, MO		yes		1950s to present
American Legion	1919	Minneapolis		yes	yes	1920s to present
American Farm Bureau Federation	1919	Chicago		yes	yes	1920s, 1940s to present
Old Age Revolving Pensions, Ltd. (Townsend movement)	1934	Long Beach, CA	1953		yes	1930s
Congress of Industrial Organizations	1938	Pittsburgh	1955		yes	1930s–1950s
March of Dimes	1938	New York				1950s
United Methodist Women	1939	Atlanta, GA				1940s to present
American Association of Retired Persons	1958	Washington, D.C.			yes	1970s to present
National Right to Life Committee	1973	Detroit, MI		yes	yes	1970s to present
Mothers Against Drunk Driving	1980	Sacramento, CA		yes	yes	1980s to present
Greenpeace USA	1988	Washington, D.C.			yes	1990s
Christian Coalition	1989	Washington, D.C.		yes	yes	1990s to present

directories and compilations enable us to track virtually all associations with national visibility; thus we can tell how very large membership associations compare to all kinds of nationally relevant groups.[15] Sources on major American ethnic groups and racial minorities allow us to map associational development for sectors of the population whose numbers made it difficult to sustain groups surpassing 1 percent of the entire adult population.[16]

What is more, in a key evidentiary step, we have analyzed locally present voluntary groups listed in late-nineteenth- and early-twentieth-century city directories.[17] In a ground-breaking 1999 article, Gerald Gamm and Robert Putnam track the spread of locally present voluntary groups across twenty-six U.S. cities between 1840 and 1940. Gamm and Putnam tally tens of thousands of groups, decade by decade, using regularly published local directories for five large cities, ten medium-sized cities, and eleven small cities, spread across all regions of the United States.[18] In about 1910 locally listed groups reached a peak of prevalence in relation to city populations. Reexamining directories for Gamm and Putnam's twenty-six cities in 1910 (or as close as possible to that date), we classified the types and organizational scale of all membership groups listed. Were most groups purely local, or were they parts of translocal federations of various sorts? Which kinds of groups were the most stable? Our findings are unequivocal.[19] The vast majority of locally present voluntary groups in the industrializing United States were parts of national or regional voluntary federations. Averaging across all twenty-six cities examined at the height of per capita voluntary group organization in 1910, we found that 78 percent of groups were parts of religious denominations, union federations, very large membership federations (in addition to churches and unions), or other membership federations spanning regions or the nation as a whole. Church congregations and chapters of the very same large membership federations listed in table 2.1 were predominant in every city and especially predominant in the smallest cities. What is more, over-time evidence also confirms the centrality of federated membership associations. Between 1870 and 1920 churches and chapters of very large federations were the most persistent of locally present voluntary membership groups, forming the stable core of organized civic life in communities of all sizes all over America. Thus as I talk about the origins and development of translocally federated voluntary associations in the pages that follow, the reader can be sure that I am talking not about the icing on the U.S. associational cake but about the cake itself.

THE ORIGINS OF AMERICAN VOLUNTARISM

An extensively organized and deeply participatory civil society took shape from the start of U.S. national life, even as the vast majority of Americans lived and worked on farms or in very small towns. In the era between the Revolution and the Civil War, voluntary groups proliferated and formed links across localities. American civic democracy emerged well before industries and metropolises.

Before voluntarily created associations could proliferate, historian Richard D. Brown explains, there had to be communities with two hundred to four hundred families and one-fifth of adult men engaged in nonagricultural occupations.[20] But demography alone did not shape early American civic destiny. Many communities surpassed this threshold before 1760, yet colonial Massachusetts (which included most of the territory of present-day Maine) had only a few dozen voluntary groups apart from churches. More than one-third of these groups were located in Boston, the colonial capital and only substantial city. This situation soon changed, however. During the struggles for American independence from Britain, voluntary groups proliferated dramatically, at a rate far surpassing population growth. Associations other than churches and for-profit groups increased from 14 in the city of Boston before 1760 to 135 groups by 1830—a roughly 760 percent increase. Beyond Boston, groups emerged even more rapidly, increasing from just 24 before 1760 to 1,305 by 1830—an explosive growth of more than 5,000 percent.[21] Most of this civic growth occurred after 1790, as the new U.S. nation took shape.

"In colonial America," Brown observes, social patterns involving choice and extralocal awareness were "a highly restricted phenomenon, limited to port towns that were also administrative centers."[22] Such patterns penetrated parts of the hinterland only via elites "who were in touch with the [colonial] capital as an occupational necessity." But by the 1830s, "localism and insularity were being challenged. . . . People remained bound to the old organiza tions of family, church, and town, but now they possessed additional ties. . . . Sometimes the contact was direct, if they traveled to a meeting or convention or if outsiders came to them as part of a political campaign, lyceum, temperance or missionary association. More often, the contact was psychological, coming from memberships in countywide or statewide organization and the publications such activities produced."[23]

Civil Society Goes National

Early America's burst of civic voluntarism happened first and most intensively in the northeastern United States, yet similar changes soon spread across the expanding new nation and involved people from many backgrounds. At first only groups such as the Masons and most churches were formally linked in translocal organizations. Even so, many other voluntary endeavors multiplied as people in one locality modeled their efforts on similar undertakings elsewhere.

Although women rarely organized separate translocal associations in this early period, recognizably similar female benevolent groups appeared in many towns.[24] At least one translocal association, the American Female Moral Reform Society founded in New York City, eventually encompassed 445 auxiliaries across the middle states and greater New England.[25] Meanwhile, male promoters disseminated explicit models and instructions for founding and operating community associations. A prime example was Josiah Holbrook, who traveled, spoke, and published to promote "lyceums," that is, voluntary community institutions intended to promote adult education, sponsor traveling lecturers, and support the emerging "common" public schools and their teachers.[26] Between the 1830s and the 1850s these institutions spread from New England into the upper South and (especially) into the Midwest east of the Mississippi River.

During the same era, vast moral crusades inspired the creation of thousands of interlinked local and state societies. Excellent examples are the temperance associations that gained enormous prominence before the Civil War.[27] By

1834 the American Temperance Society (ATS) claimed some 5,000 societies and one million members in the East and Midwest, but this group proved too top-down to sustain its popular appeal and soon evolved into a national center for publishing and lobbying (operating much like a modern professional advocacy group). In the 1840s the Washingtonian crusade reached out for working-class members and reformed "drunkards," briefly claiming some 600,000 members and 10,000 societies.[28] Washingtonians did not believe in formal national organization and experimented with radical, bottom-up democracy (much like the 1960s New Left). But such arrangements did not outlast the initial popular fervor, and temperance supporters soon joined orders with state and national institutions. Founded in 1842, the Sons of Temperance grew by 1860 into a truly continent-spanning federation boasting some 2,398 local "divisions" and 94,213 members spread across more than three dozen state divisions in the North and South and across the Mississippi River into Iowa and California.[29] During the 1850s, the Independent Order of Good Templars (IOGT) likewise began its climb to national prominence.[30] Open to women as well as men for leadership positions as well as membership, the IOGT claimed by 1860 more than 50,000 members grouped into about 1,200 lodges spread across 20 states, including Alabama and Mississippi in the Deep South.

Fraternal orders devoted to mutual aid and rituals of brotherhood also spanned the fledgling United States, despite the outburst of a fierce but temporary furor against Masons and other "secret societies" that peaked in the 1830s.[31] From colonial times Masonic lodges sunk roots everywhere in America; local lodges were founded immediately on the arrival of military garrisons in each new territory, and new "sovereign grand" lodges were chartered as states joined the U.S. union.[32] National, state, and local political elites were very often members of the Masonic fraternity. Yet Masonry also incorporated men from many other walks of life. From the 1810s to the present Masonic membership has always surpassed 1 percent of the U.S. adult male population.

America's second great fraternal association, the Independent Order of Odd Fellows (IOOF), was fashioned under the direction of brothers in Baltimore, Maryland, between 1819 and 1842. After immigrants established a few outposts of English orders, Odd Fellows in the United States took an organizational step that the (basic, "blue lodge") Masons never did. They established a three-tiered federal structure capped by a national-level "sovereign grand lodge" formed from representatives sent from state-level "grand" lodges with jurisdiction over local lodges.[33] Perfectly suited to American conditions, this new IOOF federated structure encouraged rapid growth. By 1830 American Odd Fellows met in fifty-eight lodges spread across Maryland, Massachusetts, New York, Pennsylvania, and the District of Columbia; and by 1860 there were more than 170,000 U.S. Odd Fellows meeting in more than 3,000 local lodges in thirty-five states in all regions of the nation.[34] As Paschal Donaldson, author of the 1852 edition of *The Odd-Fellow Text Book*, proudly declared: "From town to town, from city to city, from state to state, has this Order spread, and thousands upon thousands of the best men of our nation have been gathered to its folds."[35]

If not on such a spectacular scale as the Masons and the Odd Fellows, other U.S. fraternals also made rapid headway before the Civil War. Founded in 1834, the racially and ethnically exclusionist Improved Order of Red Men consisted of white Christians who dressed up like Indians and dated their order from 1492, when Columbus arrived in America. By 1860 almost 10,000 Red Men were meeting in 94 "tribes" spread across the "reservations" of Maryland, Pennsylvania, Virginia, Ohio, New Jersey, Missouri, Kentucky, Delaware, and the District of Columbia.[36] Not to be outdone, in 1836 Irish Americans founded the American branch of the Ancient Order of Hibernians, which was organized in eight states of the East, South, and Midwest by the outbreak of the Civil War.[37] During the 1840s, German Americans in New York City launched the Order of the Sons of Hermann and the Order of Harugari, two (eventually transstate) beneficial and cultural federations dedicated to furthering German culture and defending German Americans from nativist attacks during widespread Know-Nothing agitations.[38] Modeling their efforts on the Odd Fellows, moreover, Czech immigrants founded the Bohemian Slavonic Benefit Society in 1854.[39]

Along with the Irish and Germans, African Americans were the other very large U.S. minority. With the exception of some temperance orders, white-dominated U.S. voluntary associations shunned blacks as members. Nevertheless, even before the Civil War, African Americans built substantial orders paralleling the groups from which they were excluded. Prince Hall Masonry originated in 1775, when British Masons chartered a Negro Masonic lodge in Cambridge, Massachusetts.[40] In early national times, free blacks spread this fraternal republic across eighteen states, including "most of the Atlantic coastal states as far south as Virginia, and many midwestern states . . . [and] Maryland,

Virginia, and Louisiana, the centers of the free Negro population" of the South.[41] Meanwhile, in 1843 African Americans in New York City under the leadership of seaman
Peter Ogden launched the Grand United Order of Odd Fellows, again with the aid of a lodge charter from England.
By the early 1860s about fifteen hundred African American
Odd Fellows were meeting in about fifty lodges scattered
across more than half a dozen eastern states.[42]

Why Did Civic Voluntarism Flourish?

Why was early American civil society so sharply and
precociously transformed—as communities of all sizes established voluntary groups with remarkable simultaneity, and
many groups became linked in translocal, representatively
governed, federated organizations? The effects of U.S. governmental institutions, and the political and religious competition they fostered, lie at the heart of the answer.

As we have glimpsed, the American break from British
imperial control fueled the growth of a democratic civil
society. The revolutionary war and subsequent struggles
over a new U.S. Constitution disrupted taken-for-granted
loyalties, brought geographically dispersed sets of Americans into contact with one another, and undermined the
sway of great cities along the Atlantic seaboard. Once victory brought independent nationhood, the ongoing political routines of the representative polity pulled Americans
into broader involvements. Elections were held for statewide and national offices, and fledgling political parties
competed for support, linking some citizens in each place
to fellow Federalists or Jeffersonians elsewhere. By the 1830s
most adult white men enjoyed the right to vote, and trans-

regional political parties were knitting together patronage machines and networks of grassroots associations capable of mobilizing popular votes in incessant rounds of elections.[43] It was no coincidence that translocal movements and civil associations flourished in the era of mass party building. Both party builders and association builders sought to mobilize a democratic citizenry.

Early America was simultaneously swept by the religious enthusiasms of the Second Great Awakening. Religious proselytization started during late colonial times and accelerated during the early national period. Distinctively, the United States soon did away with governmentally established church monopolies—and that turned out to be the best possible situation for popular, energetic, independent-minded religions to flourish. "Beginning with Virginia in 1776 and ending with Connecticut in the 1840s, all American states eventually broke the traditional ties that had bound church and state together."[44] Under the Constitution and the Bill of Rights, competing denominations were free to preach and proselytize.[45] Indeed, because churches lost governmental sponsorship, each denomination had to organize and attract devoted congregants or risk eclipse. Soon traveling organizers, especially newly energized Methodists and Baptists, spread out across the land. Traveling preachers founded new congregations and inspired local leaders, including laypeople, to keep them going.[46] Women as well as men were involved in these religious movements.[47] Because they were the majority of churchgoers, women were likely to be drawn into reform crusades grounded in religious ideals and networks; and they had room to assert themselves amid the contending denominations. As historian Kathryn Kish Sklar explains,

"beginning in the 1820s, women were able to form vigorous pan-Protestant lay organizations, which challenged
the authority of ministers and generated an autonomous
social agenda."[48]

Translocal associations flourished in early America in significant part because people were constantly on the move.
Recent demographic research shows that long-distance
geographic mobility peaked in the mid-1800s, especially
among young men.[49] As waves of migration spread across
the continent, new arrivals established familiar kinds of
lodges or clubs at the same time that they built farms, businesses, and churches.[50] Once settled, moreover, people visited or wrote to relatives and friends in their places of origin, learning in the process of new kinds of associations
that they might help to establish in their new communities.

But Americans on the move might not have been able
to cooperate had not a very centralized and active arm of
the early U.S. government, the U.S. Postal Service, facilitated the efficient social communication that allowed citizens to create interconnected groups for political, religious,
and moral purposes. Before the American Revolution the
colonies had a rudimentary postal system comparable to
that of many European countries, with larger cities loosely
tied together, especially along the Atlantic coast. This
changed soon after the founding of the republic, when
Congress passed the Post Office Act of 1792, which "admitted newspapers into the mail on unusually favorable
terms, . . . prohibited public officers from using their control over the means of communication as a surveillance
technique," and "established a set of procedures that facilitated the extraordinarily rapid expansion of the postal network from the Atlantic seaboard into the transappalachian

West."[51] "By 1828," as historian Richard John points out, "the American postal system had almost twice as many offices as the postal system in Great Britain and over five times as many offices as the postal system in France. This translated into 74 post offices for every 100,000 inhabitants in comparison with 17 for Great Britain and 4 for France."[52] In the 1830s and 1840s the system accounted for more than three-quarters of U.S. federal employees, and most of the 8,764 postal employees in 1831 and the 14,290 employees in 1841 were "part-time postmasters in villages and towns scattered throughout the countryside."[53]

The postal network was shaped by U.S. government institutions. Congressional representation based in states and local districts gave members of the Senate and the House of Representatives a strong interest in subsidizing communication and transportation links into even the remotest areas of the growing nation—yet in a carefully calibrated way. Legislators wanted mail and news to be carried into even the smallest communities; and they also wanted to be able to travel to and from the national capital. Hence they subsidized stagecoach travel and set cheap postal rates. Postal rules also allowed for the free exchange of newspapers among editors, so that small newspapers could pick up copy from bigger ones. But at the same time, rate structures were fine-tuned to prevent eastern seaboard papers from outmarketing provincial news sheets.

To take advantage of politically engineered postal subsidies, voluntary groups as well as political parties disseminated their messages in "newspaper" (and later magazine) formats. Civil organizing was greatly facilitated—and, not infrequently, voluntary associations became engines of political reform. One of the first great moral reform movements

in America—briefly embodied between 1828 and 1832 in
the General Union for Promoting the Observance of the
Christian Sabbath—was devoted to trying to stop the opening of post offices and transportation of the mails on Sundays.[54] Ironically, this movement depended on the federal
postal system it sought to challenge, because it relied on the
mail to spread tens of thousands of pamphlets and petitions! The same was true of other great voluntary crusades
in the pre–Civil War era, including the temperance movements and the popular drive against slavery that helped to
spark the Civil War.[55] The early U.S. state, in short, created
favorable conditions for associations, social movements,
and mass-mobilizing political parties—all of which, in turn,
continuously roiled and transformed national politics and
government.

The Federal Representative State as a Civil Model

There was a final way in which U.S. governing institutions influenced association building: the structure of government served as an organizational model. The United
States was put together by the Founding Fathers as a federal republic, and the nation and the states had written constitutions that spelled out rules for voting and representation; explicitly parceled out administrative, legislative, and
judicial functions; and assigned levels of sovereignty to
national, state, and local government. From early national
times American civil associations began to use governmental federalism as an organizational model (see table 2.1).
Constitutions establishing national, state, and local units
tied together by representative procedures were adopted
by three-fourths of the ultimately large voluntary groups

launched in the decades before the Civil War (and by a similar preponderance of those launched in the late 1800s).[56]

Political considerations encouraged many groups to adopt constitutional arrangements paralleling the U.S. state. Social movements often adapt their organizational structures and routines to national "political opportunity structures."[57] The U.S. political system rewarded movements and associations able to coordinate efforts at the national, state, and local levels. From temperance movements and antislavery crusades to farmers' groups, women's movements, and nativist agitations, groups aiming to shape public opinion and influence elected legislators learned the advantage of such cross-level organization. Serving as bridges between local sets of citizens and elected officials, associations could influence both Congress and state legislatures. Operating across levels, moreover, groups could pursue both sociocultural and political change; and they could go toe-to-toe in battles with one another. "Our order," explained the Right Worthy Grand Templar of the Independent Order of Good Templars, "is organized to destroy the evils growing out of the drink traffic, and the individual use of alcoholic drinks." Because the "drunkard-makers have strong Local, State, and National Organizations," subordinate lodges reach out to save individuals and agitate public opinion, while "against the State Liquor Union" the IOGT arrays the state-level "Grand Lodge; and against the American Brewers' Congress and National Distillers Union" it deploys the national-level "R.W.G. Lodge."[58]

But the response of civic activists to political openings and challenges is not a sufficient explanation, because many associations not dedicated to political goals also adopted federal representative constitutional arrangements. Accord-

ing to institutionalist theorists of organizational development, organization builders who face complex challenges
in conditions of uncertainty may draw inspiration from
well-understood, already legitimate models in their environment.[59] Innovative adaptations of this sort are often
made by ambitious but somewhat marginalized people,
such as foreign immigrants arriving in a new country.[60]
Thus Odd Fellows arriving in America seem to have reorganized themselves in imitation of the divisions of powers
and local, state, and national levels of the U.S. state because
the Constitution offered a prestigious and well-understood
model for spreading lodges and coordinating their activities on a national scale. As chronicler Henry Stillson explains,
immigrant Odd Fellows with "superior discernment" realized "the impracticality" and "especial unfitness for this
country" of English-style fraternal governing arrangements,
which coordinated local lodges through national committees of notables. Instead, the transplanted Odd Fellows
soon "found their model in the political framework of the
United States."[61] The preamble of the fraternal constitution
newly devised by the American Odd Fellows unmistak-
ably echoed the U.S. Constitution:

> Whereas, it has been found expedient, and of great
> importance to mankind, to perpetuate those institutions
> which confer on them great and essential benefit. There-
> fore, the GRAND LODGE OF THE UNITED STATES . . . ,
> for the more effectual purpose of binding each other in
> the bond of one common Union, by which we will be
> . enabled to insure a co-operation of action, . . . and to
> secure unto ourselves and posterity more effectually the

blessings which are to be derived from so valuable and beneficial an institution, do ordain and establish the following as the CONSTITUTION . . . OF THE INDEPENDENT ORDER OF ODD FELLOWS.[62]

Many other groups soon followed in the footsteps of the Odd Fellows. So prestigious was the U.S. constitutional model that immigrant-ethnic fraternals often established a full complement of state and national representative arrangements at a stage when they barely had enough members to fill a small number of local lodges scattered across several cities. Everyone, it seemed, wanted associations patterned on America's new representative federal government.

Just as U.S. national and state constitutions specified residency rules for voting, the constitutions of civil associations included explicit rules about the establishment of state and local units and the recruitment of resident members into them. Unlike fraternal groups in other nations, for example, U.S. fraternals and their female partner groups required a potential member to apply to the lodge nearest his or her residence.[63] Traveling members had to have formal documentation from their lodges of origin to be admitted as visitors or to "transfer" their membership elsewhere. Associations other than fraternal groups did not always follow such formal rules, but they too managed the flow of people across places. U.S. voluntary federations certainly sustained ties across vast distances and let people move around. But rootless cosmopolitanism was not allowed— not in associational life any more than in the U.S. version of representative democracy.

THE MODERNIZATION OF CIVIC AMERICA

If waves of ambitious voluntary group formation occurred before 1861, even greater bursts gathered force after the Civil War, expanding some older associations and giving birth to hundreds of new popular voluntary federations, including dozens of groups that were destined to become very large and persist through much of the twentieth century. The late nineteenth century was an extraordinary period of civic creativity. But what kinds of groups emerged, and what forces shaped the innovations? Associational life might have been upended and divided by class as the United States became a metropolitan industrial powerhouse, yet this was not the whole story—not even the main story line. As the economy modernized, American associational life retained and expanded preindustrial forms, even as new kinds of groups emerged.

Social scientists often presume that big changes in the economy will automatically bring similar shifts in everything else. Standard explanations for associational change thus focus on emerging actors responding to new stresses and opportunities offered by corporate industrialization and the growth of big cities. Some scholars maintain that class conflict spurs workers to form unions and capitalists to band together in business groups. Others view modern associations as mechanisms of social integration, substituting for ties of family and neighborliness in preindustrial villages. One version of such reasoning appears in Robert Wiebe's influential synthesis, *The Search for Order, 1877–1920*, where the key actors are rising "new middle class" professionals and business people who fashioned new associations and service groups in "response" to the unsettling transformations of immigration, industrialization, and urban concentration.[64]

Certain facts fit these expectations. Gamm and Putnam's study of voluntary groups listed in directories for twenty-six cities between 1840 and 1940 documents that labor unions proliferated sharply in the late 1800s and early 1900, while business and professional groups also increased in number relative to city populations.[65] From more qualitative sources, we also know that elite "service groups"—Rotary clubs, Exchange clubs, and Lions clubs for men and smaller groups for business and professional women—also spread across cities in the early twentieth century.[66] Emphasizing fellowship and service to the broader community, such clubs accepted modest numbers of leaders from each business or profession (although "professions" could be defined very narrowly to expand membership). Some scholars believe that elite service clubs replaced cross-class fraternal associations, as business and professional people grew tired of evening-long rituals, preferred shorter lunchtime meetings, and wanted to network among themselves rather than reaffirm "brotherhood" with blue-collar wage earners and white-collar employees.[67] But this was not the whole story, because as America industrialized certain old-line fraternals renewed themselves; and rising fraternal groups such as the Elks, Moose, Eagles, and Knights of Columbus grew to unprecedented prominence, relying on simplified rituals and new solicitude for community outreach.

If we focus on isolated types of voluntary groups one at a time, it is all too easy to be fooled into thinking that as new kinds of associations emerge, older types must be in decline. That is why *systematic* data about the changing big picture is needed. Gamm and Putnam's overview of groups listed in city directories shows, for example, that religious groups and fraternal associations not only were more prevalent than economic groups *before* the United States became a metropolitan-industrial nation; religious and fraternal groups also proliferated *during* industrialization.[68] In per capita terms, fraternal associations exhibited an especially sharp upsurge between the 1870s and the turn of the twentieth century. Data on national foundings of larger and smaller popular membership associations confirm this picture. The very large membership associations my colleagues and I have studied necessarily had many members from nonelite backgrounds, and most of these groups were launched in the late 1800s (see table 2.1 above and fig. 2.4 below). Historical directories tell us that hundreds of smaller cross-class federations were born and attracted members during the same era.[69]

As industrialization transformed the national economy, in short, Americans did not simply sort themselves out into class-segregated and occupationally based associations. Of course, trade unions, business associations, and professional groups proliferated and attracted new members. But spreading and growing during exactly the same period were churches, religious associations, fraternal and women's groups, and many other long-standing kinds of voluntary associations that attracted members across class lines.

The Formative Impact of the Civil War

Apart from the American Revolution itself, no watershed had a greater impact on the development of U.S. civil society than the Civil War of 1861 to 1865. Scholars often presume that "basic" causes must be economic, but wars

and political conflicts also shape polities and societies—
and nowhere was this more true than in the modernizing
United States. More voluntary associations destined to
attract very large memberships were launched at the conclusion of the Civil War, in the late 1860s, than in any other
five-year period in all of U.S. history. Dozens of additional
foundings of eventually large groups followed across the
immediate post–Civil War decades, while prewar federations also ballooned in size.[70] The Progressive Era of the
early twentieth century is often cited as the seedbed of
modern American civil society, but this is off the mark.
Union victory in the Civil War spurred the formation and
expansion of many of the very large, popularly rooted
membership federations to which the extraordinarily
numerous local lodges, clubs, and labor union locals of the
early twentieth century were connected. The national- and
state-level centers of these ambitious federations were
almost always founded well in advance of the local chapters that flourished within them. National- and state-level
organizers and leaders fashioned rules and institutions
that fostered local chapters and allowed them to flourish in
constant touch with one another.[71] American voluntary
group formation was not primarily local or attributable to
"spontaneous" grassroots organizing. Local people and
leaders certainly mattered, but they were called into action
by and worked hand in hand with, nationally ambitious
leaders—bold and visionary men and women who launched
and spread the great voluntary federations that would
serve as the institutional holding environments for U.S.
associational life well into the twentieth century.

    That the Civil War encouraged ambitious association
building seems, at first thought, counterintuitive. Tocque-

ville feared that prolonged warfare would squelch civic freedom.[72] And the cataclysm of 1861 to 1865 was by far America's most destructive war, involving more casualties per capita and much more civilian destruction for the United States than the great wars of the twentieth century. The Civil War tore apart preexisting voluntary federations like the Odd Fellows and the Sons of Temperance; diverted adult energies and took hundreds of thousands of lives; and left much of the South economically prostrate. Yet the Civil War also brought "philanthropic results," as one contemporary observer marveled.[73] People committed themselves to service; and massive wartime efforts reinforced the practicality of popularly rooted federalism as America's preeminent model for large-scale association building. Especially for leaders, wartime experiences created ideals, network connections, and models of citizen organization that encouraged ambitious association building long after the fighting ceased.

Civic results flowed from *how* this huge conflict was fought, especially on the winning Union side. Well before 1861 Americans were familiar with federated voluntary associations; they knew how to "combine" for purposes big and national as well as particular and local. Government, however, was less well prepared than the citizenry for the gargantuan efforts internecine warfare would demand. When South Carolinians fired on Fort Sumter, the U.S. federal government had little in the way of a standing army. The federal military consisted of a mere sixteen thousand soldiers—most coping with Indians "in seventy-nine frontier outposts west of the Mississippi"—led by a small corps of West Point–trained professionals, about a third of whom, including leading lights like Robert E. Lee, soon "went

South on us" to serve the rebellious Confederacy.[74] Both sides in the war between the states relied of necessity on civilian as well as elected leaders to assemble local volunteers into community and state units and then combine those assemblages into great armies and civilian relief operations. The Civil War was fought by volunteer groups organized across class lines. Educated and privileged citizens and other officers who rose through the ranks "led by example, not prescript."[75]

Voluntarism was especially deep and persistent in the North. Even though there were Union military drafts from 1862 on, at least 87 percent of the men who fought were volunteers, usually marched off to war by officers from their own states, towns, and ethnic groups.[76] On the home front, women and civilian men coordinated medical, social, and spiritual support for the troops through the U.S. Sanitary Commission (which evolved from the Women's Central Association for Relief), the YMCA-sponsored Christian Commission, and other volunteer federations. The U.S. Sanitary Commission was "the largest voluntary organization yet formed in a country noted for such enterprises," explains historian James McPherson; it "grew from a fusion of local soldiers' aid societies that had sprung up within days of the firing on Sumter. Women took the lead in forming these associations, drawing upon their sense of commitment and previous experience in societies advocating the abolition of slavery, women's rights, temperance, education, missions, and the like."[77]

After the Confederates surrendered at Appomattox, spirits soared on the Union side. Inspired by a new sense of national purpose and thoroughly familiar with federated models of popular mobilization, northern men and women who grew to maturity in the late 1800s launched many new mass-based voluntary federations. These were bold organizational creations, intended to span the nation and tie localities and states together. I noted earlier that ultimately very large U.S. membership associations launched after the Civil War (like those founded before 1860) were usually organized as representative national-state-local federations. The aspirations of the founders of ultimately large membership associations also reveal the impact of the Civil War. Figure 2.1, using data for all U.S. voluntary membership associations that ultimately recruited 1 percent of men or women or both genders as members, summarizes data about the scope of operations originally envisaged by associational founders.[78] Some ultimately large associations were originally "local," in the sense that they were initially understood as city or state groups and only later evolved into widespread national associations. Others, like the Masons, the Odd Fellows, and the YMCA, commenced on American soil as local "outposts" of transnational associations arriving from Europe. Still other ultimately very large associations, like the General Federation of Women's Clubs, were formed as "combinations" of preexisting groups.[79] But these three paths taken together account for only two-fifths of the foundings of ultimately very large U.S. membership associations across all eras of national history. Three-fifths of all such associations were launched by ambitious leaders who, from inception, envisaged creating national organizations, even if it took them some time to realize their plans. And notice that the Civil War era, from 1860 to the turn of the twentieth century, stands out as having a very high number and proportion of nationally ambitious foundings (64 percent of the foundings between

FIGURE 2.1

The Original Scope of Very Large U.S. Membership Associations Founded in Different Eras

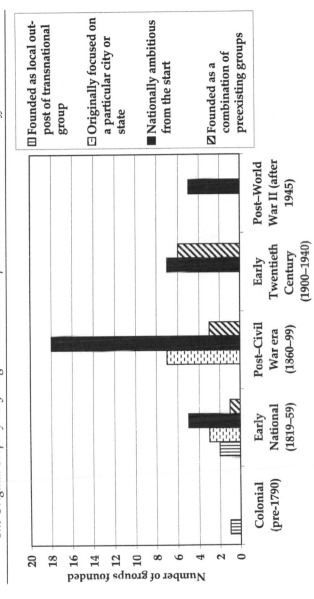

SOURCE: Civic Engagement Project data on 58 U.S. associations with memberships that ever exceeded 1% of men and/or women.

1860 and 1899 were nationally focused). Not only were a greater number of ultimately very large associations launched in the decades after the Civil War than in any other era of U.S. history, association builders of this watershed era were more likely to have planned national projects from the start than were founders of ultimately very large associations active in any other (comparably long) period before World War II.

The founding stories of particular groups suggest how wartime Union mobilizations encouraged subsequent association building. In 1868 railroad workers who met during the Civil War launched the Ancient Order of United Workmen (AOUW) in Meadville, Pennsylvania. They formed the nation's first insurance-oriented fraternal group, a model for other associations soon to come.[80] Founders of the AOUW aimed to bridge class divisions thought to have been sharpened by the war, by offering cultural uplift as well as regular insurance benefits to all workingmen. Soon to grow into America's third largest fraternal association, the Knights of Pythias was launched from Washington, D.C., in 1864 by young clerks who met in the war-swollen federal civil service and devised a ritual of sacrificial brotherhood that appealed not only to former soldiers but also to all Americans hoping to reknit North and South.[81]

Another regionally disparate group of federal clerks started the Patrons of Husbandry (or Grange) in 1867.[82] This happened after Minnesota native and federal agricultural official Oliver Kelley was commissioned by President Andrew Johnson to assess the rural needs of the devastated South. Using Masonic ties to make personal contacts in the defeated region, Kelley soon realized that farmers too could benefit from a nationwide fraternity. Working with fellow federal officials—each of whom, like him, moved back and forth between Washington and his home region—Kelley designed a federation that incorporated some existing farm groups and stimulated the founding of thousands of additional local granges.

Union Civil War experiences also heightened the aspirations and increased the civic capacities of American women.[83] Oliver Kelley's niece, Carrie Hall, persuaded him to make females equal and full members of the Grange.[84] Along with the famous wartime nurse Clara Barton, many other women and men who had been active in wartime relief activities agitated from the 1860s to 1881 for congressional charter of the American Red Cross.[85] Meanwhile, women moved to the fore in the massive temperance movement. Willing to accept women leaders and members on equal terms, the IOGT held its own during the war and burgeoned afterward, prodding the Sons of Temperance to accept females too.

Temperance-minded American women nevertheless wanted an even more dominant role to meet challenges they understood in gendered terms. They were anxious to counter male drunkenness, which had been exacerbated by military service, and determined to fight government policies favorable to the liquor industry, which had become a lucrative source of tax revenues during the war. Female reformers convened in Cleveland, Ohio, in 1874 to launch the Woman's Christian Temperance Union (WCTU). Some of these women had met in Union relief efforts; all of them applauded the women's crusades against saloon keepers that spread in the Midwest during the early 1870s.[86] Grassroots protests were hard to sustain, however, so women gathered at a summer camp for the National Sunday School Assembly hatched a plan to institutionalize "the grand temperance uprising." In cadences resonant with the "Onward Christian Soldiers" rhetoric of Union victory, a "Committee of Organization . . . consisting of one lady from each state" issued a "Call" to organize the national WCTU. "In union and in organization," proclaimed the Call, "are . . . success and permanence, and the consequent redemption of this land from the curse of intemperance."[87]

Wars can bring together people on all sides of the conflict, yet the winners are likely to reap the most enduring civic gains. Before 1860 many American voluntary groups were founded and maintained their headquarters in Baltimore, an eastern seaboard city at the juncture of North and South. What is more, despite their predominantly rural character, southern areas held their own within national federations. But after the war new associations with national ambitions were launched from large or medium-sized northeastern and midwestern cities and later from a few far western sites, while southern membership lagged in previously established national federations like the Odd Fellows (see fig. 2.2 below).[88] Although Union veterans' federations (including the eventually dominant Grand Army of the Republic) were launched right after the war, local groups of Confederate veterans did not come together to form the United Confederate Veterans until 1889. As losers in the great conflict over the demarcation of American nationhood, white southerners found it harder than the victorious northerners to organize or participate in large-scale civic endeavors in the postwar era.

An exception to pure northern predominance in U.S. associational growth after the Civil War confirms the rule

FIGURE 2.2

White and Black Odd Fellows Lodges in the North and South before, during, and after the Civil War

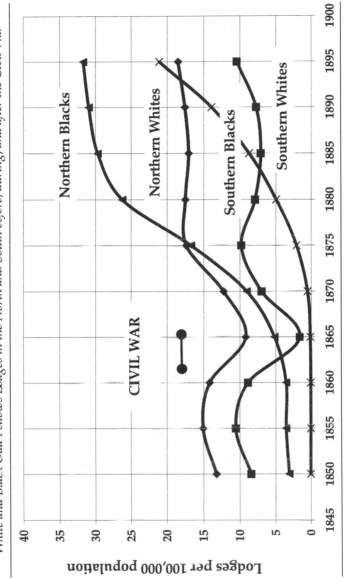

SOURCE: Annual Reports of the Independent Order of Odd Fellows; estimates from lodge foundings and death rates in Charles H. Brooks, *The Official History and Manual of the Grand United Order of Odd Fellows in America* (Freeport, N.Y.: Books for Libraries Press, 1971; reprint of 1902 ed.).

that winning a mass-mobilizing war boosts civic energy. Along with northern whites, after all, African Americans in the South and North alike were big winners of the Civil War. Some 180,000 African American men served in the Union armies, contributing to the victory that ultimately broke the legal shackles of slavery for all blacks. The moment southern slaves started to become emancipated, transregional African American associations expanded in numbers and membership. Dozens of new African American fraternal and mutual aid federations, many of them involving women along with men, were launched in the decades after the Civil War. Such federations were often launched from cities in states of the upper South. Along with pre–Civil War fraternal groups like the Prince Hall Masons and the Grand United Order of Odd Fellows, emerging African American fraternal federations such as the United Brothers of Friendship and Sisters of the Mysterious Ten, the Independent Order of Saint Luke, the Knights of Tabor and Daughters of the Tabernacle, and the Mosaic Templars of America established lodges and attracted new members at an extraordinary rate.[89] Rapid growth occurred even in rural parts of the Deep South where African American freedmen and women were economically impoverished and little educated. After the end of Reconstruction in 1876, blacks faced increasingly fierce repression if they tried to vote or join labor unions, yet they never lost their right—or their will—to form and join churches and fraternal groups. Indeed, the spotty evidence that exists suggests that African Americans of the late nineteenth and early twentieth centuries were even more likely than privileged Caucasian Americans to organize and join churches and fraternal groups. For one very telling piece of evidence, figure 2.2 traces the incidence of African American and white Odd Fellows lodges in the South and the North through the Civil War. Note that after the Civil War both northern and southern lodges of the African American Grand United Order of Odd Fellows proliferated in relation to population much more rapidly than even the fast-proliferating *northern* lodges of the white Independent Order of Odd Fellows. White southern Odd Fellows, tellingly, were by far the laggards in forming and maintaining lodges in proportion to their share of the adult male population.

VOLUNTARY FEDERATIONS PROLIFERATE

African Americans exemplified the exuberance of association building characteristic of the post–Civil War era. Following well-worn organizational grooves, all sorts of federated, cross-class membership associations continued to proliferate across the United States through the turn of the twentieth century. Established models were copied and elaborated by multiple waves of association builders, including female civic activists, organizers offering fraternal insurance, and clashing nativists and ethnics.

Women formed many new national associations in the decades around 1900.[90] Often after years of struggles (which revealed that female fraternalists were anything but passive), auxiliaries open to women relatives were added to almost all of the major male fraternal and patriotic groups.[91] Professional women, though few in numbers, formed their own federations. And two new, giant independent women's membership federations appeared: the General Federation of Women's Clubs, founded in 1890, and the National Congress of Mothers (later the National Congress of Parents and Teachers [PTA]), founded in 1897. For these cross-class federations, the WCTU, formed during the immediate post–Civil War era, was an organizational model. Many women who had been active in the WCTU helped to found and spread the General Federation and the Congress of Mothers as well. By the turn of the twentieth century, American women not only participated avidly in local communities; they also influenced state and national legislation through an interlocking system of membership federations.

Another turn-of-the-century dynamic was the rise—and often quick demise—of fraternal groups aiming to provide insurance to members. Fraternal insurance orders established after 1880 usually adopted more businesslike methods than the pioneering Ancient Order of United Workmen. They tailored their dues assessments to the age of members and built up financial reserves to cover projected benefit payments. But many small insurance orders never grew very large, because they were deliberately limited to potential members thought to be relatively healthy or because they formed in the first place by breaking away from previously established insurance orders. Youthful westerners, for example, frequently broke away to avoid paying dues to cover benefits for aging easterners. And still other small insurance fraternals, like the Order of the Iron Hall of 1881–91, represented little more than thinly disguised Ponzi schemes that proved actuarially unsound and hence short-lived. Tellingly, only a handful of the fraternal groups that grew very large and survived over many decades were *primarily* focused on provision of social insurance—except among African Americans, where major orders almost invariably sponsored insurance. Among whites, leading U.S. fraternal groups normally did better when they focused on social ties and moral suasion, while relegating insurance provision, if any, to adjunct programs that were optional for members.

A final point is worth emphasis, given the tendency of today's analysts to treat voluntary groups as pure manifestations of social cooperation. In real life, people often associate to exclude, fight, or defend against others. Certainly, fierce ethnic and religious conflicts fueled much association building in the late-nineteenth-century United States. In response to waves of new immigration from eastern and southern Europe, voluntary associations appealing to native-born Americans asserted Protestant folkways, championed public schools, and demanded laws to limit the influx and political influence of hyphenated Americans.[92] In turn, ethnics under attack pulled together their own voluntary federations aiming to unite local groups for self-defense and assert their legitimacy as Americans. Unsurprisingly, peak periods of nativist association building and political agitation in U.S. history—such as the 1840s and 1850s, the 1890s; and the 1920s—are the same periods when large numbers of ethnic American groups were launched or expanded.[93]

CIVIL SOCIETY IN THE TWENTIETH CENTURY

By the dawn of the twentieth century, the United States was awash with chapter-based membership federations recruiting men or women (or, occasionally, both together) across lines of class as well as place. Dozens of ultimately very large voluntary federations, and hundreds of smaller ones too, were launched between 1865 and the early 1900s. Local chapters linked to these federations soon spread into even the smallest towns. Sheer numbers of local chapters of large and small voluntary federations probably peaked during the 1900s and 1910s. After that a certain consolidation occurred, as many insurance-oriented fraternals faltered and other voluntary federations completed their nationwide chapter networks. Twentieth-century American membership associations were also more likely than their earlier counterparts to stress large units with many internal subgroups rather than sheer proliferation of separate units. Thus expanding twentieth-century fraternal groups, such as the Elks, the Eagles, the Shriners, the Knights of Columbus, and the Moose, had rules allowing only one or a few lodges per city, instead of encouraging the formation of dozens of lodges in each place, as had the Odd Fellows, Knights of Pythias, and other fraternal federations that grew to national prominence in the nineteenth century.[94]

Federations and Government in World War I

The surprisingly beneficial impact of big wars on American civic voluntarism did not end with the Civil War, for similar dynamics happened again during and immediately after the great, mass-mobilizing world wars of the twentieth century. As Tocqueville believed, war can be deleterious for organized civic life, especially when authoritarian bureaucrats take over all aspects of economic and social life and suppress voluntary efforts. But this was not the way big wars were fought in the United States. During America's greatest wars—the Civil War, World War I, and World War II—federal authorities needed help from voluntary groups willing to jump into the fray. Participation on the winning side of such wars in turn enhanced the legitimacy and bolstered the resources of cooperating voluntary groups.

Great, mass-mobilizing wars also taught American elites the value of organizing their fellow citizens and drawing them into full participation in shared endeavors. Along with competitive elections run by parties committed to popular mobilization, great wars encouraged American elites to be democratic. In big wars as well as in the competitive electoral politics of the nineteenth century, U.S. elites discovered that they could not get the job done unless they organized and involved masses of ordinary citizens in cooperative endeavors.

World War I was America's first centrally managed war, with men selected to fight by the Selective Service and economic production coordinated by federal agencies.[95] Even so, this war, like the Civil War before it, stimulated and reinforced organized voluntarism in the United States. The federal government of the 1910s deployed professionals and managers in Washington, D.C.—many more, certainly, than it used in the 1860s—but government could not reach into local communities and homes. Only popularly rooted voluntary federations could do that, so federal war managers needed them. Because partnerships with popularly rooted voluntary groups were so necessary to war mobilizations, World War I helped to consolidate an organized U.S. civil society grounded in nation-spanning federated associations.

To be sure, most of the brand new associations established during and right after World War I were business and professional bodies.[96] To manage the economy between 1917 and 1919, federal authorities fostered innovative kinds of cooperation among business and professional leaders; and elites who met on wartime boards often established more permanent associations.[97] While dozens of new business and professional groups formed in the late 1910s and early 1920s, only two new large-scale popular federations were born. In 1919 military officers launched the American Legion as a nationwide federation representing World War I veterans of all ranks.[98] That same year the American Farm Bureau Federation (AFBF) was founded, taking advantage of the wartime cooperation among local and state farm bureaus encouraged by federal Agriculture Department officials, who had preferred not to rely on the somewhat pacifist Grange or other preexisting farm federations.[99] In most areas of wartime activity, however, federal authorities had no need to encourage new popular voluntary federations, because so many were already flourishing and were eager to cooperate and lend their preexisting networks of local units to the national effort. For example, table 2.2 enumerates the dozens of associational networks and thousands of congregations and voluntary chapters that participated in food conservation drives in the single midwestern state of Iowa. Iowa may have been an especially civic state, yet similar voluntary mobilizations occurred all over the country.

Dramatized in the ubiquitous posters adorning homes and public places during the Great War (see fig. 2.3 for an example), partnerships between federal government agencies and leading nationally federated membership associations figured in every aspect of social and economic mobilization.[100] The Red Cross, the YMCA, the Knights of Columbus, and the Jewish Welfare Board (including the Young Men's Hebrew Association) worked with the War Department to provide social supports to the troops.[101] This partnership of Protestant, Catholic, and Jewish associations was especially important, because for the first time in

TABLE 2.2
Federated Groups Engaged in World War I Food Drives in Iowa

CHURCH CONGREGATIONS:

Methodist: 783	Presbyterian: 202	
Catholic: 480	German Lutheran: 121	
Lutheran: 337	German Evangelical: 56	
Christian: 324	Swedish Lutheran: 53	
Congregational: 237	Episcopal: 40	
Baptist: 221	Evangelical Lutheran: 19	Total: 2,873

ASSOCIATION CHAPTERS:

United Commercial Travelers: 34 lodges
Travelers Protective Association: 14 lodges
Iowa State Traveling Men's Association: 235 lodges
Gideons: 324 lodges
Knights of Pythias: 235 lodges
Benevolent and Protective Order of Elks: 32 lodges
Loyal Order of Moose: 50 lodges
Knights of Columbus: 47 lodges
Ancient Order of United Workmen: 118 lodges
Fraternal Order of Eagles: 25 lodges
Independent Order of Odd Fellows: 685 lodges
Brotherhood of American Yeomen: 500 lodges
Homesteaders: 140 lodges
Woodmen of the World: 400 lodges
Modern Woodmen of America: 982 lodges
Masons: 531 lodges
Sons of Herman: 1,500 lodges
Foresters: 22 lodges
Royal Neighbors of America: 575 lodges
Order of the Eastern Star: 419 lodges
Woodmen of the World Circle: 190 lodges
Rebekahs: 600 lodges
Pythian Sisters: 144 lodges
Women's Clubs: 600 clubs
Woman's Christian Temperance Unions: 400 unions
Daughters of the American Revolution: 75 chapters

TABLE 2.2 (cont.)

Colonial Dames: 100 chapters	
Grand Army of the Republic: 600 posts	
Sons of the American Revolution: 25 chapters	
Ad Men's Clubs: 14 branches	
Rotary Clubs: 14 clubs	Total: 9,630

SOURCE: Ivan L. Pollock, *The Food Administration in Iowa*, vol. 1 (Iowa City
State Historical Society of Iowa, 1923), pp. 188–89.

U.S. history interdenominational cooperation was officially sanctioned and made nationally visible. From this time, Americans could begin to think of the nation in more religiously inclusive terms. Beyond the leading associations of the United War-Work Campaign, moreover, the Boy Scouts helped the Treasury Department to sell liberty bonds.[102] Women's voluntary federations and fraternal groups worked with the Food Administration to ask every home to use less wheat, meat, and other food products needed for export to starving Europe.[103] And the American Federation of Labor cooperated to manage war production.[104] Close to the entire panoply of nation-spanning voluntary federations that had grown up since the Civil War came into play as partners helping the U.S. federal government to fight America's first world war. In the end the federations that worked most closely with national agencies during World War I— including the Red Cross, the YMCA, the Knights of Columbus, the Elks, and the PTA—were the ones most likely to attract members right after the conflict. These groups, in turn, ended up well positioned to withstand economic downturns in the 1920s and 1930s.[105] (An exception was the American Federation of Labor, which gained during

FIGURE 2.3. World War I window poster, from the author's personal collection

the war but lost ground in the 1920s due to severe corporate and federal repression.)

World War I was not good for all voluntary groups, however. Socialist and radical groups suffered during as well as
after the war, as did ethic associations whose identities were
misaligned with wartime enmities and alliances.[106] Unable
to be enthusiastic about a conflict in which the United States
was allied with Ireland's enemy, Great Britain, the Irish
American Ancient Order of Hibernians went into decline in
the World War I era.[107] Previously vibrant German American
associations fared even worse.[108] After Congress convened
hearings to investigate its alleged disloyalty, the German-
American Alliance decided to disband and hand over what
remained in its treasury to the Red Cross.[109] And this was
but the tip of the iceberg. From World War I, the approxi-
mately one-tenth of the U.S. population who were of German
descent mostly switched to non-ethnic-identified groups—or
relabeled long-established associations in ostentatiously
"American" ways. Fraternal groups disallowed long-standing German-language lodges; "German" churches went in-
cognito; and German flags and national colors disappeared
from group emblems.

From nineteenth- into twentieth-century America, in sum,
great wars pulled many Americans into stronger civic com-
mitments. Some groups were marginalized, to be sure,
especially white Southerners after 1860 and German Americans after 1917. On balance, however, both the Civil War
and World War I—the great martial bookends of American
industrialization—invigorated organized civil society. Both
great wars reinforced local and national participation in
large-scale cross-class federated membership associations—
and such federations, in turn, helped to prevent Americans

from dividing into class-segregated associational worlds as the country modernized.

Voluntarism in the Modern U.S. Polity

By the 1920s the United States had become an industrial nation, and the data in figure 2.4 make it clear that some two dozen large-scale membership federations coexisted thereafter, though there was some shrinkage in the ranks of very large associations during the Great Depression of the 1930s. Of course, the exact mix of large U.S. voluntary associations was considerably transformed over time. Some older groups such as the Sons of Temperance and the IOGT and the GAR declined or went out of existence, while other associations were never more than temporary. Some brief-lived associations died after reform crusades, whether abortive (as in the cases of the Knights of Labor and the Colored Farmers' Alliance) or successful (as in the case of the National American Woman Suffrage Association). Other short-lived groups—such as the American Protective Association, the Junior Order of United American Mechanics, and the second Ku Klux Klan—became huge only briefly during periods of heightened ethnic or racial tension. In the final accounting, however, as some massive voluntary federations declined or disappeared, others emerged and grew, including the American Legion and the Veterans of Foreign Wars, the PTA and the General Federation of Women's Clubs, and the Knights of Columbus, the Shriners, the Eagles, the Moose, and the Elks.

Political parties and voluntary federations met somewhat different fates in the early twentieth century. As organizations, U.S. political parties changed in striking ways after

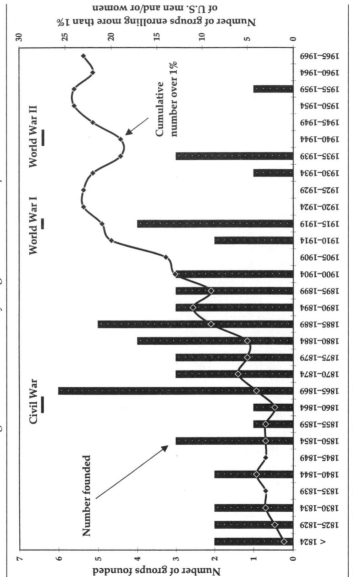

FIGURE 2.4

Foundings and Accumulation of Large U.S. Membership Associations

SOURCE: Civic Engagement Project data

the end of the nineteenth century. Although the Democratic Party acted as an agent of mass mobilization during the 1930s, both the Democrats and the Republicans gradually turned toward more "educational" styles of electoral campaigning.[110] In many states and localities, party organizations gradually withered and stopped organizing and contacting voters at the grass roots. In contrast, civil associations other than political parties remained much more stable as locally rooted federal networks. The basic features of the membership-based federations examined throughout this chapter proved surprisingly persistent—through industrialization and depression, through war and peace—from the early 1800s through the middle of the twentieth century.

As is well known, the New Deal marked a period of heightened electoral mobilization leading to new federal government initiatives to help people and businesses cope with the Great Depression. The Townsend movement flourished at this juncture, demanding new efforts to aid America's elderly. And labor unions (including industrial as well as craft workers) finally gained a major foothold in U.S. civil society during the 1930s and 1940s. Yet the 1930s were stressful for many other voluntary associations, because economic times were so hard for the working and middle-class men and women who paid dues to them. Most voluntary federations experienced membership downturns during the Great Depression, sometimes very sharp declines. But most also revived along with the economy in the late 1930s; and nearly the same panoply of national federations that cooperated with the federal government to fight World War I turned up to cooperate again during World War II. The aftermath of that great conflict brought renewed growth and energy to the nation's voluntary membership federations, larger and smaller ones alike. In his important book, *Bowling Alone*, Putnam goes so far as to present the immediate post–World War II decades as the high point of modern American civic voluntarism, a veritable golden age for the nation of joiners.[111]

Conservatives frequently assert that the growth of "the modern welfare state" crowded out U.S. voluntary efforts, citing as a prime example the diminution of social insurance provision by fraternal groups.[112] But the timing of associational change does not fit this hypothesis, because many major fraternal groups abandoned or marginalized their social insurance programs well before the New Deal of the 1930s; and hundreds of small insurance fraternals died or merged into commercial insurance companies in the 1910s and 1920s.[113] Besides, we cannot just look at voluntary associations as social service providers. Their roles as organized voices for citizens, their political activities, need to be considered as well. Many of America's greatest voluntary membership federations pressed for public social programs in the first place and then prospered by helping government to reach citizens with new benefits and services for millions of people.

In the late 1800s the GAR grew along with generous state and national provisions for Union military veterans and survivors.[114] From the late nineteenth through the mid-twentieth century, the Grange and the AFBF were closely involved with state and federal programs to aid farmers.[115] Independent women's associations—including the WCTU, the General Federation of Women's Clubs, and the National Congress of Mothers—advocated and cooperated to implement local, state, and national public policies to help mothers, children, and families.[116] The Townsend movement pressed for federal benefits for the elderly during the 1930s and 1940s; and more recent associations of retirees have grown along with the resulting public programs.[117] Labor unions needed the U.S. government's help fully to establish themselves—and in turn became champions of New Deal economic and social programs.

A leading fraternal order, the Fraternal Order of Eagles (FOE), championed mothers' pensions in the 1910s and led campaigns for old-age pensions in dozens of states during the 1920s. Indeed, so central was the FOE in the struggle for old-age provision that the Grand Eagle himself was one of the dignitaries given an official pen when President Franklin Roosevelt signed the Social Security bill into law in 1935.[118] And finally, we must never forget that the nation's most generous social program for young workers and families, the G.I. Bill of 1944, was drafted and championed by a vast voluntary membership federation, the American Legion.[119]

From the Civil War through the post–World War II era, voluntary membership associations and the U.S. version of the modern welfare state were thoroughly intertwined. Leading membership federations gained by being associated with bold national efforts that concretely helped millions of citizens. And of course the U.S. Congress and state legislatures responded when widespread voluntary associations mobilized members and chapters to shape public opinion and press for the legislative enactment of inclusive public programs. Civil society and government thus worked hand in hand to fashion and sustain America's version of the modern welfare state, which historically consisted of educational, veterans', and social insurance programs intended to extend opportunity and guarantee a modicum of security to millions of individuals and families. Popular social programs in the United States were never "welfare" handouts for the poor alone. They were inclusive benefits or services, exactly the kinds of government activities likely to be favored by massive voluntary federations that spanned places and bridged classes.

VOLUNTARISM AND DEMOCRATIC GOVERNANCE

This chapter has taken us on a historical whirlwind tour, and we have learned that the true story of American voluntarism is very different from the myth of apolitical localism projected onto the nation's civic past by so many of today's pundits. Most voluntary groups active in American communities from the mid-nineteenth through the mid-twentieth century were more than strictly local entities. Membership associations usually enjoyed a strong local presence, to be sure, yet most emerged and flourished as parts of regional and national federations that were, as Schlesinger suspected, "voluntary bodies of sizable membership, reasonably long duration, and fairly large territorial extent."[120] Deliberately built by civicly ambitious men and women with national vision and power aspirations, membership federations grew with unusual vigor in the wake of the nation's biggest wars, and many of them supported and drew legitimation from their support of expansive—and expensive—public social programs.

Once we get beyond the blinkered thinking of recent times, there is nothing in the findings of this chapter that should really surprise us. As so well understood by wise observers—ranging from Alexis de Tocqueville and James Bryce in the nineteenth century to Arthur Schlesinger Sr. in the 1940s—civic voluntarism in the United States was the creation of citizen-organizers with national ambitions as well as an understanding that the organizations they built needed to put down strong local roots. At once luxuriant and contentious, American civic voluntarism always flourished as a vital part of muscular representative democratic governance—and never was in any sense a substitute for it.

CHAPTER 3

JOINERS, ORGANIZERS, AND CITIZENS

NATIONWIDE MEMBERSHIP FEDERATIONS flourished through much of U.S. history, yet why should we care? It is all well and good to trace the emergence and spread of vast associational networks, but what did voluntary federations mean to the civic organizers who launched and led them; and how did they function for the millions of men and women from various walks of life who joined and sustained them? Equally important are the consequences for U.S. democracy. If classic American voluntarism was (in the words of Arthur Schlesinger) the "greatest school of self-government," how exactly did that work? To bring the civic past more fully to life, this chapter explores how voluntary federations actually worked in the lives of American joiners, organizers, and citizens.

People who died long ago cannot speak with us or respond to pollsters, so we cannot rely on contemporary social science's favorite sources of data to learn why our forebears led and joined associations or to comprehend what participation meant to them. A great deal can nevertheless be learned by combining systematic data from associational records with hints gleaned from the remnants of personal lives. Go into any slightly junky antique store, and you will find the material traces from lifetimes of membership, objects and documents that people kept and treasured and passed to their children. Those traces stayed in families, until one day the grandkids unloaded them, not remembering or caring what they once meant. There are tiny, well-worn booklets spelling out the constitutions, procedures, programs, and ceremonies of associations like the Odd Fellows, the Federated Women's Clubs, the Grand Army of the Republic, and the Independent Order of Good Templars. There are meticulously handwritten log books, documenting minutes, attendance records, and finances, week by week and month by month. There are dog-eared old song books for groups like the Grange and the Woman's Christian Temperance Union, full of hokey lyrics about associational efforts and values.

My favorite artifacts are beautiful ribbon badges, proudly worn for parades and other celebratory occasions—and sometimes worn on a reverse, black and silver side as "In Memoriam" badges commemorating the funeral of a group member. Figure 3.1 shows an 1840s ribbon badge for the Washington Temperance Society, emblazoned with the touching motto: "We bear a patriot's honored name. Our country's welfare is our aim." This figure also shows late-nineteenth- or early-twentieth-century badges for Odd Fellows Lodge Number 412 in Kane, Pennsylvania, and for Division Number 9 of the Ancient Order of Hibernians of Newburyport, Massachusetts. As the illustrations suggest, membership badges could be quite elaborate, decorated with the mottoes and symbols of particular voluntary federations and often festooned with patriotic symbols as well. By the late 1800s ribbon badges usually also included the name, town, state, and number of the local club or lodge, so individuals could simultaneously proclaim their

FIGURE 3.1. Membership badges from the Washington Temperance Society, Odd Fellows, and Ancient Order of Hibernians

affiliation with a nationwide federation and their membership in a specific local chapter. In a dazzling array of colors, sizes, and designs, membership ribbon badges like these belonged to millions of individual club or lodge members—as did ribbons printed for specific conventions and pins and medals presented to current and past officers at the local, state, and national levels. In about 1900, so many ribbon badges were bought and worn by citizens of the "nation of joiners" that big companies—such as the Whitehead and Hoag Company of Newark, New Jersey; the M. C. Lilley Company of Columbus, Ohio; and the B. Pasquale Company of San Francisco, California—specialized in their manufacture, vying to attract the large purchases made by lodges, posts, and clubs across the land.

The sources of evidence I use in this chapter are thus a bit unusual for a political scientist. My data come not only from university libraries and computer disks but also from the dusty archives and basements where associations store their records, from regular bidding in "eBay" on-line auctions of old items, and from my personal travels to antique shops and "paper ephemera" shows all across the country. Unorthodox as my tactics for data-gathering may have been, the resulting evidence allows us many glimpses into what membership and leadership meant in the nation's associational past. We also gain insights into the many ways membership federations contributed to the vitality and drama of American democracy.

THE MEANINGS OF MEMBERSHIP

What was it that people got out of groups like the Grange, the Odd Fellows or the Rebekahs, the Fraternal Order of

Eagles, the (African American) Prince Hall Masons, the American Legion, and the Federation of Women's Clubs? Local chapters linked to these federations met regularly, so people clearly enjoyed the personal interactions. In addition, Americans placed a high value on connections to larger undertakings. Members of America's classic voluntary membership associations could have it both ways: they could strengthen their ties to friends, neighbors, and family members in the local community and at the same express values and an identity shared by large numbers of other people they never met personally. From the broader solidarities even more than from intimate ties, moreover, flowed shared capacities and social clout that mattered enormously for U.S. democracy.

Local and Intimate Solidarities

As social capital theorists might stress, people attended local meetings of federated associations to socialize repeatedly with familiar others. Most of America's large membership associations, especially those founded before the mid-twentieth century, were chapter-based groups whose members met weekly, biweekly, or monthly. Participants usually came from a single town or area of a city, so they often saw one another regularly in other walks of life as well. We should not imagine, however, that all interaction in chapter meetings involved people from geographically circumscribed areas. Because members of nationwide voluntary federations participated in a widely shared identity and were committed to well-institutionalized rules and procedures, travelers could quickly connect with groups meeting in places they visited. A club or lodge might well welcome a visiting brother or sister to its regular meeting. What is more, even regular members could live in wide dispersion around a core area. Sociologists Jason Kaufman and David Weintraub have examined residential addresses for the members of seventeen Knights of Pythias lodges operating in Buffalo, New York, in 1894.[1] Most lodges, they find, included members with out-of-town addresses. Also, depending on the lodge, between one-fifth and one-half of members with Buffalo addresses lived more than a mile from the lodge hall. Buffalo lodges with disproportionately more white-collar Knights were especially likely to have geographically dispersed memberships.

Even lodges in small, noncosmopolitan towns could have surprisingly far-flung memberships. In a mining area of southern West Virginia, for example, nearly two-thirds of the members of the Odd Fellows lodge in Oak Hill were not city residents but from camps and communities in sur-rounding areas.[2] And another striking instance came to my attention when I found handwritten 1890s minutes and attendance records for the Odd Fellows lodge in Greenville, Maine. Today it takes at least forty-five minutes to travel by car over poor roads between Greenville and Jackman; yet more than a century ago, when travel was by horseback, canoe, and train, New England Lodge No. 225 included a full complement of regularly attending officers and members from both Greenville and Jackman. Clearly, the interpersonal ties strengthened by membership in this "local" group reached across vast expanses of water and woods.

Friendships were forged and expressed in local chapter meetings. In the rare instances in which both sexes were members of the same groups, local meetings of voluntary chapters might be one of the few venues where prospective husbands and wives could meet outside of family homes watched by parents. Lodges of the Independent Order of Good Templars opened and closed very frequently over the post–Civil War decades, and some scholars have guessed that new lodges were continually created in thousands of communities by successive cohorts of young men and women who were happy to have a morally proper place to meet.[3] Usually, however, men met with other men and women with other women (although some fraternal groups for females, such as the Rebekahs and the Eastern Star, made provision for male relatives to join as well if they were members of the related fraternal group). The vast majority of clubs and lodges in classic U.S. voluntary federations were primarily focused on the roles and identities of either men or women. Even gender-integrated groups like the IOGT and the Grange recognized distinct gender roles in their rituals and procedures.

Separate gatherings for each gender reinforced solidarities apart from nuclear families, especially for males. When fraternal groups were at their height in the early 1920s, super-joiner husbands could attend a different lodge meeting every night of the week. At the same time, however, many voluntary federations established interlocking complexes of groups built around family roles. Male fraternal lodges, veterans' groups, and union brotherhoods usually had partner groups open to wives, mothers, and sisters. The women practiced similar rituals and celebrated many of the same values and special occasions as their male relatives—and, of course, ladies often provided food and companionship before or after meetings of male-only groups. Voluntary federations also sponsored junior affiliates, making it possible for fathers and mothers to convey norms of membership to sons and daughters. In a few associations, adults and older children actually met together. Perhaps because they appealed to families accustomed to working cooperatively on farms, the Grange and the American Farm Bureau Federation included fathers, mothers, and older children in shared webs of activities. The "farm family" was for all practical purposes the typical membership unit in voluntary federations centered in rural areas.

From fraternal groups and unions to granges and women's clubs, the rituals, values, and programs of classic voluntary federations almost invariably featured—and thus reinforced—differentiated gender roles and family obligations. Female nurturers were supposed to care for the sick and the poor, support their husbands, and guide children. Thus the ritual of induction into the Rebekahs, the female degree of the Odd Fellows, celebrated courageous and family-oriented biblical women such as Esther, Rebekah, Sarah, Miriam, Ruth, and Naomi, holding them up for emulation instead of the "Earth's mightiest" women, such as "Elizabeth, Cleopatra, Catherine, or Isabella[,] . . . who signalized their lives . . . by bloody victories on fields of carnage" or "the charms of personal beauty."[4] Women were certainly not enjoined to be weak, but the definitions of feminine strength and virtue favored by classical American voluntary groups stressed the value of female nurturance and compassion and celebrated women's contributions—not just to their own families but also to the larger social order—through their conscientious activities as wives, mothers, sisters, and daughters. Also praised was hard work at home, and thus the beehive was an emblem frequently used by women's groups on their badges and programs. Celebration of traditional womanly virtues happened across the board, from churches and fraternal orders to independent women's associations such as the WCTU, the General Federation of Women's Clubs, and the National Congress of Mothers and its successor, the PTA, though as time passed, the independent female-led federations increasingly stressed the ideal of "educated motherhood" as the key to the well-being of individual families and the broader society.[5]

Male members of voluntary federations, meanwhile, were enjoined to act as protectors. Again and again, symbolic representations of the medieval "knight" were featured in the rituals of fraternal and veterans' groups. Many groups simply labeled themselves this way, for example, the Knights of Columbus, the Knights of Pythias, the Knights of the Maccabees. Other groups used knighthood imagery in group ceremonies—for the knight, decked out in full medieval armor, was the idealized protector. On the one hand, knighthood invoked the ideal of military service to defend society as a whole. "History tells no more fascinating tale than that of the Knights of the Crusades who were inspired by purely unselfish motives to drive the Turk from the land he had defiled," declares the ritual of the Veterans of Foreign Wars in a section explaining why the group uses the Crusaders' Cross of Malta in its badge and group insignia. "My Comrades," the ritual continues, "the Cross of Malta glorifies the tattered shirt of the poorest working man and beautifies the coat worn by those highest in the land, binding all with the same spirit of comradeship which existed among the veterans of the old crusades."[6] On the other hand, knighthood symbolized virtuous men who, in times of peace as well as war, protected the vulnerable and cared for families. Making this common theme fully explicit, the ribbon badges and insignia of the Knights and Ladies of Security, a midwestern fraternal insurance group, portrayed a fully armored medieval knight standing hand in hand with an American woman in nineteenth-century dress![7] Functioning as modern-day fraternal knights during times of peace, married breadwinners were enjoined to shelter and provide for wives and children.

Indeed, entire fraternal brotherhoods dedicated themselves to honor and succor widows and orphans. Pooling resources in states, even across the nation as a whole, fraternal groups built orphanages to care for children left behind by men who died young. Perhaps the best-known example was Mooseheart, a vast orphanage complex maintained by the Fraternal Order of Moose in Mooseheart, Illinois, which during World War I was also advertised as a haven for war orphans.[8] In addition, local chapters might promise continuing care of a more personal sort. For example, the Masons of Guthrie, Oklahoma, presented an elaborately engraved certificate to Rebecca Smith in October 1900, affirming that she was "the Widow of our late beloved Brother H. L. Smith, who was a Master Mason and Member of our lodge in good standing at the time of his Death. As such, we commend her to the care and protection of the whole Fraternity." Mrs. Smith framed the certificate and hung it on her wall to display her continuing tie to the community of men so meaningful for her late husband.[9]

As this example indicates, associational ties were clearly intended to help members and their families deal with illness and death. Because group assistance could make a big difference for families hurt by the loss of a breadwinner, some scholars believe that classic U.S. voluntary federations were principally about social insurance, more or less formally provided. According to this account, fraternal groups can be understood in cost-benefit terms and flourished only until commercial life insurance came along. It is certainly true that mutual aid to families was a central part of the appeal of all nineteenth-century fraternal groups. And around 1900 hundreds of groups advertised as sources of insurance coverage to breadwinners in return for regular payments of increasingly carefully calculated dues. But many groups—including leading fraternal groups such as the Masons and the Elks—did not stress insurance. Or, like the Knights of Pythias, they eventually decided to segregate insurance provision in optional programs that were fiscally self-contained. In any event, many of the people who joined voluntary membership groups offering insurance benefits spent much more on ritual regalia, social activities, and membership dues than they could ever hope to get back in any emergency. Nor did men abandon fraternal groups right after commercial life insurance and public Social Security became available. Particular fraternal federations declined, of course, but others rose in popularity, and U.S. fraternalism flourished through the first two-thirds of the twentieth century.

Much evidence suggests that the appeal of America's most successful membership federations went far beyond individual economic calculation. Even when insurance groups offered insurance benefits planned in actuarially careful ways, they stressed social and civic purposes as well. In the early twentieth century, a major insurance-oriented fraternal group issued the pamphlet to explain to potential recruits "Why You Should Join the Maccabees." Of thirteen reasons listed, "provision while the member lives to care for those dependent upon him or her when he or she is gone" was placed last. More emphasis was placed on broader moral and patriotic concerns: "Because it is founded upon the principles of good citizenship" such as the "fatherhood of God and brotherhood of man; Loyalty to the flag that protects you; Faithfulness in performance of obligations of the home"; and "Generosity with those less fortunate than yourself."[10] Like other classic membership federations, the Maccabees were rooted in a blend of religious and patriotic ideals meant to appeal to broad solidarities stretching across class lines. The appeal went far beyond individual market calculations, even if the latter were also at work.

Part of Something Bigger

As the Maccabees pamphlet underlines, classic American voluntary federations, including fraternal groups, transcended primary solidarities among family members, neighbors, and friends. The reasons people participated and cared so much went beyond the personal, the familial, and the local, for membership in translocal federations offered connections to—and organizational routes into—broader social and political movements. The genius of classic American associational life was that joining something small connected members of local chapters to much grander organized endeavors.

Local bonds and participation in larger collectivities felt mutually reinforcing to members of classic federations. The seamless blend is nicely captured in the lyrics of "Long Live the Grange," which was song number 20 in *The Patron's Pride*. My dog-eared copy of this widely disseminated publication once belonged to a local grange in Machias, Maine.[11] "The work within the Grange our social bonds unite," sang the men and women of Machias Valley

Grange No. 360. "Its teachings ever pure/Will selfish bonds unbind. . . . May sweetest joys abound/Within this hall so grand." Face-to-face social capital was certainly celebrated here. Yet there was something more, as the Machias grangers called for the "joys" and "thoughts" of their politically engaged movement to "spread throughout the land." "May we united stand/In cause we know is just;/Go bravely forward hand in hand/And put in God our trust." As was true in this instance, Americans avidly joined chapters of widespread voluntary associations that they knew were simultaneously engaging the loyalty and energy of many thousands of others "spread throughout the land." People exulted in their sense of belonging to larger brotherhoods and sisterhoods. We know this not just from qualitative evidence but also because very large membership federations tended to persist and flourish more effectively than their smaller competitors, which often fizzled after they failed to attain a major regional or national presence.[12]

Lodge or club magazines and minutes books reveal that federation members paid attention to group doings at extralocal as well as local levels. Federation leaderships orchestrated visits back and forth among sister or brother chapters; and much excitement accompanied the sending of delegations from local chapters to attend district meetings, annual state conventions, and yearly or biannual national conventions. Membership dues were used to subsidize travel, so that even officers and representatives without great personal means could afford to go to the higher-level meetings. For months in advance, newsletters or association magazines covered the buildup to such gatherings. At the conventions themselves, Americans from various parts of states or parts of the country met one another, learned about the other people's homes, and exchanged ideas about group and civic affairs. After conventions were over, officers and delegates returned home to regale everyone with stories about the city where the meeting was held and tell what happened—what ideas were discussed and what decisions made. Local leaders and chapters were inspired and reinvigorated.

Interpersonal ties between local areas were formed at higher-level federation meetings, because delegates who met one another could keep in touch across considerable distances. "This is my Grange," Mrs. Mildred Hazelton of West Paris, Maine, wrote on a photo postcard showing her local grange hall sent in 1955 to Mrs. Ethel Jackson in Belfast, Maine, well over a hundred miles away. The rest of the message makes it clear that these were two family women, both incumbents of the office of Lecturer in their local granges. They met at a Maine Grange conference and were looking forward to the possibility of meeting again at a regional gathering: "I have intended to write before but been pretty busy with 2 weddings in the family. . . . We had a good time at lecturer Conf. Didn't we[?] I hope I can go the N. England [Lecturers' Conference]. . . . Write when you can."[13]

Constant rounds of meetings beyond the local level did much to build and sustain voluntary associations. Around the turn of the twentieth century, for instance, a movement called Christian Endeavor spread rapidly. Like so many classic federations, the Society of Christian Endeavor was rooted in thousands of local groups—in this case, linked to Protestant church congregations. Yet the society also staged regular district meetings and had state, national, and international institutions that convened recurrent conventions.

As Christian Endeavor's founder and president, Reverend Francis E. Clark explained, extralocal union brought "suggestions, inspiration, and fellowship":

> IN THEIR SUGGESTIONS.—"If the members of the local society never look or go beyond themselves, they are in danger of growing short-sighted, narrow in their conception of duty and privilege, formal and routine in their "endeavor," and are liable to languish if not die of discouragement.

> IN INSPIRATION.—"Bring together three or five hundred young Christians in a Local Union [district] meeting and from one to three thousand at a State convention; let them look into each other's faces; let them warmly grasp each other's hands; let their voices unite in song; let them hear each other pray; let them report the Lord's doing with them in their several societies and churches; let them listen to personal testimony; above all, let them bow in humble confession and consecration; and the *inspiration is untold*. Those who are present usually go back to their local societies and churches quickened and equipped for aggressive Christian work.

> IN FELLOWSHIP.—"Young Christians, especially, need this. Living in comparative isolation, as many of them do, working in their own local field, which is often, as they feel, limited and little hopeful, the danger is that they will become lonely and disheartened. Bring them into contact with fellow-Christians of their own age and "endeavor"; they will see that a common bond of sympathy unites them."[14]

Reverend Clark explained the functions of federation in the language of his association's religious purpose, yet his rationale nicely captures what members and leaders of many kinds of classic voluntary federations understood so well: Local intimacy might be comforting, but it was equally important—and much more stimulating!—to be part of something bigger.

ORGANIZERS RECRUITING ORGANIZERS

Most local voluntary membership groups in nineteenth- and early-twentieth-century America would never have come into existence in the first place had they not embodied translocal worldviews and identities and had they not promised local people access to broader, outward-looking social ties. We know this because data on the chronological development of U.S. associations shows that national leaderships and supralocal representative institutions usually were established first. In major U.S. voluntary federations, national associational centers, usually supplemented by state or regional bodies, were established *before* most local chapters were founded and existed before the buildup of large individual memberships. Figure 3.2 displays such patterns of development for four important associations with varied origins. The Independent Order of Odd Fellows was America's second-largest fraternal group, which started as a local offshoot of a British order and then became a U.S. federation that spread across the nation before the Civil War. The Knights of Pythias, which became the third-largest U.S. fraternal group, was launched as a national project in 1864. The Knights of Columbus became the nation's largest Catholic voluntary association within decades after its start in 1883 as a local New Haven, Connecticut, group. Founded in 1890 as a combination of city groups, the General Federation of Women's Clubs evolved into of one of

FIGURE 3.2

*The Spread of State Organizations and Growth of Local Chapters and Individual
Membership in Four Major U.S. Voluntary Federations*

(a) Independent Order of Odd Fellows, 1819–1940

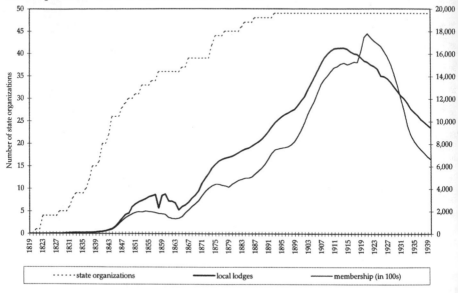

(b) Knights of Pythias, 1864–1940

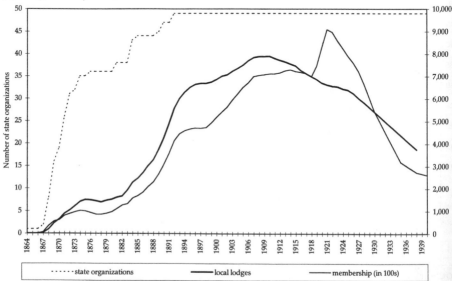

Knights of Columbus, 1882–1940

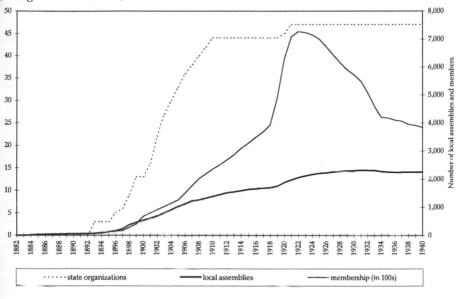

- - - - - state organizations — local assemblies — membership (in 100s)

General Federation of Womens Clubs, 1890–1940

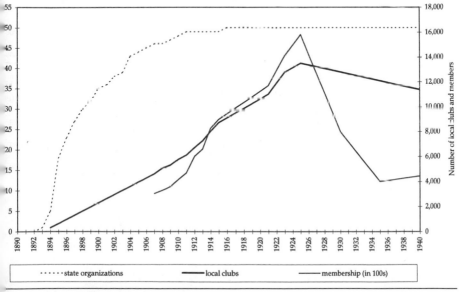

- - - - - state organizations — local clubs — membership (in 100s)

SOURCE: Civic Engagement Project data

America's largest and most important independent women's associations. Despite their diverse origins, constituencies, and purposes, all of these federations established national centers and spread state-level associational units well ahead of most local chapter formation and individual membership growth. Nor are these atypical instances; similar graphs could be presented for most of the great voluntary federations that grew up between the mid-nineteenth and mid-twentieth century.[15]

Here is how the process of building a national U.S. voluntary federation regularly worked. First, leaders came together to launch a national organizing effort. This might happen for a brand-new nationally ambitious federation, as when temperance women assembled in Cleveland in 1874 to proclaim plans for the Woman's Christian Temperance Union. Or it might happen when formerly local-minded leaders proclaimed new plans to spread their organization, as happened in the Knights of Columbus by the 1890s. Either way, ambitious national organizers fanned out over the country, contacting a dispersed network of other potential leaders. Federation builders encouraged the creation of local units in each state and then handed the job of membership organizing to native state leaderships elected by the earliest few local chapters. Vast interlocking networks of leader-organizers were thus quickly put into place; and thereafter each state leadership could be depended on to compete with leaderships in other states to see who could recruit the most new members and found and sustain the most new local chapters. In much of political science, from James Madison through Theodore Lowi, U.S. federalism is portrayed as a cumbersome institutional system designed to frustrate sudden or concerted action.[16] But that is not the way federalism worked in the historical construction of many U.S. voluntary associations. Instead, federalism made it easier for national, state, and local organizers to work together to spread voluntary chapters into every nook and cranny of the United States. National purpose could be coordinated with local variety. What is more, federalism encouraged a process of what I call "competitive emulation," in which people from one state vied with those in other states to see who could do a better and faster job of spreading the shared associational undertaking. Could the women from Illinois build the WCTU faster than the women from Michigan? Could the men from Missouri spread the Knights of Pythias faster than the men from Arkansas? And so forth. Competition encouraged the spread of similar, interconnected, chapters, so that a federation could span the country in a remarkably short time.

From the vantage point of regular Americans—who not only lived in communities across the nation but also migrated and traveled widely—higher-level national and state leaders devoted to spreading voluntary federations could provide significant assistance in forming and sustaining emergent "local" chapters. Each of the following excerpts from primary testimony reveals notable feats of local collective action by Americans on the move who were encouraged by the national and state organizations and translocal networks of leaders that were characteristic of classic U.S. voluntary federations.

From the history of the Independent Order of Odd Fellows:

The first Odd Fellows' lodge established in the Western Mississippi valley was Travellers' Rest Lodge, No. 1, in the city of St. Louis, for which a charter was granted by the Grand Lodge of the United States on the 18th of August, 1834. . . . St. Louis was then an insignificant frontier town, with about 7000 inhabitants. There were seven petitioners for this lodge "made up" of transient members then in and about the city: one from England; two from Kentucky; three from Pennsylvania; and one from Maryland. By the time the lodge was instituted all but one of the original signers of the petition had disappeared and others had to be substituted. . . . Samuel Miller of Harmony Lodge, No. 3, of Baltimore, who was about to remove to Alton, Illinois, was commissioned [by the U.S. Grand Lodge in Maryland] to institute the lodge. . . . At the close of the first year the lodge had 115 members.[17]

From the history of the Knights of Pythias:

Being an account of the introduction of the Order of Knights of Pythias in the Grand Domain of Minnesota by . . . David Royal who has been a continuous member of Minneapolis Lodge No. 1 for 27 years. In November 1868 I joined Wilmington Lodge No. 2 Wilmington Delaware. In the spring of '69 I arrived in this City [Minneapolis] and shortly after was employed as a car builder for the C.M.& St. Paul Railways at their Shops in this City. In the winter of '69–70 I talked up Pythianism among the workmen and soon had a list of 13 names. I opened up correspondence with Supreme Chancelor Read [of New Jersey] who sent me some Blank applications for a dispensation [to open a lodge] and full instructions how to procede. About the first of June I received a letter from Supreme Chancelor Read stating that Bro[ther]

Jacob H. Heisser of Marrion Lodge No. 1 of Indianapolis Ind had recently arrived in Minneapolis and had also written him about starting a Lodge. I was requested to drop Bro Heisser a line through the Post office and unite our efforts which request was complied with. . . .

Saturday evening June 25 1870 a preliminary meeting was called [to apply for a charter]. . . . I was chosen President and Bro Heisser [who had recruited two potential members was chosen] Secretary. . . . Supreme Chancelor Read arrived July 9th 1870. . . . At Odd Fellows Hall Minneapolis Minn July 11 1870 agreeable to a call of the Supreme Chancelor of the Knights of Pythias Samuel Read of New Jersey a number of Knights and Citizens of Minneapolis and vicinity assembled for the purpose of organizing a Lodge of the Order.[18]

From the history of the Knights of Columbus:

The call to Columbianism [i.e., organization as part of the Knights of Columbus] had already been heard from the great Middle West, and National Organizer Cummings was sent to Chicago to answer the call. . . . On July 10, 1896, Chicago Council No. 182 was instituted by State Deputy Delaney, of New York. Thomas S. Kernan was the first Grand Knight to hold office in Illinois, and the character of membership in this first Mid-West Council is indicated by the fact that the first thirty councils in Illinois had Grand Knights chosen from among the members of the Chicago Council. On March 19, 1899, a council was instituted in Springfield, the capital of Illinois, and from thenceforward, at brief intervals, new councils were established throughout the state.

[Illinois] State Deputy P. L. McArdle . . . presided at most of
the ceremonies . . . [and then] introduced Columbianism
into the neighboring state of Missouri.[19]

From the history of the General Federation of Women's Clubs:

There are now [in the 1890s] seventy [women's] clubs in the
Nebraska State Federation, and applications for membership constantly arriving. . . . To fully understand what state
federation has done, it is well to consider that more than
two-thirds of the clubs now auxiliary to it were coexistent
with it, and would never have been formed at all but for the
permanence of organization and the wider range of thought
which union with it and the [national-level] General Federation promised. In one town of about fifteen hundred inhabitants there had been no literary organization of any kind for
ten years previous to this movement. The same is true for
many other towns on these prairies, each with its quotient of
intelligent, well-educated people, transplanted from the cul-
tured atmosphere of the older States, who had become dis-
couraged by the difficulties of their environment, but who
are now developing State pride, and are enthusiastically
alive to all the privileges of federated clubs.[20]

As these testimonies illustrate, representatively governed national and state voluntary institutions helped the
modernizing United States to become a nation of associational organizers as well as joiners. Supralocal centers provided resources and created incentives for the leaders of
voluntary federations to reach out and help to establish new
local units. Nationally standardized and shared institutional models also made it possible for every associational

member to become an organizer, should the need or opportunity arise—as it did, for example, for David Royal and Jacob Heisser after they separately migrated to Minneapolis. By making it easier for Americans to "combine" *even when they did not know one another personally*, supralocal institutions furthered associational vitality in an expanding and mobile nation. Scattered local groups bubbling up sporadically and informally from below could never have achieved the same widespread and stable civic results. Ultimately, voluntary groups in the smallest American communities were even more likely than those in larger cities to be chapters within regional or nation-spanning federations.[21] This made sense, because associational organizers and elected leaders tried to spread their federations' networks into even very small places and because Americans—who were highly mobile geographically—wanted to join or help to found familiar groups near homes or work. In the apt words of the above-quoted 1890s report from the Nebraska State Federation of Women's Clubs, federated chapters linked their participants to "the permanence of organization and wider range of thought . . . promised" by "union with" representative state and national centers of federation activity.

Classic American voluntary associations were *not*, therefore, expressions of small-is-beautiful localism. On the contrary, multiply tiered national federations were the key institutional supports of American voluntarism because they simultaneously sustained intimate solidarities and facilitated connections to wider worlds. Viewed dynamically, U.S. voluntary membership federations were nationally ramified networks of membership organizers recruiting other membership organizers. That is how civic leadership was understood and functioned through much of the nation's history.

For most of America's history, civic leadership was about drawing fellow citizens in to shared endeavors and helping many local groups to sustain themselves within a common institutional and cultural framework.

PATHWAYS TO DEMOCRATIC CITIZENSHIP

Voluntary membership federations may have simultaneously reinforced intimate connections and linked local people to broader movements, but how did they contribute to U.S. democracy? At first glance, much of classic American voluntarism may seem focused on religious morality rather than democratic politics. Attempting to include Jews along with Christians, some membership federations stressed classical Greco-Roman myths and generalized Enlightenment or biblical morality. Yet explicitly Christian orientations were also very common—as for Protestant-inspired groups such as Christian Endeavor and the Woman's Christian Temperance Union and Catholic-linked associations such as the Ancient Order of Hibernians and the Knights of Columbus. Even if not directly linked to churches or religious movements, moreover, almost all of America's classic membership federations resembled the American Legion in loudly proclaiming themselves to be "For God and Country."

Yet the Legion's motto reminds us that unabashed patriotism was central to the rituals and ceremonies of classic membership federations. To cite a typical example, ceremonies to open a Grange meeting start with the opening of a Bible prominently displayed on an altar in the center of the hall, followed by collective recitation of the Pledge of Allegiance as the U.S. flag is ceremonially unfurled next to the Bible. Historically, patriotic loyalties were invoked as a matter of course by fraternal groups, women's auxiliaries, independent women's groups, unions, recreational groups, and church-linked associations. "The heart, the mind, the soul and the sinews of America are the Eagles' incomparable heritage," declared a 1948 article about the first half century of the Fraternal Order of Eagles, making a comment that could be repeated about virtually all of the nation's historically important membership associations. "The Eagles are American democracy. They seek no part of anything else."

In chapter 2 we learned that U.S. federated voluntary associations emerged before the Civil War in tandem with competitive, mass-mobilizing political parties. After the Civil War extraordinary numbers of new voluntary federations were launched during an era when voter mobilization reached its peak. And between the 1870s and the mid-twentieth century voluntary federations flourished in close relationship to the institutions and activities of U.S. representative government. Now we can examine more concretely what the interlacing of government, politics, and civic voluntarism meant for Americans as citizens of a democratic republic. In myriad ways—ranging from practices of politically relevant socialization used by virtually all groups to deliberate political steps undertaken by more than half of the historically large associations—membership federations forged myriad pathways into active citizenship for Americans of many backgrounds.

Citizenship Skills and Leadership Opportunities

Inside the clubs or lodges or posts of America's vast voluntary federations, millions of people learned about group operations and collective debate and decision making. Most basically, members became familiar with the "constitutional rules" that governed their association. Local chapters printed up copies of constitutions and by-laws so every member could have a copy to carry and consult. These booklets were usually plain and functional but occasionally as ornate as the 1854 booklet from Olive Branch Division No. 67 of the Sons of Temperance in New York, whose cover and first page are reproduced in figure 3.3.

Because mimicry of U.S. rules of taxpaying and representative governance was so central to group procedures, what association members learned was also relevant to what they needed to know as U.S. citizens. "Let a Neighbor attend his Camp regularly," explained *The Woodman's Hand Book*, put out in 1894 by the massive Modern Woodmen of America, "and he will become better qualified to discharge his duties as a citizen of the republic," for "the proceedings of a Camp are conducted in conformity with the rules prescribed for the deliberation of congress, and familiarity with the affairs of a Camp qualifies a man for any public business."[22]

Not just by precept but in practice, members and officers of voluntary federations were tutored in the organizational skills they would need to participate effectively in democratic politics. "Very few Americans are unconnected with some fraternity, and in these societies they are subject to a discipline" that "prepares them for a wider field of action."[23] Parliamentary procedures, formalized in Roberts Rules of Order, were standard fare, routinely taught and used in lodge proceedings—and also in women's club gatherings and union meetings. Likewise, many groups took pains to teach norms of participatory discussion. Consider, for example, the pledge made by young men and women when they

CONSTITUTION.

To maintain uniformity, the National Division of the United States ordain the following Constitution for the government of Subordinate Divisions, at the same time empowering them to make such By-Laws as do not contravene it or the Rules of the Order.

PREAMBLE.

We whose names are annexed, desirous of forming a society to shield us from the evils of intemperance, afford mutual assistance in case of sickness, and elevate our characters as men, do pledge ourselves to be governed by the following Constitution and By-Laws.

CONSTITUTION.

ARTICLE I.—*Name.*

This Association shall be known as OLIVE BRANCH DIVISION, No. 67, OF THE SONS OF TEMPERANCE, of the State of New York.

CONSTITUTION AND BY-LAWS OF OLIVE BRANCH DIVISION, No. 67, SONS OF TEMPERANCE, OF THE STATE OF NEW-YORK.

FIGURE 3.3. 1854 Constitution from a Local Division of the Sons of Temperance, from the author's personal collection

joined local unions of the Christian Endeavor movement, which enjoined democratic participation along with individual righteousness. "As an Active member," declared the pledge, "I promise to be true to all my duties, to be present at and take some part, aside from singing, in every meeting unless hindered by some reason I can conscientiously give to my Lord and Master, Jesus Christ."[24] Along similar lines, fraternal lodge constitutions listed detailed "rules of order" to guide behavior in group deliberations, such as the rule typical for Odd Fellows lodges declaring that "a member shall not speak more than once on the same subject or question, until all the members wishing to speak shall have had an opportunity to do so."[25] "The spirit of good-will diffused throughout a Camp," observed *The Woodman's Hand Book*, "encourages a Neighbor to take part in its proceedings. If he makes a mistake, he is not laughed at, and he is not afraid to try again. Many an awkward, blundering Neighbor has been drilled into a graceful, prompt, and adroit debater."[26]

Writing in 1850, Frederick A. Fickardt celebrated the Sons of Temperance as an "educational organization" well suited to a democratic republic. Colleges were open only to the few, he pointed out, but in the weekly meetings of some five thousand "divisions" of the Sons of Temperance, a quarter of a million men attended a democratically open "school for popular debate and eloquence":

> Its spirit . . . is uncompromisingly *republican*. Before it, ages and outward conditions are fraternised and equal. Within it, wealth has no influence, station no prestige, nor professional any privilege. . . . Each individual is assured of the just respect of his fellows. . . . Before a band of brothers who look

indulgently and encouragingly on every true effort, young
speakers do not long hesitate to take the floor in support or
defense of the positions they may assume. . . . Thus in a time,
often surprisingly short, young speakers obtain a footing on
the rungs of the ladder that leads to the higher exertions and
rewards. . . . They . . . gain collectedness, promptness, and
that enviable faculty of the right debater and orator, that
"conditio sine qua non," with the American people, the
power of "thinking whilst on their feet," and speaking their
thoughts firmly whilst looking in the eyes of their audience.[27]

"Accordingly," Fickardt concluded, "*our* young men . . . go
out into the general field prepared to do themselves, and
whatever cause they may espouse, full and honorable justice. . . . It is indeed gratifying to observe this elevating
influence so widely and universally diffused. It is not that
the Order of Sons of Temperance is a school for the few—
but that it exalts the *many* that makes it admirable. . . . This
self-education of citizens . . . is beyond price" and makes
the order "a proud means of good, and *a blessing to the
country.*"[28]

By pointing to the ways in which the Sons of Temperance prepared large numbers of men for effective democratic engagement, Fickardt in fact identified features that
long remained true of organized civic voluntarism in the
United States. From the 1800s to the mid-twentieth century, ordinary Americans going to the grange, the lodge, or
a women's club meeting gained the kinds of organizational
skills that today non-higher-educated people may be able
to learn only in church-related small groups if at all.[29] In the
past there were many participatory venues open to average
Americans, where men or women of various backgrounds

could learn skills of expression and organization relevant to civic and political life more generally.

Capacities for representative, majoritarian leadership, as well as politically relevant personal political capacities, were honed by voluntary federations. In the local chapters of most membership federations, new sets of officers and committee members were elected and appointed at least once a year, sometimes as often as every three months. Of necessity, rotating leaders learned how to run meetings, keep record books, make speeches, and organize events. After local officers were elected, moreover, they were often installed in solemn ceremonies. The precise duties of each office were carefully spelled out in such rituals, the repetition of which must have served to teach countless numbers of Americans what it meant to be a presiding officer, a secretary, a treasurer, an elected chaplain, a representative of a local group to a higher representative body, and so forth. The solemnity of official responsibility was hammered home, for installation ceremonies invariably stressed that the new officers must conscientiously learn their duties and set aside selfish, individualistic urges in order to redeem the trust placed in them. "You are now entrusted with the well-being and moral reputation of the Household," declared the ritual "Charge" to new officers in the African American Household of Ruth, "and you should have a thorough knowledge of the laws and usages by which it is governed. . . . [I]t would be a breach of honor to abuse the confidence and respect shown toward you by those who have elected you; we trust therefore that you will perform your duties conscientiously, and that at the expiration of your term of office, the Inmates [i.e., members of the local chapter] may feel that they were right in their choice."[30] Officer positions were frankly understood to be status attainments and stepping-stones to higher office. "You[,] . . . no doubt, hope at some future period to merit a higher distinction," acknowledged the "Charge" of the Household of Ruth.[31] Yet the inviolability of the collective trust was stressed at the same time, and the new officer was implicitly warned that she would not move up if she misbehaved in her current position.

In 1892 Walter B. Hill wrote a piece for the *Century Magazine* purporting to explain to a foreign friend how the United States could function smoothly when "it is the birthright of every American boy to have the chance to be President, and of every girl . . . to be the President's wife," yet "positions of political distinction are relatively very few compared to the vast multitude of possible aspirants."[32] The answer, Hill explained, lay in the organization of millions of ordinary Americans "into social, business, religious, and other associations, all of them elaborately officered." "Take a city directory," he suggested, "and examine the list of organizations. . . . [Y]ou will see ample provision for the local ambitions of all the inhabitants. . . . But mere local precedence does not satisfy the more aspiring minds; hence, nearly all of the thousand and one Societies have State and national organizations" with "an enormous supply of official positions . . . commensurate in territorial magnitude with our great country." "Here then we have the great American safety-valve—we are a nation of presidents."

Hill was exaggerating for humorous purposes, of course, but he also had a point. Federated voluntary associations—especially those with three tiers—had enormously proliferated officer ladders. Each local club or lodge usually elected and appointed a complement of eight to twelve or more officers and committee chairs each year. Members could start small and move up. After successfully serving as the head of the local unit, one could work one's way up the ladder of state offices and, with enthusiastic support from ones local and state colleagues, perhaps get onto the national ladder as well. National leaders, invariably, knew what it was like to run local affairs and win the respect—and votes— of constituents. They were thoroughly grounded in the workings of a democratic civil society.

Modern pundits have tended to pooh-pooh the democratic credentials of classic voluntary federations on the grounds that officer positions were often held by business or professional men, or their wives. To be sure, elite men and women were frequently elected to officer positions, not just in local clubs and lodges, but especially at the state and national levels. Still, many lowly clerks and farmers and skilled workers, or their wives, also attained leadership posts. This was especially true for local posts—which led to subsidized opportunities to attend higher-level associational meetings and perhaps to opportunities to serve in state or national offices. Some clubs and lodges were overwhelmingly blue collar, so their officers routinely came from humble backgrounds. Yet even in mixed-class chapters, a person of lesser occupational status could work his or her way up the ladder, all the way to the top.

To investigate whether Arthur Schlesinger was correct to declare U.S. voluntarism a "school for democracy," political scientist Douglas Rae has investigated the occupational backgrounds of the officers of all sorts of voluntary groups, except for churches, in the city of New Haven, Connecticut, in 1913.[33] At this time locally present voluntary groups— including a preponderance of chapter-based federated associations—were close to their per capita peak, so Rae's study gives us important clues about patterns of associational leadership throughout classic civic America. Of 334 New Haven associations, 28 groups, or percent, were headed by men who were heads of companies. Only slightly more than one-half of 1 percent of the New Haven population at that time were presidents of business firms; consequently, such "potentates at work," as Rae dubs them, were over-represented among associational heads. But most of these businessmen officers headed "upscale clubs" and "heavily capitalized public charities," while "only four ordinary fraternal or sororal organizations" had "top business leadership at the helm."

"By the wildest stretch of the evidence," Rae writes, "one could not make out a case for business and the learned professions heading up anything much beyond a fifth of the organizations constituting the civic fauna" of New Haven in 1913. Although there were some ambiguous cases, Rae finds that slightly more than one-third of New Haven's associations were clearly "headed by people in working class jobs," and another third were led by white-collar employees, most of whom were not "figures of great authority during the workweek." According to Rae, even allowing for incomplete data that might shift these percentages somewhat, "we can conclude with complete certainty that a *major ity of all civic organizations were headed by regular folks for whom high office was not the routine expectation in life.*" Schlesinger was "broadly correct about the operation of civic life," Rae concludes. "This analysis certainly confirms the broad reach of civic life in this period, and understates it by ignoring the thousands of less visible tasks being performed by committees, and by lesser officials of civic organizations."

Elites in Cross-Class Voluntary Groups

Were we to investigate the occupational backgrounds and educational credentials of national-level and state-level officers in voluntary federations, we would no doubt find much more overrepresentation of the privileged than occurred in the leadership of local chapters such as those Rae examined in New Haven. But, I would argue, even when men or women of relatively high social status served as officers popularly rooted voluntary federations had a democratizing impact by encouraging a style of civic leadership oriented toward fellowship and the recruitment of fully participating members from various walks of life. Federations were special in that they encouraged two-way linkages between members and leaders and rewarded leaders for organizing other persons of good character regardless of occupation. Here we come to the heart of the difference these translocally organized associations made for U.S. democracy. In part, local-state-national federations constituted mobility ladders with rungs reaching down to the modest reaches of society. At the same time—and perhaps more tellingly—these associations required leaders and would-be leaders, no matter how privileged in the larger society, to interact with a wide range of their fellow citizens.

Although the local lodges, posts, and clubs of America's largest voluntary federations varied in social composition depending on where each chapter happened to be located and who joined at various times, virtually all chapters included men or women of different occupational and class backgrounds. Evidence to this effect is entirely consistent, whether it comes from scholarly studies or from assorted old lodge or post rosters I have found that happen to list members' occupations.[34] "We have among us merchants and mechanics, employers and employees, men of wealth as well as men of modest means," explained a brief description of Baltimore Lodge No. 70 of the Loyal Order of Moose published in 1918. "All are alike and equal in the precincts of a Moose lodge, the only difference existing being in the endeavor to excel in carrying out the fundamental principles of the Order."[35]

That high-status Americans were historically very likely to participate in voluntary federations, which also included people from humbler occupational backgrounds, had important democratic consequences. "As I looked over this audience tonight," William Jennings Bryan explained in a speech he gave in Lincoln, Nebraska, on May 6, 1903, to the Modern Woodmen of America, of which he was a member, "I could not help thinking of the representative character of the men here assembled. . . . [I]n the camp we learn that worth does not depend upon the amount of money a man has, that it does not depend upon the degrees he receives from college, that it does not depend on his pedigree or the distinction of his ancestors. We learn in the camp . . . to measure men by the manner in which they discharge the duties of citizenship, and this fraternity and fraternities like it have been doing a wonderful work, not only here, but everywhere, in bringing the people together and making them know each other."[36]

Scholars often presume that higher-status people exert "social control" over others when they participate in and lead organizations. But we should not lose sight of the value of ongoing interactions between people of various statuses and socioeconomic backgrounds, especially in settings like churches and voluntary membership groups where there is presumption of shared citizenship and sisterhood or brotherhood. The ceremonies and rituals of veterans' and fraternal groups, women's associations, temperance groups, and many other associations celebrated American citizenship and brotherhood or sisterhood under God. Lest we think these messages silly or hypocritical, we might want to reflect on how rarely they are heard nowadays as part of associational or institutional routines, except in religious congregations. Part of the reason that early-twentieth-first-century U.S. politicians make such a big fuss about religion—especially during presidential election campaigns—is that there are virtually no other associational spheres in which people of various class backgrounds participate together. Brotherhood, sisterhood, and fellow citizenship used to be more variously embodied in an array of interlocking associations, some religious and others bridging religious denominations. Today fellowship groups other than religious congregations have atrophied or disappeared—and certainly are no longer fashionable among American elites.

Read biographical sketches of prominent men and women of the past—businesspeople, politicians, professionals, prominent wives, society figures, and so forth—and you will see proudly proclaimed memberships and officerships in a wide array of the same fraternal, veterans', women's, and civic associations that also involved millions of nonelite citizens. In the past prominent institutional leaders considered active participation in the Masons, the Odd Fellows, the Grange, the WCTU, and the General Federation of Women's Clubs, the Elks, and the major veterans' groups a vital part of successful lives—or, for Catholics, it was the Ancient Order of Hibernians, the Knights of Columbus, and the Catholic Total Abstinence Union. High-status men and women worked their way up local-state-national leadership ladders, interacting with other members in the process. What is more, because enrollment numbers and group meetings mattered in all the classic voluntary associations, those who were leaders—or who wanted to use officerships in these groups to symbolize or validate broader societal leadership—had to care about inspiring large numbers of fellow members. Members counted; and leaders had to mobilize and interact with others from a wide range of backgrounds, or they were not successful. To get ahead within associations, ambitious men and women had to express and act on values and activities shared with people of diverse occupational backgrounds.

Involvements in cross-class membership federations also contributed to U.S. electoral campaigns and helped democratic politicians to legitimate their aspirations for governmental leadership. The reasons were both reputational and organizational. Reputationally, actual or aspiring elected officials used associational ties to proclaim democratic sentiments and moral rectitude. Like many U.S. presidents and congressmen of his era, President Warren Harding made a public show of his fraternal memberships.[37] When he joined the Loyal Order of Moose while in office, he "was inducted into the order by his own chauffeur, an arrangement designed to underline the democratic principles of the order"—and, of course, the democratic propensities of Harding as well.[38] Similarly, when Anton Cermak ran for mayor of Chicago in the 1930s, he distributed "A. J. Cermak for Mayor" tokens to potential supporters, each engraved on the back with the names of the fraternal lodges of which he was a member: Medinah Temple of the Shriners;

Lawndale Lodge No. 995 of the Masons; Chicago Elks Lodge No. 4; and Odd Fellows Lodge No. 5. No doubt Cermak hoped that fellow Shriners, Masons, Elks, and Odd Fellows would vote for him; but he also proclaimed his memberships as a badge of honor, so the entire electorate could see his involvement with groups well known for uniting men of good character across occupational lines.

Organizationally, associational networks helped people aspiring to public office in the earliest stages of their campaigns. It should come as no surprise that Irish machine politicos, such as Mayor Michael Curley of Boston, launched their campaigns with endorsements from the Ancient Order of Hibernians.[39] Ethnic fraternal groups played similar roles in vetting politicians from other hyphenated-American backgrounds. Yet elite, WASP, reformist politicians could also make good use of federated fraternal networks. Franklin Delano Roosevelt's political manager, Jim Farley, used his active participation in the Benevolent and Protective Order of Elks to "judge political sentiment" for FDR's possible run for the presidency, first in travels around New York State, and then on a trip out West, when the 1931 Elks national convention happened to be held in Seattle, Washington.[40] Likewise, one of America's earliest female reform politicians, Senator Margaret Chase Smith of Maine, built her civic reputation through participation in women's groups and ran for office with the support of the Woman's Christian Temperance Union, the Daughters of the American Revolution, and the Maine Federation of Business and Professional Women.[41] Leadership in voluntary membership federations not only helped a man or woman to gain the skills and reputation to run for elected public office. It also required a person to travel around and thus led to the development of geographically widespread contacts. In the civic world patterned by classic American membership federations, an associational leader necessarily participated in and helped to build extensive interpersonal networks not confined to particular occupational or social circles. Later these networks could be used to assess electoral prospects, disseminate political messages, and mobilize popular campaign support.

Fostering Citizenship and Civic Virtues

Moving from organizational side effects to more substantive impacts on democracy, we can start with ways in which membership federations inculcated the core values underpinning republican citizenship. In their rituals and programs virtually all voluntary federations stressed basic values of charity, community, and good citizenship. To be sure, only a minority of the federations were overtly politically partisan in the Democrat versus Republican sense. But all celebrated "American" identity, republican governance, and service to the nation. "Our Order is no political association," declared the author of the *Odd-Fellows Textbook*, first published in the 1840s, but "[w]e are bound by our obligations to perform all the duties which can be required of good citizens; and a violation of any of those laws, if proven against a member of our Fraternity, will subject him to immediate expulsion from our Society."[42] On the positive side, members who loyally served community and country were honored—especially those who served in the military. Every lodge and grange and club hall had wall hangings for each major war, with blue stars to symbolize members on active military duty and gold stars to memorialize individuals who died while serving.

But didn't ethnocultural barriers negate many of these civic effects? As we learned in chapter 2, much association building in the United States in the late nineteenth and early twentieth century arose from ethnic antagonisms and proceeded in furrows worn by religion and race. We might conclude, therefore, that any democratizing impact of voluntary federations—any espousal of the virtues of good citizenship—was counteracted by intolerant and exclusionary messages. Whites refused to meet with African Americans; Protestants and Catholics organized to struggle against one another; and ethnic groups were often at loggerheads even within the broad ranks of Protestants, or Catholics, or Jews.

Ethnocultural exclusions and intolerance were not the whole story, however. Let us not forget that nationally ambitious federations had many incentives to build social bridges, for these groups aimed to recruit and retain millions of dues-paying members. Thus leading fraternal federations often allowed ethnic Americans or Jewish Americans to join mixed lodges or form their own social lodges in full fellowship with others in the order. What is more, federations built cross-partisan and cross-denominational ties, especially among Protestant Americans. "We become members regardless of the church to which we belong, and without regard to the political parties with which we affiliate, and we learn to respect each other's rights and each other's independence," explained William Jennings Bryan in his 1903 speech to the Modern Woodmen.[43] Occasionally, too, racial differences were bridged at least to some degree—as in the great national veterans' groups such as the Grand

Army of the Republic, the Veterans of Foreign Wars, and the American Legion, all of which allowed African American soldiers to either join integrated posts (in parts of the North) or form their own posts within the order (in much of the South).

Even when mobilization and countermobilization occurred between mutually exclusive groups, moreover, similar civic lessons could be learned from voluntary participation. Despite racism and fierce religious and cultural rivalries, African American and ethnic voluntary groups stressed the same values and engaged in organizational practices very similar to those of native-born, Protestant-dominated groups. Every group claimed to represent good Americans and godly men and women. Group badges and banners featured the U.S. flag—or, in the case of many immigrant associations, a U.S. flag crossed with the flag of the nation from which members hailed (as, for example, in the Hibernian ribbon badge pictured in fig. 3.1). Table 3.1 lists the watchword virtues of a range of classic membership federations, and we can see that groups espoused remarkably similar patriotic and ethical ideals. Thus the white Independent Order of Odd Fellows had the same watchword virtues as the African American Grand United Order of Odd Fellows. And there were important similarities as well between virtues featured by Protestant-dominated and Catholic fraternal groups and by groups with various ethnic identities.

Associations with clashing constituencies also organized along the same institutional lines, paralleling U.S. federalism. White and black, native and ethnic—voluntary federations of all sorts and sizes fostered interconnected local chapters and ran their affairs under constitutions written

TABLE 3.1
Virtues Celebrated by Various American Fraternal Orders

FRATERNAL GROUP	FEATURED VIRTUES
Independent Order of Odd Fellows	Friendship, Love, Truth
Grand United Order of Odd Fellows (African American)	Friendship, Love, Truth
Improved Order of Red Men	Freedom, Friendship, Charity
Ancient Order of Hibernians (Irish American)	Friendship, Unity, True Christian Charity
German Order of Harugari	Friendship, Love, Humanity
Order of Sons of Temperance	Love, Purity, Fidelity
Independent Order of Good Templars	Faith, Hope, Charity
Junior Order of United American Mechanics	Virtue, Liberty, Patriotism
Knights of Pythias	Friendship, Charity, Benevolence
Knights of Pythias of North America, South America, Europe, Asia, Africa (African American), and Australia	Friendship, Charity, Benevolence
Ancient Order of United Workmen	Charity, Hope, Protection
Benevolent and Protective Order of Elks	Charity, Justice, Brotherly Love, Fidelity
Knights of Columbus	Unity, Charity, Brotherly Love
Loyal Order of Moose	Purity, Aid, Progress
American Woodmen (African American)	Protection of the Home, Brotherhood of Man
Order of Vasa (Swedish-American)	Truth, Unity
Western Bohemian Fraternal Association	Truth, Love, Faithfulness
Catholic Order of Foresters	Faith, Hope, Charity
National Slovak Society	Liberty, Equality, Fraternity
Fraternal Order of Eagles	Liberty, Truth, Justice, Equality

SOURCE: Civic Engagement Project, Harvard University

to imitate the U.S. Constitution. Classic U.S. membership associations, in short, may often have restricted membership and battled one another, but every category of the population combined into similarly organized cross-class federations expressing much the same Judeo-Christian and patriotic worldviews. Ironically, this had the effect of pulling American citizens together—teaching them shared values and similar citizenship practices—even when they did not intend to be united.

Public Discussion and Political Mobilization

Rules of official nonpartisanship such as those enshrined by the Odd Fellows were adopted by most classic American membership associations. The purpose of such rules was to allow members of different party persuasions to work together and to rule out direct subordination of the group to a political party in a way that might tear the association apart. Nonpartisanship did not mean withdrawal from politics, however. Not only could groups still foster good citizenship and encourage discussion of public issues; many also launched what might be called "transpartisan" efforts to achieve legislative goals. "The American Legion has no place in partisan politics, and partisan politics, thank God, have no place in the American Legion," declared the Legion's national commander, Paul V. McNutt, in a speech to the Maine legislature on January 24, 1929. Commander McNutt nevertheless outlined a whole series of legislative and civic initiatives that the Legion was supporting. And he supplemented his rejection of partisanship with a rousing affirmation of active citizenship. We "say to our members, 'You have obligations as citizens, a definite obligation

to exercise the right of suffrage, and you have an obligation beyond that, namely, to arouse the intelligent interest
of all those with whom you come into contact'" about
important public issues of the day.[44]

More was involved here than sheer exhortation of individual members to "educate themselves" politically. The
translocally federated structure of most U.S. membership
groups was ideal for fostering group discussion of public
issues. Local groups in translocal federations were, ipso
facto, connected to channels of programmatic information,
to a circulation of ideas among representatives and leaders. Local people went to district, state, or national meetings; heard speeches by experts, civic activists, or politicians; and then returned home brimming with plans for
entertaining and informative local meetings. During their
terms in office, officers were enjoined to visit local chapters
in their states or regions—and in the process they carried
program ideas from lodge to lodge, grange to grange, union
local to union local, and club to club. Benefiting from such
linkages, local voluntary groups in even very tiny or out-
of-the-way locations could end up talking about the most
sophisticated matters, including the pressing legislative or
political issues of the day.

For just one example among countless instances I could
develop from the yearly program booklets I have collected
for local chapters of federated groups, consider the women's
Progressive Study Club of the tiny town of Henry, South
Dakota, organized in 1897 and federated in 1900. Twelve
members of the Henry club are pictured in figure 3.4,
women obviously ranging in age and looking much as any
ordinary group of women in midwestern farm towns might
have appeared in the early twentieth century. But consider

FIGURE 3.4. Members of the Progressive Study Club, Henry, South Dakota. Courtesy of Elinor Ostrom.

the subjects these women covered in just four months of meetings in early 1916. As we learn from the programs reproduced in figure 3.5, discussions ranged from lighthearted topics and projects of cultural enrichment to state-level legislation ("South Dakota Laws of Interest to Women and Children," "Ten Questions on Needful Legislation for Married Women in South Dakota") to the largest topics of national and international concern ("Our National Defenses Today," "Our Immigration"). The range of issues covered would put any modern university faculty to shame. And we can be sure that many of the programmatic ideas came to Henry through channels of interchange fostered by the South Dakota Federation of Women's Clubs and the national-level General Federation of Women's Clubs.

Even when classic voluntary groups emphasized ritual activities, they could create space for discussions of public issues. Such "space" was physical as well as social, because so many groups raised the resources to build meeting halls— used not only by their own members but by other groups in town as well. Normally occupied for weekly meetings or social gatherings, these halls could host political discussions too. Consider the example of the Knights of Pythias hall in Auburn, Maine, in 1934. Set into a minutes book from the Eureka lodge—a dusty old records journal I found in an antique mall—was a request on lodge stationery from four members dated November 22, 1934, "respectfully" applying for "the use of this Hall free of charge Wednesday evening November 28. For discussion of Townsend Old Age Pension plan."[45] At the height of the Great Depression and the New Deal, some Auburn Pythians used their fraternal hall to orchestrate a discussion of one of the most controversial public policy issues of the day. Similarly, on

Education of a Music Lover
JANUARY FOUR

Hostess—Mrs. Pease
Roll Call—My Favorite Instrument and Why?
Lesson — Chapter IX, "The Problem of Expression
                    Mrs. Murphy
Review—Orchestral Music
                    Mrs Morris
Magazine—Three Four-minute Articles   Mrs. Martin

❦

JANUARY EIGHTEEN

Hostess—Mrs. Martin
Roll Call—What Women Elsewhere are Doing
Travalogue   Mrs. Snyder
Review—Womans' Progress
                    Mrs. Goepfert
Magazine—Three Four-minute Articles   Mrs. O. H. Tarbell

MARCH FIRST

Hostess—Mrs. Hopkins
Roll Call—Favorite Musical Selection
Musicale   Mrs. Martin
Review—New Methods of Child Education   Mrs. L. B. Parsons
Magazine—Three Four-minute Articles   Mrs. Whooley

❦

MARCH FIFTEEN

Hostess—Mrs. H. A. Tarbell
Roll Call—South Dakota Laws of Interest to Women and Children
Discussion—Ten Questions on Needful Legislation for Married Women of South Dakota   Mrs Kreger
Magazine—Three Five-minute Articles   Mrs. Parsons

❦

MARCH TWENTY-NINE

Hostess—Mrs. Baker
Roll Call—Current Events
Discussion—Our Immigration
                    Mrs. Pease
Review—America's Policy in Regard to Contraband Goods   Mrs. Brown
Magazine—Three Four-minute Articles   Mrs. Babcock

FEBRUARY ONE

Hostess—Mrs. Goepfert
Roll Call—An Incident in the Life of a Musician
Lesson—Chapter X to close (History and Biology)
                    Mrs. Duffner
Review—American Scientific Investigation   Mrs. Pease
Magazine—Three Four-minute Articles   Mrs. Kreger

❦

FEBRUARY FIFTEEN

Hostess—Mrs. Babcock
Roll Call—Patriotic Quotation
Lesson—Fathers' of the Constitution   Mrs. Whooley
Review—"Our National Defenses Today"   Mrs. Snyder
Magazine—Three Four-minute Articles   Mrs. Baker

APRIL TWELVE

Hostess—Mrs. Snyder
Roll Call—Scenic Wonders of the United States from Personal Observation
Fashions of Different Periods
                    Mrs. H. A. Tarbell
Ten-minute Monologue
                    Mrs. Murphy
Magazine—Three Four-minute Articles   Mrs. Stutenroth

❦

APRIL TWENTY SIX

Hostess—Mrs. Brown
Roll Call—Words Usually Mispronounced
Our Expositions and their Benefits to Our Country
                    Mrs. Goepfert
Review—Synopsis of a Standard Popular Book   Mrs. Neill
Magazine—Three Five-minute Articles   Mrs. Murphy

FIGURE 3.5.   Biweekly Meeting Programs of the Progressive Study Club, Henry, South Dakota, 1916. Courtesy of Elinor Ostrom.

November 21, 1933, the Parent-Teacher Association at Girls'
High School in Atlanta, Georgia, departed from its usual
focus on topics directly related to education and child training. At its regular monthly meeting in the high school audi-
torium, this local PTA scheduled for discussion an address
by Mr. Eugene Gunby on "The N.R.A.," the National
Recovery Administration, which was the main New Deal
national economic recovery initiative of the early 1930s.[46]
National public concerns were woven seamlessly into the
flow of discussion of local matters related to the school.

Like the American Legion and the Federated Women's
Clubs, nearly three-fifths of the voluntary associations that
ultimately enrolled 1 percent or more of Americans went
further than simply fostering discussion of public issues.
Thirty-four of the fifty-eight large associations listed in table
2.1 mobilized their members to work for explicitly political
causes—ranging from opposition to slavery and temperance reforms to women's suffrage and a range of social and
ethnic programs.[47] Once in a while the usual barriers
against partisan electoral involvement were breached. In
1920, for example, the Woman's Christian Temperance
Union of Iowa could not resist endorsing native son Herbert C. Hoover for president. "Shall This Iowa Boy Become
President?" asked the pamphlet they issued, which pictured Hoover when he was a child and answered in the
affirmative:

> It is now time to elect a new President of the United States.
> Let us have a farmer boy who knows what the farm needs.
> Let us have a good business man who can teach us how to
> make money and save because he has done so. Let us have
> a Christian man, for this is a Christian nation. Let us have a

man who loves our Constitution and says he will keep it safe. Let use have a man who does not drink intoxicants and who promises to enforce the prohibition law. LET US HAVE HERBERT C. HOOVER FOR HE IS ALL THIS.[48]

More often, however, national and state leaders of voluntary federations coordinated campaigns on behalf of favored legislation. They contacted state and national elected officials to press their case and urged local chapters to spread the word and contact elected representatives. Sometimes in concurrence with legislative campaigns, sometimes apart from them, federations also worked to influence public opinion on behalf of moral or political goals thought vital to the nation's well-being.

In chapter 2 I mentioned numerous instances of federations campaigning for public social programs. Federated voluntary associations have been uniquely positioned to influence legislation and public opinion, because their structures often parallel legislative and congressional districts. As American women's federations splendidly demonstrated in their campaigns for mothers' pensions and the Sheppard Towner Act in the 1910s, campaigns coordinated across many states and localities can have a decisive impact on elected representatives, regardless of party.[49] The same kinds of successes were achieved in the same ways by the Grange and the American Farm Bureau Federation agitating for land grant college programs and benefits for farmers and by the great military veterans' associations lobbying on behalf of services, pensions, and (ultimately) the G.I. Bill for former servicemen. In all these instances and many others, voluntary federations could simultaneously shape public opinion and influence the priorities and votes of legislators

across party lines. They could be enormously influential
actors in U.S. state and national politics, even as they
engaged millions of Americans in local community life.

RETROSPECT AND PROSPECT

Directly, therefore, as well as in a number of indirect ways,
America's traditional voluntary membership federations
fostered active citizenship and made a difference in politics and governance. Federations were especially vital in
building an American democracy in which ordinary people
could participate, gain skills, and forge recurrent ties to one
another—not just locally but also across communities,
states, and regions of a vast and expanding nation. Federations allowed ordinary Americans to interact with powerful
societal leaders. And they nurtured a style of public leadership based on majority election and the responsibility of
officeholders to engage and mobilize their fellow citizens.

Over the long run of U.S. history, voluntary membership
federations have both complemented and rivaled political
parties in setting the course of politics and government.[50]
By coordinating and inspiring so many people across the
myriad districts that elect representatives to U.S. state and
national legislatures, voluntary federations have been able
to exert democratic leverage. Federations combine state
and national reach with local presence, the best way to
influence U.S. elected officials. Of course, the political goals
of membership associations have not always been good. To
give one egregious example, the Ku Klux Klan was a tem-
porarily massive group that pursued racial domination
and religious exclusion, in part through extralegal violence
and in part through legislative campaigns. Similar (if usually

less virulent) nativist goals figured in the programs of many historically important voluntary federations. So I am not arguing that social tolerance and maximally inclusive citizenship have invariably been furthered by associations with large memberships.

What is more, smaller and more agile voluntary groups willing to take courageous stands on matters of principle have often promoted important democratic goals. Obvious examples include relatively small membership associations such as the National Association for the Advancement of Colored People (NAACP) and professional advocacy groups ranging from the abolitionists to the Children's Defense Fund. A complete account of democratic civil society in the United States cannot dwell only on associations with large memberships. Through much of our national history, however, major membership federations consistently weighed in on issues of moral and material concern to vast sectors of the American population. For millions of citizens, federations offered ways to work together—to "combine" nationally as well as locally—and thereby had an impact on public opinion and the actions of government. In many instances, the democratic responsiveness of the U.S. government was enhanced by the efforts of vast voluntary federations.

In about 1960, when Gabriel Almond and Sidney Verba asked citizens of five national democracies about their civic involvements and attitudes, they discovered a highly engaged U.S. citizenry.[51] American men and women alike reported high degrees of involvement as officers and committee members in voluntary groups, and Americans were unusually confident in their ability to make a difference in national and local public affairs. In their snapshot social survey, Almond and Verba captured the subjective side of a democratic U.S. civil society centered in locally rooted yet nationally organized voluntary membership federations.

But as so often happens in social science, scholars figure things out and nail down the facts just as the phenomena in question are about to change. As *The Civic Culture* was published in 1963, unsettling and exhilarating civic transformations were just over the horizon for Americans. A U.S. civic universe centered in federated membership associations, built and elaborated over so many decades, was about to change fundamentally. In the next three chapters we will consider what changed in late-twentieth-century American civil society, why the changes happened, and what difference civic reorganizations make for our democracy. Our appreciation of contemporary transformations will be greatly enhanced by the understanding we have already gained of classic civic America—the nation of joiners and membership organizers that flourished from the 1800s through the middle of the twentieth century.

CHAPTER 4

FROM MEMBERSHIP
TO MANAGEMENT

AN AMERICAN RIP VAN WINKLE who slept from 1960 to the turn of the new millennium would hardly recognize his country's civic life. A civil society once centered in nationally active and locally vibrant voluntary membership federations—such as the American Legion, the Elks, and the PTA—went the way of the once-popular television program *Leave It to Beaver*. There may still be reruns, but they seem rather quaint. By now Americans are no longer such avid joiners, although they may be organizing more civic endeavors than ever before. Professionally run advocacy groups and nonprofit institutions now dominate civil society, as people seek influence and community through a very new mix of largely memberless voluntary organizations.

Some Americans, to be sure, find community in the enveloping life of evangelical churches. But many others volunteer sporadically for projects run by nonprofit institutions of which they are not members and send checks to public affairs groups run by professionals. Aiming to speak for—and influence—masses of citizens, droves of new national advocacy groups have set up shop, with the media amplifying debates among their professional spokespersons. The National Abortion Rights Action League debates the National Right to Life Committee; the Concord Coalition takes on the American Association for Retired Persons; and the Environmental Defense Fund counters business groups. Ordinary Americans attend to such debates fitfully, entertained or bemused. Then pollsters call at dinnertime to glean snippets of what everyone makes of it all.

Understanding civic America's recent transition from membership activities to professionally managed institutions and advocacy groups is vital if we are to reflect wisely on prospects for our democracy. Shifts in mass attitudes, individual behaviors, and patterns of voter turnout are routinely probed by scholars and pundits. Important as these matters may be, changes in *organized* public activities and strategies of civic leadership deserve equal or greater attention. More than at any time since the civically generative decades just before and after the Civil War, recent times have witnessed extraordinary changes in the ways Americans create and use associations. In the 1960s and 1970s massive social movements bypassed federated membership associations and set the stage for the proliferation of new kinds of professionally run civic undertakings.

OLD FEDERATIONS AND NEW SOCIAL MOVEMENTS

Consider the largest American membership associations of the 1950s. Table 4.1 lists twenty-three associations that enrolled as "members" 1 percent or more of men, women, or men and women in 1955. This list provides a fascinating window into the integument of American civil society in that time, because these giant membership associations had local units in communities all across the land. Included are occupationally based membership federations—the

American Federation of Labor and Congress of Industrial Organizations (which merged in 1955) and the American Farm Bureau Federation—as well as a number of recreational associations, plus two national service institutions (the Red Cross and the March of Dimes).[1] Dominating the list, however, are male-led fraternal and veterans' groups and female-led religious and civic associations. Millions of Americans in all regions not only participated in religious congregations linked to major denominations; they also belonged to chapters affiliated with nationally prominent voluntary federations.

The largest membership groups of the 1950s were old line and well established, with U.S. founding dates ranging from 1733 for the Masons to 1939 for the United Methodist Women (formed through a merger of several "missionary" societies with roots in the nineteenth century). Like most of the large membership associations throughout American history, many of the associations enjoying large enrollments in the 1950s recruited members across class lines. Local chapters held regular meetings and sent delegates to periodic assemblies at the state (or regional) and national levels. Engaged in multiple rather than narrowly specialized pursuits, many of these associations combined social or ritual activities with community service, mutual aid, and involvement in national affairs. American patriotism was a leitmotiv, so perhaps it is not surprising that during and after World War II—a passionate and victorious national endeavor to which voluntary federations lent enthusiastic support—these associations expanded their memberships and reinvigorated their local and national activities.[2]

To be sure, very large groups were not the only voluntary associations that mattered in wartime and postwar

TABLE 4.1
U.S. Membership Associations Enrolling 1 Percent or More of American Adults in 1955

Name (Year Founded)	Membership	Percent of Adults who Belonged	Number of Local Units
AFL-CIO (1886)	12,622,000	12.05	NA
National Congress of Parents and Teachers/PTA (1897)	9,409,282	8.99	40,396 local PTAs
American Automobile Association (1902)	5,009,346	4.78	464 clubs
Ancient and Accepted Free Masons (1733)	4,009,925	7.86 (m)	15,662 lodges
American Legion (1919)	2,795,990	5.48 (m)	16,937 posts
Order of the Eastern Star (1868)	2,365,778	2.26	12,277 chapters
Young Men's Christian Association (1851)	2,222,618	2.12	1,502 local YMCAs
United Methodist Women (1939)	1,811,600	3.37 (w)	NA
American Bowling Congress (1895)	1,741,000	3.41 (m)	43,090 leagues
American Farm Bureau Federation (1919)	1,623,222	1.55	3,000 local farm bureaus (est.)
Boy Scouts of America (1910)	1,353,370 (est.)	1.29	53,804 local troops
Woman's Missionary Union (1888)	1,245,358	2.32 (w)	65,132 church WMU organizations
Benevolent and Protective Order of Elks (1867)	1,149,613	2.25 (m)	1,720 lodges
Veterans of Foreign Wars (1913)	1,086,859	2.13 (m)	7,000 posts (est.)

Loyal Order of Moose (1888)	843,697	1.65 (m)	1,767 lodges
General Federation of Women's Clubs (1890)	857,915	1.6 (w)	15,168 clubs
Knights of Columbus (1882)	832,601	1.63 (m)	3,083 councils
Nobles of the Mystic Shrine (1872)	761,179	1.49 (m)	166 temples
Fraternal Order of Eagles (1898)	760,007	1.49 (m)	1,566 aeries
Women's International Bowling Congress (1916)	706,193	1.31(w)	22,842 leagues
Independent Order of Odd Fellows (1819)	543,171	1.07 (m)	7,572 lodges
American Red Cross (1881)	*	*	3,713 chapters
March of Dimes (1938)	*	*	3,090 chapters

NOTES: (m) indicates men only; (w) indicates women only; (est.) indicates best available estimate.
NA indicates data not available at this time.
* Membership data are not given for the Red Cross and March of Dimes, because they include contributors as well as participants.

SOURCE: Civic Engagement Project, Harvard University

America. Also prominent were somewhat smaller, elite-dominated civic groups, including male service groups such as Rotary, Lions, and Kiwanis and long-standing female groups such as the American Association of University Women and the League of Women Voters.[3] Dozens of ethnically based fraternal and cultural associations flourished, as did African American fraternal groups like the Prince Hall Masons and the Improved Benevolent and Protective Order of Elks of the World.[4] Yet all of the aforementioned operated along lines similar to the largest membership federations; and most likewise experienced membership gains and renewals of energy from the 1940s into the immediate postwar era.

When Gabriel Almond and Sidney Verba queried Americans and citizens of four other nations about memberships in various types of associations in 1959 and 1960, U.S. respondents were unusually likely to claim memberships in fraternal, church-related, and civic-political associations.[5] Almond and Verba also found that Americans were more likely than any of the other citizenries to report membership in several associations. American women were more involved than women elsewhere, and associational involvement was less differentiated by educational status in the United States than in the other four nations.[6] All of these individual-level findings fit the picture of a postwar civic universe dominated by religious, fraternal, and civic voluntary federations that involved large numbers of male and female members from diverse occupational backgrounds.

For membership federations of all kinds, the mid-twentieth century was a golden era of national as well as community impact. In 1960 two-fifths of associational members in the United States told Almond and Verba's interviewers that they believed an organization of theirs was involved in political affairs. Because so many Americans were members of groups of all sorts, this meant that a higher proportion of U.S. citizens claimed involvement in politically active associations, despite the fact that fewer Americans than Britons or Germans were affiliated with trade unions.[7] The immediate postwar era was certainly a time when U.S. labor unions, business groups, and professional associations exerted a lot of influence in state and national policy debates. But so did many community-based federations that recruited people across occupations and income strata. The American Legion and the Veterans of Foreign Wars advanced veterans' programs;[8] the Fraternal Order of Eagles championed federal social security programs;[9] the Grange and the American Farm Bureau Federation joined other farmers' associations to influence national and state agricultural policies;[10] and the National Congress of Parents and Teachers and the General Federation of Women's Clubs were influential on educational, health, and family issues.[11] As suggested in Figure 4.1, which reproduces a graphic from *Your Farm Bureau*, a 1958 civics manual for AFBF members, voluntary membership federations served as two-way "highways" connecting citizens in local communities and state and national government. The results could be decisive, as exemplified by the pivotal role of the American Legion in drafting and lobbying for the G.I. Bill of 1944, one of the most generous and socially inclusive educational and family policies ever enacted by the U.S. federal government.[12] The world of American membership federations was riding high from the late 1940s through the mid-1960s.

FIGURE 4.1
The Farm Bureau's Policy Highway

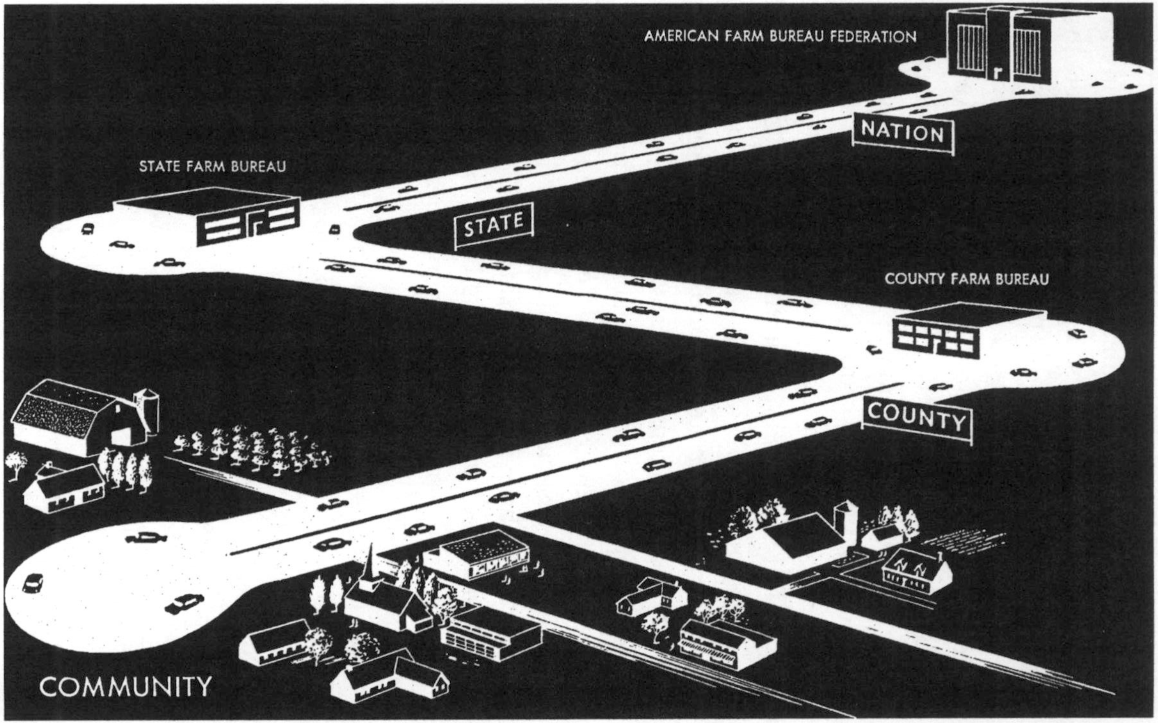

The Long 1960s

But then, suddenly, old-line membership federations were no longer where the action was. Upheavals shook America during "the long 1960s," stretching from the mid-1950s through the mid-1970s. The southern Civil Rights movement challenged white racial domination and spurred national legislation to enforce legal equality and voting rights for African Americans.[13] Inspired by civil rights achievements, additional "rights" movements exploded in the sixties and seventies, promoting equality for women, recognition and dignity for homosexuals, the unionization of farm workers, and the mobilization of other nonwhite ethnic minorities.[14] Movements also arose to oppose U.S. involvement in the war in Vietnam, to champion a new environmentalism, and to further a variety of other public causes. At the forefront of these groundswells were younger Americans, especially from the growing ranks of college students and university graduates.

"Social movements" are vast and somewhat unstructured endeavors whose participants express new ways of thinking and agitate for institutional transformations. Never the work of just one organization, movements are pushed forward through shifts in public opinion spurred by the efforts of many contending as well as cooperating groups. Actors comfortably situated in previously dominant institutions and associations rarely spearhead movements for fundamental social change. Instead, new leaders take the initiative—sometimes working through previously existing but somewhat marginalized organizations but often launching brand-new associations.[15] Activists in movements for social change are notable for their moral determination,

strategic agility, and capacity to help people combine in
new ways. Such leaders, and the redirected or newly created associations through which they work, are vital agents
of democratic revitalization. Again and again in American
history, this has been true.

Innovation and fresh leadership certainly marked the
great American social movements of the long 1960s. The
southern Civil Rights movement of 1955 to 1965 was sparked
by direct actions—the "freedom rides," the Montgomery
bus boycott, the Greensboro sit-ins, and citywide nonvio-
lent demonstrations—sustained and pushed forward by a
remarkable combination of African American church networks and leadership cadre groups.[16] Ordinary people
became engaged through social ties within church congregations, while strategic innovation came from the Southern Christian Leadership Council (SCLC), a coordinating
group of African American ministers founded in 1957; and
the Student Non-Violent Coordinating Committee (SNCC),
a coordinating association of student activists founded in
1960. Previously, the NAACP, an interracial federation
founded in 1909, had been the nation's leading civil rights
organization. Although the NAACP was decisive in legal
advocacy, before the civil rights upheavals it never recruited
more than 2 percent of African Americans, mostly professionals and ministers. When activists shifted to new, direct-
action tactics, particular NAACP chapters and Youth Councils played key roles, but the SCLC and SNCC moved to the
fore as coordinators of the spreading mass protests.[17]

The feminist movement of the late 1960s and 1970s was
propelled by a combination of loosely interconnected circles,
assorted cadre organizations and single-issue groups, and
a few newly launched membership associations.[18] Launched

during the Civil Rights movement, radical "women's liberation" efforts were grounded in consciousness-raising and direct-action groups. Reform-oriented "women's rights" feminism took shape when participants in government commissions decided in 1966 to launch the National Organization of Women (NOW) as an activist and chapter-based association.[19] The vanguard of feminist reform included the Women's Equity Action League (founded in 1968) and the National Abortion Rights Action League (created in 1973 through a reorientation of an earlier group)—both leadership groups that eventually developed mailing list memberships of modest size. Although a number of them joined in support of feminist projects during the 1970s, old-line membership federations such as the American Association of University Women, the Young Women's Christian Association, the General Federation of Women's Clubs, and the League of Women Voters did not initiate or drive the new feminism. Describing "feminist mobilization" in 1982, Joyce Gelb and Marian Lief Palley concluded that the "groups [of] the past twenty years have tended to be leadership and not membership based."[20]

Nationwide demonstrations for the first Earth Day in 1970 symbolized the emergence of the modern environmental movement, which took shape as long-standing concerns about land conservation and the protection of particular animal species broadened into ecological awareness. Along with Rachel Carson's famous book *Silent Spring*, new advocacy associations established by lawyers, scientists, and dissident breakaways from earlier environmental groups propelled this transition.[21] Spark plugs included the Environmental Defense Fund, formed in 1967 amid "the battle to ban DDT"; the Friends of the Earth, founded

founded in 1969 by a former Sierra Club director fired for independent activism; Environmental Action, founded in 1970 by the student organizers of Earth Day; the National Resources Defense Council, founded in 1970 out of "an environmental law firm run by lawyers"; and Greenpeace, launched internationally during the 1970s by activists who eschewed legislative lobbying for more colorful direct actions.[22] From the 1970s to the 1990s, modern environmentalism burgeoned as a large and disparate set of associations with varying strategies, histories, and bases of support. Cadre groups continued to proliferate, redefining issues and pursuing fresh tactics. At the same time, such old-line membership federations as the Sierra Club (founded in 1892), The National Audubon Society (Founded in 1905), the Wilderness Society (founded in 1935), and the National Wildlife Federation (founded in 1936) reoriented their efforts and became major players in the new environmentalism.[23]

The great social movements of the long 1960s thus synthesized grassroots protest, activist radicalism, and professionally led efforts to lobby government and educate the public. Some older membership associations ended up participating and expanding their bases of support, yet the groups that sparked movements were more agile and flexibly structured than preexisting membership federations. What is more, many of the key groups were not membership associations at all. They were small combinations of nimble, fresh-thinking, and passionate advocates of new causes.

ADVOCACY EXPLOSIONS

Still, we can wonder about what happened next. Once the protest movements of the long 1960s achieved victories and began to wane, associational innovation might have subsided in the late-twentieth-century United States; and civic currents might have flowed back into long-established if widened channels. Extraordinary times of civic ferment and political agitation had happened before in American history, only to spur the replacement and renewal of membership federations rather than their displacement. The upheavals of the sixties might have left behind a reconfigured civic world, in which some old-line membership associations had declined, some new federations had emerged, and still others had reoriented and reenergized themselves to take advantage of new issues and sources of support. Within each great social movement, memberships might have consolidated and groups coalesced into new (or renovated) omnibus federations able to link the grass roots to state, regional, and national leaderships, allowing long-standing American civic traditions to continue in new ways.

But for the most part, this is not what happened. Instead, the 1960s, 1970s, and 1980s brought an extraordinary proliferation of new and different civic organizations. The total number of national associations listed in the *Encyclopedia of Associations* grew almost fourfold from 1959 to 1999 (see table 4.2 below). In 1959 there were 5,843 groups, and that number almost doubled to 10,308 groups by 1970. Some of this initial increase can be attributed to discovery by the *Encyclopedia* editors of previously existing groups; but later increases included only a few groups founded much earlier.[24] By 1980 there were 14,726 national groups in existence; and the total reached 22,259 in 1990. During the decade of the 1990s, America's expanded universe of national associations reached a plateau, as the total number of groups stabilized between 22,000 and 23,000. Most group proliferation happened before 1990, especially in the 1970s and 1980s, when foundings of new groups far outran U.S. population growth.[25] What is more, innovation was as important as proliferation in this civically fecund period—for *new kinds of groups* took front and center stage, including many professionally led advocacy associations focused on policy lobbying and public education.

What Jeffrey Berry aptly calls the "advocacy explosion" happened in several overlapping waves.[26] Groups advocating for the rights of formerly marginalized categories of Americans were in the lead, closely followed by many new citizen advocacy groups arguing for fresh conceptions of the public interest. The ranks of advocacy associations were swelled further by additions to already numerous occupational and business associations.

Rights Advocates

Many movements of the long 1960s championed people marginalized in classic civic America, and new associations both sparked and emerged from these efforts. Debra Minkoff has studied "organizing for equality" in some depth, using listings in yearly volumes of the *Encyclopedia of Associations* to identify some "975 national minority and women's membership associations that were active at some point between 1955 and 1985."[27] Overall, groups acting on behalf of the rights or welfare of women, African Americans, and Hispanic or Asian Americans multiplied sixfold—from 98 groups in 1955 to 688 groups in 1985.[28] According to Minkoff's data, the immediate aftermath of Civil Rights victories in the mid-1960s was a time when many groups speaking for African Americans were launched, while the ranks of groups advocating equality for women and ethnic minorities expanded a bit later, especially during the 1970s.[29] Actually, Minkoff's study understates the proliferation of rights-oriented groups, because her database includes only associations with constituencies of some sort, setting aside "government bodies and staff-run not-for-profit organizations such as research centers and operating foundations."[30] All the more telling, then, are Minkoff's findings about the changing mix of organizational strategies used by the constituency groups she surveyed.[31] Between 1955 and the late 1960s about half of the groups focused on women and racial or ethnic minorities provided social services, and another fifth emphasized cultural activities (such as sponsoring arts festivals or preparing media materials). But as the universe of rights groups expanded dramatically during the 1970s and 1980s, the mix shifted sharply toward policy advocacy groups and service providers also engaged in policy advocacy. Rights groups focused primarily on political protest were always few, and their number remained relatively constant from 1955 to 1985. Still, as Minkoff explains, "when 10 of 183 organizations were pursuing protest at the end of 1965," this was "likely more noticeable than when 10 of 678 groups" engaged in protest in 1985.[32] Among associations furthering causes identified with women, African Americans, and other racially distinctive ethnic minorities, protest as a strategy was overtaken by policy advocacy.

Minkoff's findings complement those of other scholars. When Kay Lehman Schlozman investigated Washington, D.C.-based associations at the beginning of the 1980s, she found that women's groups—especially those with a rights orientation—had been founded very recently yet already used the same mix of professional advocacy methods as other Washington pressure groups.[33] The feminist "groups that emerged as a social movement in the late 1960s," Gelb and Palley concur, "evolved in the later years of the 1970s into a stage of political development that emphasized interest-group organization and professionalization."[34] Feminist associations appeal to general public sympathy while pursuing legal, research, and lobbying activities. "Like their black civil rights counterparts," Gelb and Palley note, "feminist groups are frequently based in Washington or New York."[35]

Citizen Advocacy Groups

Another wave of late-twentieth-century advocacy involved "public interest" or "citizen" groups seeking to shape public opinion and influence legislation.[36] Citizen advocacy groups espouse "causes" ranging from environmental protection (for example, the Sierra Club and the Environmental Defense Fund) to the well-being of poor children (the Children's Defense Fund [CDF]) to reforming politics (Common Cause) and cutting public entitlements (the Concord Coalition). According to Berry, these associations make claims about the public interest, not about the occupational or material self-interests of their adherents. Citizen advocacy groups often speak on behalf of constituents, but even if they are labeled "members" such constituents are as likely to be other organizations or sets of social service professionals as they are to be individual citizens. Many citizen associations claim no members at all; and groups founded in recent times are unlikely to include networks of local chapters or to rely heavily on dues-paying individual members.[37]

Although many citizen advocacy groups were launched by activists who got their start in the social movements of the long 1960s, large numbers of additional organizations functioning as public interest advocates proliferated through the 1980s, founded amid ongoing policy struggles in Washington, D.C. and in the nation's media. In a survey of eighty-three public interest groups active in Washington in the early 1970s, Berry found that almost half had been launched between 1968 and 1973.[38] Kay Lehman Schlozman and John C. Tierney analyzed groups listed in a 1981 lobbying directory, noting that 40 percent were founded after 1960 and 25 percent after 1970.[39] In the most comprehensive study, Jack Walker and his associates examined 564 groups based in Washington, D.C., in the early 1980s and found that 30 percent were launched between 1960 and 1980, with citizen groups increasing much more sharply than other kinds of lobbying organizations.[40] The first waves of citizen advocates were liberal, but newly founded conservative groups soon joined the fray, especially during the 1980s.[41]

As "avowedly political" groups, citizen associations deploy "substantial financial resources to hire large staffs of lobbyists and researchers."[42] Political tactics vary, and many groups use shifting blends of tactics. Some may focus on "inside lobbying," contacting public administrators and congressional staffers to make the case for rules or legislative provisions. Others litigate in the courts. And still others orchestrate public relations campaigns or try to stir up far-flung constituencies to contact Congress. Regardless of tactical emphases or blends, however, citizen groups need expertise to devise and disseminate persuasive arguments. Practicing politics in much the same way as the business and professional lobbies against which they often square off in policy disputes, citizen associations develop strong professional staffs. An excellent example is the environmental movement, in which the number of nationally active groups more than tripled from 119 in 1961 to 396 in 1990, and the combined national staffs swelled by nearly tenfold, from 316 people in 1961 to 2,917 in 1990.[43] Professionalization proceeded across the board, affecting both old-line groups likely to have large memberships and recently founded groups more likely to forgo or deemphasize individual membership and local chapters.

Business Associations

The last wave of the recent U.S. advocacy explosion has been, at least in part, a response to the previous two. From the early through the mid-twentieth century, trade and professional associations were a growing presence in U.S. politics and associational life. Spurts of new foundings coincided with World War I, the early New Deal, and World War II, junctures when the federal government actively sought to cooperate with or manage the national economy.[44] After the mid-1960s rights groups and citizen advocates markedly increased their presence on the national scene; but previously dominant interests did not just sit idly by. Business groups are of special interest, because they are often thought to be the mainstays of conservative coalitions opposed to taxes, expensive social programs, and new regulations of the sorts that environmentalists or rights advocates might support. During the 1970s and 1980s, segments of the business world formed more specialized associations, and new groups appeared to do battle with citizen groups. What is more, many corporations and preexisting business associations opened offices for the first time in Washington, D.C., the better to monitor government and counter the newly mobilized rights groups and citizen associations.[45] In the advocacy arms race, action has led to counteraction very rapidly.

Even so, the late twentieth century witnessed a sharp change in the balance between business groups and other civicly active associations. According to tallies in the *Encyclopedia of Associations*, arrayed in table 4.2, the combined numbers of "trade, business, and commercial" associations and "chambers of commerce, trade, and tourism" accounted for a remarkable 40 percent of all U.S. national associations in 1959, just before the era of the advocacy explosion. Over the next four decades, the absolute numbers of such business groups grew—from 2,309 in 1959 to 3,831 in 1999. But the *share* held by business groups in the overall universe of national associations was reduced by more than half, to just 17 percent. Meanwhile, the fastest-growing category of groups, "public affairs" associations, expanded from 2 percent to 9 percent of all U.S. associations. And the combined total of "social welfare," "educational and cultural," and "health and medical" associations grew from just over one-fifth of national groups in 1959 to one-third of them in 1999. Not all groups in these categories are exactly what Minkoff or Berry would call "rights" or "citizen" associations. Many speak for social service institutions or relatively elite professions. But it remains very telling that by the 1990s the overall share of these fast-growing categories substantially surpassed the share of business associations among all nationally active groups.

TABLE 4.2
National Associations in the United States, 1959–1999

Number of Associations Listed in

Type of Association	1959	%	1970	1980	1990	1999	%	Ratio of Growth
High to Very High Growth								
Public affairs	117	2%	477	1,068	2,249	2,071	9%	19.2
Hobby and avocational	98	2%	449	910	1,475	1,569	7%	16.0
Social welfare	241	4%	458	994	1,705	1,929	8%	8.0
Athletic and sports	123	2%	334	504	840	821	4%	6.7
Veterans, hereditary, and patriotic	109	2%	197	208	462	769	3%	7.1
Educational [a]	563	10%	1,357	976	1,292	1,311	14%	5.7
Cultural [a]				1,400	1,886	1,912		
Health and medical	433	7%	834	1,413	2,227	2,485	11%	5.7
Fan clubs [b]	—	—	—	—	551	485	2%	—
Close to Average Growth								
Legal, governmental, public administration, and military	164	3%	355	529	792	786	3%	4.8
Engineering, technological, and natural and social science	294	5%	544	1,039	1,417	1,353	6%	4.6

Fraternal, foreign interest, nationality, and ethnic	122	2%	591	435	572	524	2%	4.3
Religious	295	5%	782	797	1,172	1,217	5%	4.1
Environmental and agricultural	331	5%	504	677	940	1,120	5%	3.4
CLEARLY SLOWER GROWTH								
Trade, business, commercial	2,309	40%	2,753	3,118	3,918	3,831	17%	1.7
Chambers of commerce, trade, and tourism [c]	100	2%	112	105	168	119	0.5%	1.2
Labor unions, associations, and federations	226	4%	225	235	253	243	1%	1.1
Greek and non-Greek letter societies	318	5%	336	318	340	333	1.5%	1.1
TOTAL	5,843		10,308	14,726	22,259	22,878		3.9

[a] The educational and cultural categories were combined before 1972. Their combined growth rate is presented in the last column.

[b] Fan clubs was not a category before 1987. No growth rate is calculated.

[c] Before 1970 thousands of local chambers of commerce were also listed in the national *Encyclopedia*. Since 1970 they have been listed separately. The 1959 figure is an estimate for the number of national groups in that year.

SOURCE: Updated version of table 6.1 in Frank R. Baumgartner and Beth L. Leech, *Basic Interests* (Princeton: Princeton University Press, 1998), p. 103. Data from *Encyclopedia of Associations*, years indicated. For 1999, the CD-ROM version; for earlier years, printed volumes.

Taking an even longer view, political scientists Frank Baumgartner and Bryan Jones calculate that in the early twentieth century, profit-oriented national associations (including agricultural as well as business groups) had a two-to-one predominance over associations based on other kinds of identities and interests. In the middle of the century, between 1930 and the 1960s, profit-oriented associations increased their advantage to more than three to one over nonprofit groups. But after the 1960s the advocacy explosions quickly reduced the profit-group advantage to well below what it had been in the early part of the twentieth century. "These data," Baumgartner and Jones reflect, "give some indication why political scientists and others studying policymaking and interests groups in Washington during the 1940s and 1950s discussed iron triangles, subgovernments, and the like, while those discussing the same topics during the 1970s and 1980s were more likely to describe diffuse policy networks and advocacy coalitions."[46] The result was not only a greater ability on the part of rights groups and citizen advocates to influence agendas of public discussion and legislation. Public policymaking also became much more conflictual, as "issues once understood in a consensual, proindustry manner became more controversial."[47]

Additional Organizational Proliferations

We should not take the expansion of the ranks of nationally active public interest groups relative to business associations as the only important organizational indicator of recent U.S. civic trends. The advocacy associations just discussed are but one among several kinds of oganizations that have proliferated to change the face of organized civic life in the United States. As figure 4.2 shows, other entities wielding money and ideas have also flourished in recent times, and business interests or the very wealthy certainly play an important role in many of them. Political action committees, or PACs, collect money from businesses or wealthy donors and then channel it to office-seeking politicians or to influence the course of public debates. Gradually dispensing assets originally donated by wealthy founders, private foundations distribute grants to chosen groups and causes. And think tanks, often similarly endowed, assemble experts to address public policy issues. PACs, think tanks, and foundations may take various stances in struggles between profit and nonprofit interests, but the concerns of business and the privileged hardly lack for effective representation by such entities. Whatever their stances in policy battles, morover, PACs, think tanks, and foundations share telling characteristics with the other kinds of recently proliferating advocacy associations. Like most contemporary advocacy groups, PACs, think tanks, and foundations are professionally run and rely on money or expertise to influence public life. All have patrons or donors, and many may have constituencies. But PACs, think tanks, and foundations do not usually have individual members in the sense that historically influential U.S. voluntary associations almost invariably did.

Another trend worth mention stretches the scope of this book, which primarily deals with national-level civic transformations. National changes nevertheless are linked to state and local developments, and nonprofit institutions of many kinds have recently proliferated in communities across America. Advocacy associations may be the key new

FIGURE 4.2
Organizations Wielding Money and Ideas in U.S. Public Affairs

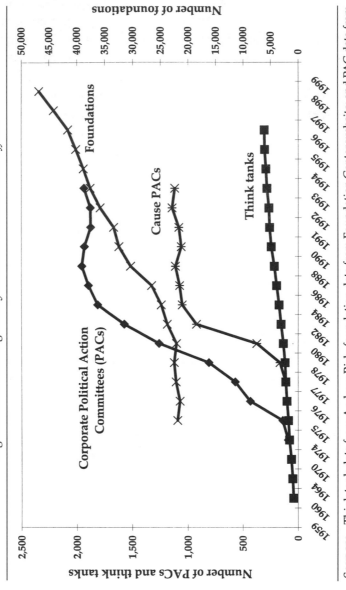

SOURCES: Think tank data from Andrew Rich; foundation data from Foundation Center website; and PAC data from M. Margaret Conway and J. Green, "Political Action Committees and the Political Process in the 1990s," in *Interest Group Politics*, 4th ed., edited by A. J. Cigler and B. A. Loomis (Washington, D.C.: CQ Press, 1995), table 7-1, p. 157.

actors in national politics and public debates, but in the states and localities, a variety of nonprofit institutions play leading public roles while at the same time delivering services to the public. Human service providers, cultural institutions, community foundations, and many other professionally run groups focused on creating public goods for states and localities are where the action is for community elites, who vie to sit on their boards. Nonprofits, Berry writes, "are at the very core of civil society," because "most Americans either volunteer for nonprofits in their communities or are clients served by them."[48] All told, "there are 1.6 million nonprofits in the United States" and "half . . . are involved in human services or provide health care." The economic output of nonprofits is "approximatedly 7 percent of the nation's GDP and nonprofits employ nearly 11 million people."[49]

Nonprofit institutions often brag of their independence from both the market and the government, but actually they are profoundly intertwined with both, especially with government. Not only do nonprofits regularly seek monetary contributions from the well-to-do, they cooperate closely with local and state governments to (as Berry puts it) "co-produce" public programs. During an era when governments are trying to do more and more without hiring new "bureaucrats," nonprofit institutions help them to implement publicly funded programs. As a by-product of their close involvement with public policy implementation, moreover, nonprofits are frequently approached by legislators and public administrators to provide research expertise and advice about policy design. With their ideas and expertise much sought after, nonprofits also speak for the needs of their "clients" in policy discussions—and in state and local politics, they may be the only groups routinely advocating on behalf of the homeless, the battered, the mentally ill, or impoverished children, even if they do not officially engage in lobbying as such.

Thus local and state nonprofits are, in an important sense, as much involved in policy advocacy as national advocacy associations. Indeed, national advocacy associations, such as the Children's Defense Fund, often represent the views of local and state social service institutions, whose leaders and staff professionals are likely to be among their most attentive constituencies. Much local service delivery has moved into the realm of professionally managed institutions, whose leaders look to professional advocates at the national level to lobby for policies that enhance the flow of resources via state government to nonprofit providers.

MEMBERSHIP GROUPS IN THE ADVOCACY ERA

The rise of professionally managed advocacy associations and nonprofit institutions is not the entire story of recent civic change. Classic membership federations enrolled huge numbers of individual Americans through the mid-twentieth century, and we must discover what has happened to them. Amid the growth of advocacy groups and nonprofits in recent years, associations rooted in individual membership—especially those with large networks of local chapters—lost visibility and clout. Even so, there are complexities to explore. Some large membership associations grew even as most classic federations dwindled. And certain kinds of local and intimate groups seem to have flourished in recent decades, quite apart from representatively governed federations.

Classic Voluntary Federations in Decline

America's once large and confident membership federations were not only bypassed in national politics after the 1960s; most of them also dwindled. Full details are presented in table 4.3, but the basic picture can be straightforwardly summarized. Most of the largest membership federations of the 1950s began to lose membership shares of the adult population in the 1960s or 1970s, with especially sharp downturns from the mid-1970s on.[50] Only a few of the leading membership associations of the 1950s held their own or gained membership shares: the YMCA, which shifted from fostering men's physical and spiritual development to managing facilities for family recreation; the American Farm Bureau Federation, which expanded its insurance programs as the farm population declined; and the Veterans of Foreign Wars, which during the 1980s and early 1990s proved appealing to many veterans who served in Korea and Vietnam. These groups were exceptions, however. Three-quarters of the associations listed in table 4.1 have experienced significant membership share losses in recent decades—including thirteen associations that lost from 20 to 90 percent of the share of the U.S. adult population they once recruited.[51]

Trade unions have plummeted, not just the percent of adults enrolled in the AFL-CIO, but the proportion of the employed labor force involved in any sort of union. More than one-third of the nonagricultural labor force was unionized in the 1950s, but by the 1990s less than one-sixth of workers were enrolled in any union.[52] Fraternal and civic membership associations have also been hard hit. Once predominant groups such as the Masons and Eastern Star, the

TABLE 4.3

Membership Change for Large U.S. Associations, 1955–1995

ASSOCIATIONS FOR MEN	U.S. MEN ENROLLED					DECADE SHIFTS				TOTAL SHIFT, 1955–95
	1955	1965	1975	1985	1995	1955–65	1965–75	1975–85	1985–95	
FRATERNAL										
Ancient and Accepted Free Masons	7.9	7.1	5.3	3.7	2.4	-10.1	-25.2	-30.1	-35.7	-69.8
Fraternal Order of Eagles	1.5	1.0	1.1	0.9	0.8	-31.2	4.5	-14.6	-11.2	-45.5
Loyal Order of Moose	1.7	1.5	1.7	1.7	1.3	-11.9	18.3	-3.6	-22.0	-21.6
Benevolent and Protected Order of Elks	2.3	2.4	2.4	2.0	1.4	7.0	-1.2	-15.2	-30.0	-37.2
Knights of Columbus	1.6	1.8	1.5	1.4	1.3	14.3	-16.8	-4.8	-8.4	-17.0
Independent Order of Odd Fellows	1.1	0.6	0.3	0.2	0.1	-44.1	-46.3	-48.7	-47.9	-92.0
Nobles of the Mystic Shrine	1.5	1.5	1.4	1.1	0.7	0.3	-6.6	-21.3	-38.9	-55.0
VETERANS										
American Legion	5.5	4.5	4.1	3.3	3.3	-17.7	-10.1	-17.5	-2.7	-40.6
Veterans of Foreign Wars	2.1	2.2	2.7	2.6	2.3	4.2	21.1	-4.7	-8.9	9.5
RECREATIONAL										
American Bowling Congress	3.4	8.1	6.5	4.6	2.7	136.2	-19.8	-28.4	-41.5	-20.6

PERCENT

ASSOCIATIONS FOR WOMEN	U.S. WOMEN ENROLLED					DECADE SHIFTS				TOTAL SHIFT, 1955–95
	1955	1965	1975	1985	1995	1955–65	1965–75	1975–85	1985–95	
RELIGIOUS										
United Methodist Women	3.4	2.8	1.8	1.4	1.0	-16.7	-34.6	-23.2	-28.4	-70.0

	U.S. Adults Enrolled					Decade Shifts				Total Shift, 1955–95
	1955	1965	1975	1985	1995	1955–65	1965–75	1975–85	1985–95	
General Federation of Women's Clubs	1.5	1.2	0.8	0.5	0.3	–22.5	–33.3	–39.7	–45.8	–83.1
RECREATIONAL										
Women's International Bowling Congress	1.3	4.4	5.0	4.3	2.2	237.9	12.8	–14.6	–47.9	69.7
MIXED-GENDER ASSOCIATIONS										
OCCUPATIONAL										
AFL–CIO	2.1	10.9	10.0	7.9	6.9	–9.2	–8.3	–21.2	–12.9	–42.9
American Farm Bureau Federation	1.5	1.4	1.7	2.0	2.1	–1.6	22.4	14.0	8.8	49.4
FRATERNAL										
Order of the Eastern Star	2.3	2.0	1.5	1.0	0.6	–11.5	–27.0	–29.9	–38.0	–71.9
EDUCATIONAL										
National Congress of Parent and Teachers (PTA)	9.0	10.0	5.0	3.4	3.6	11.2	–49.6	–32.8	6.3	–60.0
Boy Scouts of America	1.3	1.6	1.2	1.0	1.1	21.8	–21.9	–23.0	17.7	–13.7
RECREATIONAL										
Young Men's Christian Association	2.1	2.8	4.3	3.3	3.5	29.6	57.1	–22.7	3.3	62.5
OTHER										
American Automobile Association	4.8	8.0	12.4	15.8	20.2	66.2	56.4	27.1	27.7	322.0

Note: Percents are rounded to one decimal point, but decade shifts are based on underlying unrounded numbers.
SOURCE: Civic Engagement Project, Harvard University

American Legion, and the General Federation of Women's Clubs persevere with shrinking memberships, cajoling people to attend less frequent meetings. Annual reports portray portly, graying men and women, because younger Americans simply have not joined such groups in the proportions their elders once did.

Table 4.3 does not tell the whole story, to be sure, because some national membership associations have been newly launched or expanded in recent times. Table 2.1 indicates the newly founded associations that managed to recruit 1 percent or more of U.S. adults as members after the 1940s. By far the largest is the American Association of Retired Persons (AARP), which now boasts more than 33 million adherents, about one-half of all Americans aged fifty or older.[53] Launched in 1958 with backing from a teachers' retirement group and an insurance company, the AARP grew rapidly in the 1970s and 1980s by offering commercial discounts to members and establishing a Washington headquarters from which to monitor and lobby about federal legislation affecting seniors. The AARP has a legislative and policy staff of 165 people, 28 registered lobbyists, and more than 1,200 staff members in the field.[54] After recent efforts to expand its regional and local infrastructure, the AARP involves 5 to 10 percent of its members in membership chapters—like the one that proudly proclaims its existence (along with traditional service, fraternal, and women's groups) on the civic billboard that graces the entrance to the town of Princeton, Illinois. But for the most part, the AARP national office—covering an entire city block with its own mail zip code—deals with masses of individual adherents through the mail. Individualized contact is also the norm for other recently enlarged membership associations such as the National Wildlife Federation (founded in 1936 but expanded after the 1960s) and Mothers Against Drunk Driving (founded in 1980), which uses advertising and direct-mail solicitations. Founded internationally in 1971, with a "USA" organization established in 1988, Greenpeace relies on door-to-door canvassing as well as direct mail.

Four additional membership associations that recently surpassed 1 percent of the U.S. adult population use such individualized recruitment methods, yet also have portions of their national memberships involved in local and state chapters. Interestingly, these groups are heavily involved in partisan electoral politics—especially on the conservative end of the political spectrum. To be sure, one liberal group appears among those recently achieving very large size. For many decades after its establishment in 1857, the National Education Association (NEA) was a relatively elitist association of public educators. But in the 1970s it became a quasi-union for public school teachers and a stalwart in state and local as well as national Democratic Party politics.[55] Meanwhile, locally rooted membership federations fared even better on the right, including the National Right to Life Committee, founded in 1973, and the Christian Coalition, launched in 1989. Both recruit members and activists from evangelical church congregations and involve them in political work in and around the Republican Party. In addition, although founded way back in 1871, the National Rifle Association (NRA) became a massive force only in the 1970s, when right-wing activists opposed to gun control changed what had traditionally been a network of marksmen's clubs into a conservative, Republican-leaning advocacy group fiercely opposed to gun control legislation.[56]

Overall, the ranks of America's very largest individual membership associations changed markedly over the last half of the twentieth century. Figures 4.3 and 4.4 trace two of the most dramatic changes, looking only at the twenty absolutely largest associations at each mid-decade point from the 1940s through the 1990s.[57] In the mid-twentieth century, as figure 4.3 shows, half to three-fifths of the very largest U.S. voluntary membership associations enrolled men or women (either exclusively or overwhelmingly). Americans of each gender met separately for fun, fellowship, and community service. But among the largest associations, gender-segregated groups lost ground steadily after the 1960s, as new integrated associations emerged and some male-only groups began admitting adult women (in the case of the Boy Scouts, as troop leaders). By 1995 sixteen of the twenty absolutely largest U.S. membership associations were fully gender integrated.

Even more striking is the changing mix of primary purposes for very large U.S. associations, displayed in figure 4.4. In the mid-twentieth century most large Amerian voluntary associations were fraternal or religious federations focused on celebrating brotherhood or sisterhood, or civic associations devoted to community service. Specialized recreational and economic groups also existed but were in the minority. By the 1980s and 1990s, however, the goals of very large assocations were much more narrowly instrumental or recreational—which corresponds to the fact that many large groups now recruit supporters through the mail with promises of economic benefits or virtual representation in Washington, D.C. The universe of very large American membership associations today is much less concerned with brotherhood, sisterhood, fellow citizenship,

FIGURE 4.3

Gender Composition of the Largest American Membership Associations, 1945–1995

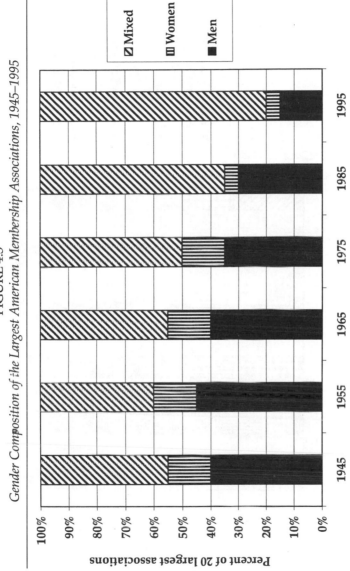

FIGURE 4.4

Primary Missions of the Largest American Membership Associations, 1945–1995

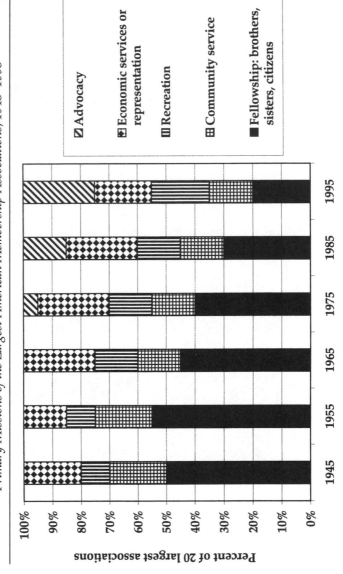

and community service than ever before in the nation's long civic history.

New Social Movements and
Chapter-based Membership Federations

To some extent, looking at only the very largest membership associations becomes misleading for the period since 1960. Certain membership associations, including federations with local or district chapters, were buoyed by the liberal social movements of the 1960s and 1970s, yet their growth has stopped well short of the absolute and population-share levels attained by classic American voluntary federations. Two previously small conservation groups caught the winds of the new environmentalism. From 1960 to 1990 the Sierra Club (originally created in 1892) ballooned from some 15,000 members into a giant with 565,000 members meeting in 378 "local groups." And the National Audubon Society (founded in 1905) went from 30,000 members and 330 chapters in 1958 to about 600,000 members and more than 500 chapters in the 1990s.[58] Another recently growing group is NOW, which reached 1,122 members and 14 chapters within a year of its founding in 1966 and spread across all fifty states with some 125,000 members meeting in 700 chapters by 1978.[59] Significantly, these environmental and feminist groups have clear partisan political leanings. Although officially nonpartisan, they are leading actors in the advocacy clusters surrounding the Democratic Party.

But notice that such "new social movement" associations do not match the organizational scope of old-line American membership federations. At its post–World War II high point in 1955, for example, the General Federation of Women's Clubs (GFWC) boasted more than 850,000 members meeting in 15,168 local clubs—with the local clubs themselves clustered into representative networks in each of the fifty U.S. states plus the District of Columbia. By contrast, at its high point in 1993 NOW reported some 280,000 members and 800 chapters, with no intermediate tier of representative governance between the national center and local chapters.[60] NOW has since contracted considerably, and its chapters are located primarily in cities and university towns in the more liberal and cosmopolitan states, whereas for most of the twentieth century thousands of GFWC chapters were scattered through communities—big, medium, small, and tiny—in all of the U.S. states. Environmental membership groups, meanwhile, frequently rely on canvassing or direct-mail for recruitment, even if a portion of their members join via local or regional chapters. When state or local groups are to be found in modern environmental associations—as, for example, in the Sierra Club and the Audubon Society—they are not as numerous or thick on the ground as chapters of classic membership federations.

Ranging from NOW to the Christian Coalition, recently enlarged national membership federations certainly matter, especially in contemporary partisan politics. But we should not imagine such groups are anything except counterexamples to dominant associational trends. Using various kinds of data, scholars have repeatedly demonstrated that U.S. associations founded after the mid-twentieth century often had no individual members and even more rarely developed national networks of local chapters.[61] I have examined the issue in yet another way. Summary statistics about 3000 "social welfare" and "public affairs" organizations founded in the 1960s, 1970s, and 1980s show that close to half indicate no "members" at all, and another quarter claim fewer than 1,000 "members."[62] In some instances a number under 1,000 indicates a modest individual membership, but it may also connote an association that has other organizations as its constituents, just as many public affairs, trade, and professional associations do.

Reconfigured by the advocacy explosion, the new universe of national American associations that emerged after the 1960s not only features proportionally more nonbusiness groups and thousands more groups overall than the federation-heavy civic universe of the 1950s. It also has many more small groups and many more memberless entities and groups with constituents attracted through the mail and the media. Specializing in this or that constituency, cause, or activity, civic entrepreneurs by the thousands have founded advocacy organizations without individual members, groups that represent other organizations, and groups that speak for modest numbers of individual adherents who respond to mass mailings or canvasses by giving money. To borrow the colorful phrase of my colleague and fellow researcher Marshall Ganz, the vast majority of recently founded civic associations are "bodyless heads." And the reconfigured civic universe is much more focused on specialized, instrumental activities than on broad expressions of community or fellow citizenship.

Are Grassroots Groups Proliferating?

Some observers insist that the explosion of professionally managed associations and the waning of national membership federations do not amount to the whole story of recent civic change in America. Membership groups still flourish, the argument goes, but they are a new breed of intimate and flexible creations, deliberately detached from overarching federated frameworks. Although "it's much harder to measure participation that is highly decentralized," argues Everett Carl Ladd, "in many sectors of national life, the trend is away from centralized, national organizations to those that are decentralized and local."[63] Ladd and other analysts point to trends that may be unfolding below the radar screen of the national surveys on which Robert Putnam relies so heavily in *Bowling Alone*. Although Putnam uses over-time data and his critics rely mostly on rich snapshots at one point in time, we cannot dismiss scholarly accounts of small group "movements." Perhaps contemporary Americans are increasingly doing all kinds of groupy things they have not brought to mind when asked by pollsters about "attending club meetings" or "devoting time to community organizations."[64]

Groups of parents involved with their children's schools are an excellent case in point according to Ladd, who tells a story of "expansive, energetic local engagement" in parent-teacher organizations (PTOs) to counter Putnam's claim that declining membership in local chapters of the National Congress of Parents and Teachers indicates a sharp depletion of America's "social capital."[65] "The real reason PTA membership fell off," Ladd writes, "wasn't that parents stopped participating; *rather, they associated increasingly with groups other than the PTA*. That is, they substituted other groups for the same basic functions." National PTA membership peaked in the early 1960s, but by the mid-1990s "less than one-fourth of all public and private K-12 schools had PTA affiliates." "Something else had to be happening." To discover what, Ladd and his associates surveyed a representative sample of principals and superintendents in Connecticut (a very wealthy and highly urban state) and Kansas (a less prosperous and more rural state). They received "excellent cooperation" and were assured that virtually all districts had parent organizations engaged in such supportive volunteer activities as providing classroom and office help, assisting in the library, computer room, or lunchroom, taking part in field trips, and organizing fund-raising drives. (Admittedly, this research method has its drawbacks: what principal would *not* say in a brief telephone interview that his or her school has an active parent organization?)

Putnam counters Ladd by arguing that membership in independent PTOs has not made up for declines in PTA affiliation over recent decades.[66] Ladd has certainly established the probable widespread prevalence of nonfederated school-support groups, but he has less to say about how these groups are structured, who initiates their activities and actually participates, and why they have proliferated apart from the once-hegemonic PTA. Sociologists Susan Crawford and Peggy Levitt show that travails over racial desegregation of the public schools—and desegregation of the national PTA itself—coincided with massive declines in membership and local chapters in the 1960s and 1970s.[67] Disillusionment with teachers' unions and disgruntlement about national PTA opposition to school vouchers and charter schools are other reasons cited for withdrawals from the nationally federated PTA.[68] "But for many parents," Ladd concludes, "'controlling things ourselves right here in town' and keeping all the dues money for local use are probably more important factors leading them to disaffiliate."[69] In his view, "this was a big deal for the PTA, and for those who believe that its lobbying efforts are important. But it has nothing to do with developments in civic America." Not just in the educational sphere, but in other areas of religious and civic participation as well, Ladd celebrates a "vast proliferation of small groups" as a key indicator that American voluntarism is more vital than ever before.[70]

While Ladd examines American politics from a somewhat conservative angle, some leftists assert with equal fervor that local grassroots participation has flourished in recent times, rendering "large groups with a national media profile . . . simply the most visible promontories in the broader landscape of contemporary social movements."[71] Favorite examples for liberals include neighborhood environmental campaigns against threats such as the dumping of toxic wastes, campaigns that are said to number in the thousands and far surpass the proliferation of national advocacy groups in the 1970s and 1980s.[72] The data supporting this claim are sketchy in the extreme, based on "contacts" with an umbrella "clearinghouse" organization, the Citizen's Clearinghouse for Hazardous Wastes.[73] But a more systematic analysis by sociologist Bob Edwards examines some 7,651 associations "working for peace" listed in the 1987 edition of the *Grassroots Peace Directory*.[74] Edwards examined the organizational characteristics and scope of operations of the 7 percent of peace groups that had budgets of $30,000 or more and of a representative sample of the 93 percent of groups with smaller annual budgets. His claims that some five hundred to six hundred national, staff-run "peace movement organizations" were but the tip of the iceberg in this large social movement, which peaked during the presidency of Ronald Reagan just before the end of the Cold War. "Small, informal, volunteer-run local groups are clearly the core of the movement," he asserts.[75]

A closer look at the evidence Edwards persents suggests a somewhat different conclusion, however.[76] Only about 27 percent of all the groups Edwards tallied were classified either as "primarily a group of friends working together for peace" or as an "organized independent group working at the local level." Roughly another 29 percent were "local affiliate[s] of a statewide or national group," which means they were parts of federations. Beyond that, another 15 percent were "peace committee[s] or task force[s] within a larger organization." All the rest of the entities that Edwards could classify were state, regional, and national groups, some parts of federations and others not. Certainly Edwards portrays a substantial social movement with a mixture of many kinds of organizations and constituencies. But local, state, regional, and national parts of voluntary federations were very numerous; and many of the less formally organized and nonfederated groups were, as Edwards explains, "peace committees and task forces within larger [religious] denominational, occupational, or political organizations. . . . In fact, a large portion of the movement is embedded within some of the most mainstream religious and occupational constituencies of American society."[77]

Read in conjunction with the bits of evidence just rehearsed, sociologist Robert Wuthnow's study of small groups focused on personal inspiration and intimate social support allows us to sharpen our picture of what is really going on.[78] Since the 1960s and 1970s, Wuthnow argues, American have searched for community and heightened spirituality in new ways, forming new kinds of groups, apart from traditional voluntary associations, to overcome the fragmentation and meet the stresses of contemporary life. Measuring movements that he believes continued to grow in the 1990s, Wuthnow found in 1991 that 40 percent of U.S. adults were regular participants in 3 million or more groups, each with about twenty-five people meeting regularly and providing caring and support for their members. Men and women, blacks and whites, old and young, Americans living in all regions and in all sizes of communities are participants in Sunday school groups, Bible study classes, self-help groups, and discussion groups of many kinds. People find intimacy, inspiration, and social support in small groups, which "have an enormous advantage in adapting to a more fluid social environment." As Wuthnow explains, small groups "require virtually no resources, other than the time their members devote to them each week, so they can start with relative ease and disband just as easily. . . . [T]here are likely to be pockets of like-minded people who can populate a group that requires only twenty members to operate, whereas the same might not be true if two hundred members were required. Besides, someone interested in slightly different issues can simply start another group."[79]

We should not imagine from this depiction that the interpersonal groups Wuthnow so thoroughly documents are freestanding entities. They may be flexible, intimate, and specifically tailored to various people's interests, but the vast majority of today's small groups (like classic local groups but in new ways) are institutionally embedded, dependent on resources, networks, and organizationally embodied meanings larger than themselves. As membership-based institutions that have historically flourished in the United States and remain extraordinarily vital today, religious institutions are the most important supporters of small groups—just as, historically, there were always great numbers of men's, women's, and children groups attached to Catholic parishes, Protestant congregations, and Jewish synagogues. In recent decades ministers, priests, and rabbis have become convinced that a wide and flexible array of such groups are keys to attracting and holding congregants. "Variety is the key to our small-group ministry," a Presbyterian minister told Wuthnow in a typical remark.[80]

Small, religiously attached groups may flourish most readily among evangelical Protestants. Since the 1960s traditional mainline Protestant denominations have lost membership shares in the still-vital universe of U.S. religious participation, while evangelical churches, many of them not tied to federated denominations, have flourished. "Mega churches" are vital centers of social activity in many suburban and rural communities all across the United States, especially in the South.[81] These huge religious communities may not encourage congregants to participate in wider community associations as readily as old-line Protestant churches once did.[82] But evangelical churches, large and small, fashion rich networks of affiliated groups attractive to all kinds of congregants— from married parents to young singles— even as old-line congregations threatened with membership decline make similar efforts to attract participation.

Religious congregations offer small groups places to meet, models of organization, materials to discuss, and, of course, a meaningful framework for joining together. As a result, religious classes, Bible study groups, and other mutual support groups connected to religious congregations account for well over half of the nearly 3 million groups Wuthnow estimates existed in 1991 and well over half of the 82 million memberships he estimates for those groups (in many cases people belong to two or more groups).[83] Yet religious professionals and congregations are not the only institutional supporters of small groups. Certain liberal and conservative foundations shepherd bevies of "grassroots" groups, supplying them with funds, ideas, and oversight. And a pioneering "twelve-step" self-help association, the nationally federated Alcoholics Anonymous, nurtures many local groups for recovering alcoholics and has offered an organizational model widely copied and adapted by many other kinds of self-help groups. Self-help groups, in turn, are encouraged by national clearinghouses, by national organizations devoted to fighting particular diseases, and by hospitals and health maintenance organizations.[84] Along with church-connected small groups, self-help groups are the other big sector in the overall small group movement Wuthnow documents, accounting for an estimated half a million groups with up to 10 million members.

In addition, Wuthnow believes there may be up to 30 million members of as many as 750,000 "special interest" groups devoted to discussing books or current events or to pursuing shared interests in sports or hobbies.[85] Perhaps these groups are the most likely to be spontaneously formed outside of institutional contexts. But here too there are umbrella associations that provide models and encouragement, just as national health associations do for health-related self-help groups. As table 4.2 documents, "hobby and avocational" and "athletic and sports" groups were two clearly membership-based kinds of "national" associations that experienced extraordinary proliferation between 1959 and 1999.

In the end we must deliver a mixed verdict about small groups in contemporary civic America. Religious groups and self-help gatherings are certainly meeting vital needs for millions of Americans. Where PTA affiliates are not in evidence, local parent groups nevertheless often help out in the schools. And some grassroots "movement" groups agitate for peace or fight environmental threats in particular settings. But how many of today's "small groups" are truly grassroots undertakings? Clergy, school principals, and health professionals often take the initiative to get specialized small groups going; and because most groups do not collect regular dues or run drives to build meeting halls, they must rely on resources borrowed from host institutions.[86] Very often, contemporary small-group governance is significantly different from classic American civic governance. Unlike chapters in classic voluntary federations, small groups linked to parent institutions usually do not elect leaders charged with attending representative meetings, building intergroup networks, or making decisions at state, regional, and national levels. Instead, they concentrate on meeting immediate personal and interpersonal goals while borrowing—and taking for granted—the resources and encompassing meanings embodied in the institutions that host them.

A RECONFIGURED CIVIC UNIVERSE

As this chapter has documented, extraordinary changes have occurred over the past half century in the ways Americans combine for civic and political purposes. To be sure, the changes have not been of a piece. Countertrends are most in evidence among political conservatives and regular churchgoers (who are, of course, partially overlapping sets of people). Right-wing voluntary federations draw people from churches and kitchens into local, state, and national politics in and around the Republican Party.[87] And contemporary intimate groups are especially likely to involve churchgoers at a time when Protestant evangelical congregations are on the rise.[88] Nor are conservative evangelicals the only Americans for whom membership-centered groups and institutions remain vital. Environmentalists, labor unions, and some community organizers have also found innovative ways to bridge intimate groups and supralocal movements. Because exceptions matter as much as master story lines in social analysis, we will do well to keep them in mind as we further explore America's recent civic transformations. Exceptions, however, are not the rule.

Figure 4.5 offers a typology of various kinds of nationally consequential voluntary associations, all of which in some sense speak for members or constituents. Some membership or constituency associations purposefully speak for the self-interests of elites, that is, for business or professional people. Other associations speak for elites who aim to serve the broader community. Still other associations represent broad public and cross-class constituencies. And a few groups, finally, speak on behalf of less advantaged or marginalized people. The types of associations arrayed in this chart also differ by governance and resource base. Some are professionally run, with resources assembled from a combination of sources, including grants from patrons and perhaps computerized mass mailings. Other associations, by contrast, are headed by elected leaders and derive a major part of their resources from regularly collected membership dues. This figure is strictly a conceptual map, yet it helps to clarify the most startling transformations in America's national civic life since the mid-twentieth century.

FIGURE 4.5

Membership and Constituency Associations in U.S. Civic Life

| | | GROUP SPEAKS FOR | | |
GOVERNANCE AND RESOURCE BASE	ELITES	ELITES SERVING THE COMMUNITY	PUBLIC OR CROSS-CLASS CONSTITUENCY	LESS ADVANTAGED
Professionally run; money from patrons, other organizations, and/or mass mailings	Business associations	Foundations and other institutions that gather $ for community purposes	Public interest advocacy groups (environmental, consumers; and good-government groups) Nonprofit agencies	Advocates for the poor, disabled, children, marginalized minorities, and other vulnerable groups
Elected leaders; high proportion of money from membership dues	Professional associations; College alumni/ae groups, Fraternities and sororities	Elite service clubs (such as Rotary, Soroptimists, Junior League)	Large fraternals (such as Elks, Masons, Moose, Eagles, and their female partners) Ethnic fraternals Women's federations (such as WCTU, GFWC, PTA) Religious associations (such as Knights of Columbus, Woman's Missionary Union) Veterans' associations and auxiliaries Inclusive farm groups	Unions Populist farmers' associations

From the 1800s through the 1950s and 1960s, U.S. civic life was dominated by a mixture of business associations (classified in the top left of the chart) plus many kinds of representatively governed membership associations (the various types of groups classified across the bottom half of the chart). Since the 1960s, however, the ranks of professionally run groups (indicated on the top half of the chart) have swelled, especially groups other than business associations. Groups dispersing contributions from the wealthy; professionally run citizens' associations; and professionally managed advocacy groups for the poor and vulnerable— all of these types have expanded their presence on the U.S. civic scene. At the same time, representatively governed voluntary federations have ceased to proliferate, and their dues-paying memberships have contracted.

A new civic America has thus taken shape since the 1960s, as professionally managed advocacy groups and institutions have moved to the fore, while representatively governed, nation-spanning voluntary membership federations—especially those with popular or cross-class memberships—have lost clout in national public affairs and faded from the everyday lives of most Americans. Why all of this happened is the question I take up in the next chapter. We cannot fully rejoin ongoing debates about the vitality of U.S. democracy until we have gained a better understanding of the convergent forces that propelled and shaped the recent great transformation from membership to management in American civic life.

CHAPTER 5

WHY CIVIC LIFE CHANGED

AFTER MORE THAN A CENTURY of civic life rooted in nation-spanning membership federations, *why* did America's associational universe change so sharply in the late twentieth century? Much hand-wringing over civic decline has concerned the individual choices of masses of Americans: Are people, especially youngsters, sitting in front of television and computer screens at home rather than voting and going out to community events and club meetings? Were the adults of the World War II generation unusually civicly engaged, so that their passing from the scene brings an inevitable if unfortunate decline in participation? The answers to both questions may be yes, as Robert D. Putnam hypothesizes.[1] But to attribute the sudden shifts in civic organizing between the 1960s and the 1990s merely to gradual processes of generational replacement is not entirely plausible and says far too little about the institutional and social causes at work.

The great civic transformation of our time happened too abruptly to be attributable primarily to incremental processes of generational replacement. And this attribution misses what we most need to understand. After all, contemporary Americans are not simply joining old associations less frequently than their forebears did. They are also organizing to an extraordinary degree, and engaging public affairs in very new ways.

Social capital theorists examine all forms of social connectedness at once, lumping together for explanatory purposes everything from bowling leagues and family dinners to the more publicly relevant forms of organizing and joining. We ought to be skeptical that one explanation fits all types of sociopolitical activity, but the vague focus should worry us even more. Publicly relevant voluntary activities are the ones of greatest relevance to the health of American democracy; and to explain transformations in these activities, a focus on changing modes of social interaction cannot be sufficient. The choices masses of citizens make about politics and civic involvement respond, above all, to available avenues of meaningful group participation and publicly relevant clout.[2] Most people need to be directly invited into public engagements, contacted personally by leaders and folks they know. People must also "see themselves" in the shared undertaking. And they must believe an undertaking will really matter—or else they won't bother. All of these considerations direct our attention to the changing roles of leaders, to shifting social identities and modes of organization, and to considerations of power, resources, and institutional leverage. We cannot explain democratically relevant shifts in civil society by focusing on mass attitudes and intimate interactions alone.

As Alexis de Tocqueville recognized long ago, people in a democracy use many of their voluntarily created associations to gain leverage and to express shared identities and widely shared values. That is why civic leaders and organizers are so crucial. They are the ones who take the initiative, who define and jump-start the arts of "combination" Tocqueville rightly considered central to democracy. The kinds of associations leading citizens launch and patronize, the shared values and identities they articulate, and the tactics civic leaders use to gain and exercise public voice and political leverage—all of these matters powerfully influence the menu of possibilities for participation available to most citizens. In a thriving democracy, leaders regularly invite many fellow citizens to join with them in important endeavors. Citizens must respond, of course, or leadership initiatives fail. But it is not foreordained that leaders will emerge to offer the most democratically propitious avenues of shared engagement. Over the sweep of history, elites have often cooperated and contended with one another above the heads of most people living in their societies. Only in special circumstances do elites turn to democratic leadership—above all, to the kinds of democratic leadership that involve mobilizing and organizing others.

Democratic mobilization becomes the norm when would-be leaders can achieve power and influence only by drawing others into movements, associations, and political battles. Elites must have incentives to organize others, if democratic mobilization is to happen regularly. Such incentives were certainly in place in earlier eras of U.S. history—when party politicians could win elected office only in close fought, high-turnout elections and when association builders could attain national influence only by spreading networks of chapters of dues-paying members all across America. Similar incentives for elites to engage in democratic organizing and mobilization may be lacking today.

Using this frame of reference, this chapter examines roots and results of contemporary shifts in organized American civic life and strategies of civic leadership. A confluence of trends and events sparked a shift from membership mobilization to managerial forms of civic organizing. After 1960 epochal changes in racial ideals and gender relationships delegitimated old-line U.S. membership associations and pushed male and female leaders in new directions. New political opportunities and challenges drew resources and civic activists toward centrally managed lobbying. Innovative technologies and sources of financial support enabled new, memberless models of association building to take hold. And, finally, shifts in America's class structure and elite careers created a broad constituency for professionally managed civic organizing. Many Americans are now relatively privileged, highly individualistic businesspeople or professionals, with formidable civic resources at their personal disposal. The most privileged Americans can now organize and contend largely among themselves, without regularly engaging the majority of citizens.

SOCIAL LIBERATION AND CIVIC TRANSFORMATION

Until recent times most American membership associations enrolled business and professional people together with white-collar folks, farmers, and craft or industrial workers. There was a degree of fellowship across class lines—usually accompanied by racial exclusion and gender separation. But then, as old social barriers were breached in the 1960s and 1970s, established associational practices were inevitably shaken to their core.

Old Exclusions Breached

Classic American membership federations typically enrolled either men or women, not both together.[3] True, women's auxiliaries or partner groups—such as the Daughters of Rebekah, the Pythian Sisters, the VFW Auxiliary, the Eastern Star, and the Ladies Auxiliary to the Brotherhood of Railroad Trainmen—operated alongside most fraternal and veterans' groups and trade union brotherhoods. Female partner associations could be surprisingly assertive: the Royal Neighbors of America, for instance, insisted that all officer posts be held by women, even though men of the Modern Woodmen of America could also join. Nevertheless, partner associations fell short from a modern feminist perspective, because they focused on helpmate roles and were usually open only to the wives, daughters, widows, or other female relatives of men who were members of the primary brotherhood.[4] Independent women's federations like the WCTU and the PTA were open to a wider range of women; yet they too stressed traditional gender roles and responsibilities in ways that most feminists would find limiting.

Racial separation was even more the rule than gender segregation in civic America before the 1960s. Giant American membership federations like the Odd Fellows and the Knights of Pythias at one time or another bridged most ethnic and religious divides—accepting Jews, for example, and allowing ethnic lodges to conduct their rituals and business in a variety of European languages. But white opposition to accepting African American members remained virtually airtight, especially in male membership federations other than national federations of military veterans.[5] As late as the period after World War II, there was nothing subtle about white racism in fraternal life. Virtually all group constitutions echoed the words of a 1950s orientation pamphlet, *What It Means to Be an Elk*: "Membership in the Order is limited to white male citizens of the United States . . . who believe in the existence of God [and] who subscribe themselves to the objects and purposes of the order."[6] When the traditional white Elks spoke of "Charity, Justice, Brotherly Love, and Fidelity," they did not mean it where African Americans were concerned.[7] African Americans built fraternal federations of their own, yet they unquestionably resented exclusion by white fraternal groups.

Given the pervasiveness of both racial separation and the gender division of labor in classic civic America, established voluntary associations were bound to be shaken after the mid-1950s, as the Civil Rights revolution, soon followed by a cascade of additional rights movements, shook American society and culture to the core. As we learned in chapter 4, most membership federations flourishing in the 1950s dwindled thereafter. Some associations lost membership and clout in the 1960s, and all but a few of the rest trended downward from the mid-1970s. Not incidentally, membership erosions accelerated as new racial and gender ideals took hold in American public life and as more and more women entered the paid labor force. Female labor-force participation mattered for male associations because, after all, the ladies of the auxiliaries had often been the ones to prepare (and clean up after) all those group suppers. Yet of course new roles for women had an even greater impact on the purposes and activities of traditional women's associations.

For example, a long-standing and important female-dominated federation, the National Congress of Parents and Teachers, struggled after the early 1960s to implement racial desegregation and cope with changing conditions of work and family life.[8] Historically, blacks and whites were organized into separate but parallel PTA federations, but in 1970 the national white PTA leadership mandated racial integration over the resistance of southern white federations that had previously vetoed this step. Nor was this the only wrenching change to hit from the 1970s. Long dependent on the activism of married homemakers, local and supralocal PTA organizations had to adapt to a society with increasing numbers of dual-career families and single-parent households. The PTA of our time has been relatively successful in adapting to new racial ideals and family conditions, yet it has lost members and local units in the process. And long-standing local chapter activities have often fallen by the wayside.

Other U.S. membership federations also struggled to adapt to new social ideals. Associations dropped explicit racial bars and undertook new public service projects. Some built new recreational facilities. Such steps kept membership losses minimal for some groups—such as the YMCA, with its shift from Christian spiritual and physical development for men and boys to community recreation for the whole family. But many federations could not stave off delegitimation and steady membership decline. Once socially segregated associations simply lost appeal to younger Americans coming of age in the 1970s and afterward, in an era of social toleration and hopes for racial and gender integration. A 1997 survey asked Americans how likely they would be to join groups with various characteristics. Fully 58

percent said they would be "very unlikely" (not just "somewhat unlikely") to join a group that "accepts only men or
women," and 90 percent said they would be very unlikely
to join a group with "a history of racial discrimination."[9]
Today American men and women are in fact much more
likely than their predecessors to participate in mixed-gender groups. Racial integration has not been achieved to the
same degree; in practice many small groups and national
advocacy associations remain largely racially homogeneous,
just as most church congregations do. Nevertheless, all
respectable associations endorse racial inclusion as the
ideal—and so it is understandable that contemporary Americans are averse to "group labels" tainted by racist legacies.

The Eclipse of Patriotic Brotherhood

As segregated groups became less appealing to potential
membership recruits, changing gender roles also cut off
long-standing routes to associational leadership. Historically, former soldiers and higher-educated women outside
the paid labor force were mainstays of voluntary membership federations. Over many decades, both of these gender
categories generated leaders who appealed to—and could
mobilize—Americans across lines of class and place. In the
late twentieth century, however, these traditional wellsprings
of gendered civic leadership dried to a trickle.

On the male side of the classic associational equation, military veterans were key leaders—and not only in obvious
groups like the Veterans of Foreign Wars and the American
Legion. Military veterans were leading and highly honored
participants in fraternal groups, which accounted for nearly
a third of very large U.S. membership associations as late as

the 1950s. Patriotism, brotherhood, and sacrifice were values celebrated by all fraternal groups, and military service was touted as the surest way to achieve and express these virtues. During and after each major U.S. war, the Masons, Knights of Pythias, Elks, Knights of Columbus, Moose, Eagles, and scores of other fraternal groups celebrated and memorialized the contributions of their soldier-members. So did fraternal women's auxiliaries, not to mention men's service clubs and trade union "brotherhoods" and granges. Associational meeting halls displayed flags honoring members who served in the armed forces. Also held up for emulation were civilian associational leaders who threw themselves into campaigns to support national war efforts.

But "manly" ideals of military service faded after the early 1960s—and did not really revive amid renewed national respect for the military occasioned by the Gulf War of the early 1990s and the military actions following the anti-U.S. terrorist attacks of September 11, 2001. America's military has remained relatively small, as recent interventions abroad have been conducted by professional solidiers and National Guard reservists, not by masses of citizens subject to a nationwide draft. Cohorts of U.S. males coming of age in recent decades are much less likely than their predecessors to have served in the military. Two-thirds or more of American men born in the 1920s and early 1930s served; but the proportion plummeted afterward, so that only one-fifth or fewer of American men born since the mid-1950s have spent stints in the armed services.[10] Nor was military service the only issue, for America's bitter experiences during the controversial and unsuccessful war in Vietnam disrupted the intergenerational continuity of male identification with martial brotherliness.

Across most of U.S. history, even sons who did not go to war idealized the martial experiences of their fathers and grandfathers. Punctuated now and again by actual mobilization into victorious wars, intergenerationally shared ideals of martial valor, sacrifice, and comradeship helped to sustain fraternal and veterans' associations as the United States became a class-divided industrial nation. From the Revolution through the Civil War and the twentieth-century world wars, veterans' associations spawned interlinked associations for the "Sons of" those who actually fought. Similarly, late-nineteenth- and early-twentieth-century fraternal associations boasted of "marching orders," in which younger men, as well as actual veterans, could dress up in military-style uniforms to drill and maneuver much as the U.S. Army did. Wars exemplified cross-class brotherhood, and sons were presumed to follow fathers. The "Loyal Order of Moose is a militantly patriotic organization," declared the 1944 pamphlet *Moose Facts*, which added that "the desire of fathers—long members—to see the day when they may witness the initiation of their sons . . . has always been a potent . . . factor in stabilizing and building the Order's membership."[11]

But by the 1970s increasing numbers of fraternal fathers did not see the initiation of their sons. Standard fraternal histories recounting events in the 1960s and 1970s show mature lodge brothers staging ceremonies to celebrate "Americanism," deplore civil disturbances, and announce support for national military efforts in Vietnam.[12] At the same time, military service lost its élan for many younger people, and a cultural chasm opened between them and the aging World War II generation.

As the Vietnam experience disillusioned many younger Americans, other late-twentieth-century developments also undercut traditional nationalism. With the end of the cold war, peaceful international outlooks and activities came to seem normal and desirable for Americans in many walks of life. After the mid-1960s, moreover, the United States admitted increasing numbers of immigrants, not just from Europe, but from Central and Latin America, Asia, and all over the world. At least until the jarring reorientations occasioned by the terrorist attacks of September 11, 2001, internationalist cosmopolitanism and domestic multiculturalism were both on the rise, and talk of national solidarity and patriotism was gauche, especially among educated elites. Yet this was a huge break from America's long-term civic heritage. As we learned in chapters 2 and 3, national patriotism was central to the rituals, purposes, and activities of many classic U.S. voluntary federations. Its eclipse during the late twentieth century thus dissolved much of the moral glue that enabled cross-class associations to flourish—particularly among men.

Breaks with long-standing fraternal and patriotic traditions occurred first and most clearly for privileged, higher-educated young people. Some support for this claim comes from the General Social Survey (GSS), which between 1974 and 1994 asked national samples of Americans about their memberships in specific types of voluntary associations. Many of the types of groups named in GSS surveys are ambiguous, but the "fraternal" and "veterans" categories clearly refer to cross-class associations traditionally at the heart of American civil society.

As figures 5.1 and 5.2 show, from the mid-1970s through the mid-1990s affiliations with fraternal and veterans' associations followed different trajectories among the most and least educated Americans. As educational levels rose for each succeeding youthful cohort, people with no more than a high school degree became a smaller and less prestigious segment of the population. We might expect such increasingly marginal people to be the first to drop out of traditionally influential fraternal and veterans associations. But, actually, Americans without college experience maintained their participation at about the same level, while people with college degrees or postgraduate attainments were the ones who withdrew from or refused to join traditionally important fraternal and veterans' groups.[13] It would be nice to have comparable surveys from earlier decades, but even these limited aggregate data paint a startling picture. The aftermath of previous wars in modern U.S. history brought rising enrollments in fraternal and veterans groups—with privileged Americans very much in the vanguard. But something very different happened after the war in Vietnam.

Another kind of data supports the hypothesis that elite Americans pulled back from traditional brotherhood associations after the late 1960s and did so remarkably suddenly. Figure 5.3 surveys affiliations with fraternal and veterans' groups of thirteen sets of forty persons—the vast majority of them college- and graduate-educated business and professional men in their forties and fifties—who have served in the Senate of the state of Massachusetts at five-year intervals between 1920 and 2000. Each year the state of Massachusetts publishes a little book that shows a picture of each public officeholder and gives specific background information, including associational affiliations, in

FIGURE 5.1
Membership in American Fraternal Groups

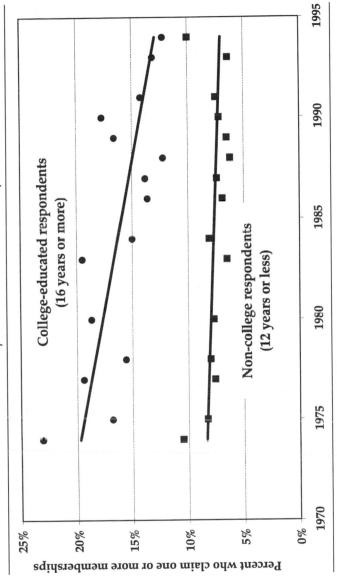

SOURCE: General Social Survey, 1974–94.

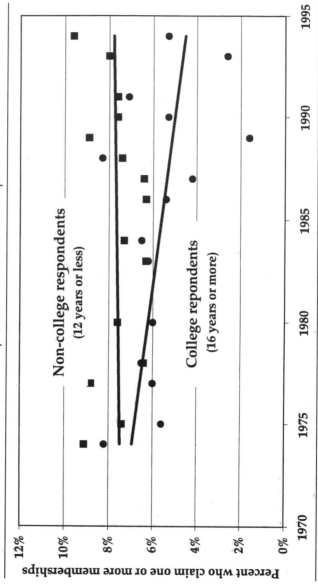

FIGURE 5.2
Membership in American Veterans' Groups

SOURCE: General Social Survey, 1974–94.

FIGURE 5.3

Fraternal and Veterans' Group Affiliations of Massachusetts State Senators, 1920–2000

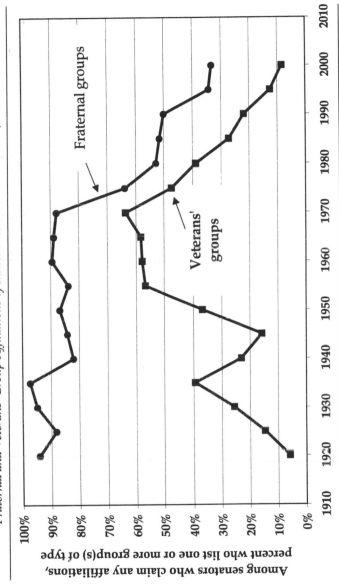

Source: *Public Officials of Massachusetts, 1920–2000.*

a format that has not changed since 1920.[14] This is a wonderfully detailed source of biographical and civic information on a consistently defined elite group.

As figure 5.3 documents, for many decades fraternal associations were by far the most common kind of voluntary group affiliation listed by Massachusetts senators (including the occasional female officeholder). Involvements with veterans' groups had ups and downs reflecting the maturation of cohorts of men who saw service in particular U.S. wars. Yet in the years immediately following the war in Vietnam, we do not see the usual increase in affiliations with veterans' associations; instead the proportion of senators claiming membership in one or more veterans' associations plummets to less than 10 percent in 2000. Even more remarkably, after the period 1965–70 long-standing senatorial ties to fraternal groups suddenly dissolved. From 1920 through 1965 more than three-ffourths of senators invariably claimed memberships in one or more fraternal groups. But the proportion of fraternalists in the Massachusetts Senate plummeted in the 1970s and declined further in the early 1990s, so that by 2000 fewer than 30 percent of senators claimed even one membership.[15]

Because, historically, Massachusetts senators frequently claimed memberships in a number of the very same large, cross-class voluntary federations in which more than 1 percent of American adults were enrolled, I have been able to compare recent rates of membership decline among male Massachusetts senators and citizens at large. My analysis focuses on four huge cross-class federations very frequently listed by Massachusetts senators. As Massachusetts senators became less likely to participate in the Elks, the Knights of Columbus, the Veterans of Foreign Wars, and the Amer-

ican Legion, were they simply reflecting trends in the Massachusetts citizenry? Or were post-1960s cohorts of senators
responding to new fashions in civic virtue, which took hold
quite suddenly among these publicly visible elites?

Figures 5.4 through 5.7 suggest that the latter hypothesis
is more plausible. Starting in the 1970s, senators were suddenly much less likely to have ties to the VFW, the Elks, and
the American Legion—and their rates of disaffiliation with
these massive associations were sharper than the declines in
membership among Massachusetts men in general. For the
Knights of Columbus, the trends stayed on a parallel course
between senators and citizens through the 1970s, but thereafter senators became much less likely to claim membership
in this group too. As Figure 5.8 suggests, instead of indicat-
ing memberships in all sorts of popular or cross-class voluntary groups, Massachusetts state senators now typically
proclaim trusteeships or other kinds of affiliations with professionally managed groups, such as cultural or social service
institutions, funds, commissions, and advocacy associations.
For relatively privileged and highly educated Massachusetts state senators, civic participation once meant membership in the same sorts of cross-class voluntary associations
in which less privileged Americans participated. By now,
however, their civic affiliations—and no doubt those of many
other U.S. elites as well—entail involvement with the management of professionally run institutions and associations.

Women's Civic Leadership Redefined

Significant as civic changes have been for men, women's
civic leadership has changed as much or more in our time.
Historically, American civic life was nourished by the

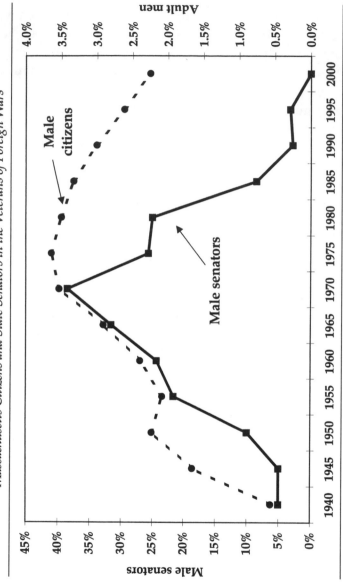

FIGURE 5.4

Massachusetts Citizens and State Senators in the Veterans of Foreign Wars

SOURCES: *Public Officials of Massachusetts, 1940–2000*; Civic Engagement Project data.

FIGURE 5.5

Massachusetts Citizens and State Senators in the Benevolent and Protective Order of Elks

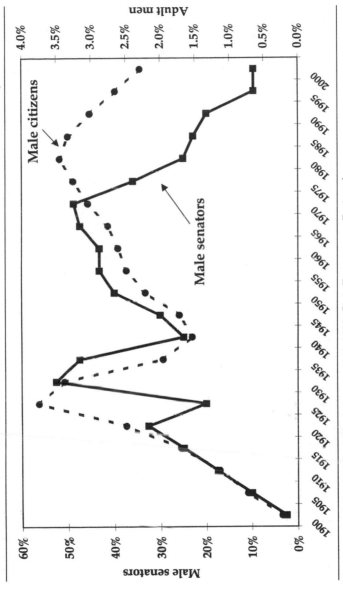

Sources: *Public Officials of Massachusetts, 1940–2000; Civic Engagement Project data.*

FIGURE 5.6

Massachusetts Citizens and State Senators in the American Legion

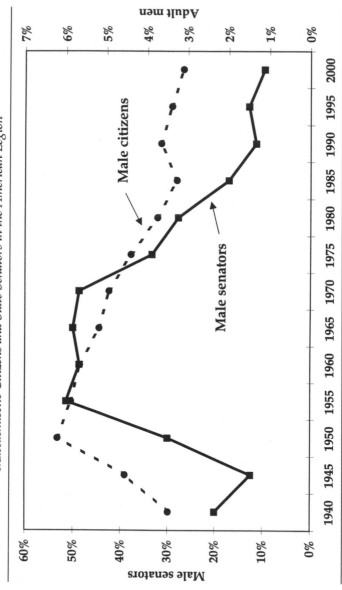

SOURCES: *Public Officials of Massachusetts, 1940–2000; Civic Engagement Project data.*

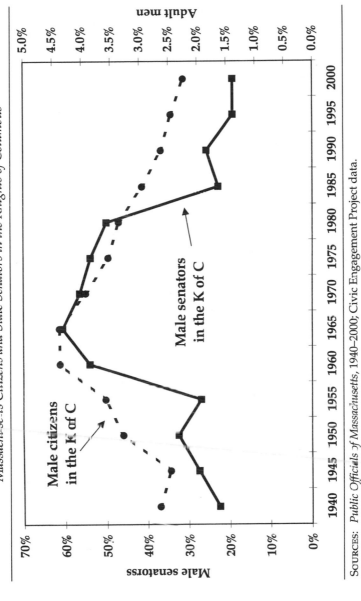

FIGURE 5.7

Massachusetts Citizens and State Senators in the Knights of Columbus

SOURCES: *Public Officials of Massachusetts, 1940–2000;* Civic Engagement Project data.

FIGURE 5.8
Civic Affiliations of Massachusetts State Senators, 1940–2000

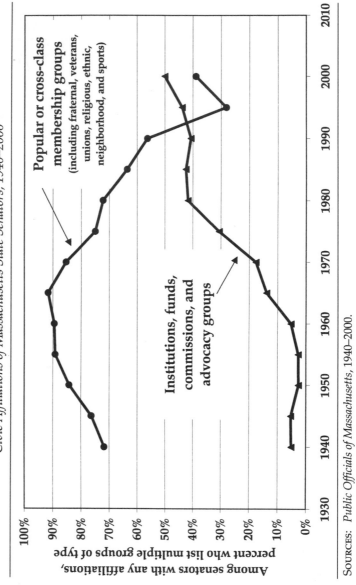

SOURCES: *Public Officials of Massachusetts*, 1940–2000.

activism of educated wives and mothers who spent most of their lives as homemakers. Although a tiny fraction of all U.S. females, higher-educated women were historically a surprisingly substantial and widespread presence, for the United States was a pioneer in the schooling of girls and in the higher education of women. By 1880 some 40,000 American women constituted one-third of all students in all kinds of U.S. institutions of higher learning; and women's share rose to nearly half at the early-twentieth-century peak in 1920, when some 283,000 women were enrolled in institutions of higher learning.[16] Many higher-educated women of the late 1800s and early 1900s married immediately and stayed out of the paid labor force. Others taught for a time in primary and secondary schools and subsequently married men in their communities and stopped teaching (either voluntarily or because school systems would not employ married women). With skills to make connections within and across places—and with spare time on their hands as children grew older—former teachers and other well-educated women were a strong civic presence in communities across America.

These days, of course, more American women than ever before are college educated.[17] By 1990 about 14 percent more women than men earned bachelors degrees; and nowadays large numbers of female college graduates go on to achieve graduate degrees and pursue professional and managerial careers.[18] Contemporary educated women face new opportunities and constraints. Paid work and family responsibilities are no longer separate spheres, and the occupational structure is less sex segregated at all levels. Today even married women with children are very likely to be employed, at least part time. In 1960, 28 percent of married women with children were employed, but by 1996 the number had risen to 69 percent.[19]

Today's educated and employed women have certainly not dropped out of civic life. On the contrary, women employed part time are more likely to be members of groups or volunteers than are stay-at-home housewives; and fully employed women are often drawn into civic activities through work.[20] New opportunities and responsibilities for women have nevertheless exacted a society-wide civic and social toll. A recent study of long-term trends in volunteering, participation in voluntary organizations, and involvement in informal social activities among American adults ages twenty-five to fifty-four shows that women's increased labor force participation has modestly contributed to declines in all three areas.[21] Nor is it adequate simply to count up group affiliations, as if all types of civic involvement were the same. America's educated women, especially, are now engaged in new kinds of activities. GSS data on types of associational memberships tell us that between 1974 and 1994 college-educated women were more likely to affiliate with professional societies but less likely to claim memberships in school-service groups, church-related groups, and fraternal or veterans' auxiliaries.

A fair guess is that female gains in higher education and career employment have hurt the very types of cross-class, broad-gauged associations in which women were traditionally active, particularly undercutting the fortunes of groups such as parent-teacher associations that once met regularly and relied on volunteer, elected leaders. Educated and employed women, like men, now join professional associations and send checks to national advocacy groups. In communities and through workplaces, an active woman may get involved intensely and episodically—running a fund-raising drive, for example—rather than attend a traditional-style club that melds sociability with community service. Similarly, a woman employed as a "helping professional" or at a non-profit agency may take part in a campaign or coalition to address a pressing social issue. As Wuthnow points out, nonprofit social service agencies, issue-oriented advocacy groups, and volunteers often work together in civic campaigns focused on specific problems or challenges.[22] Both men and women participate, of course, yet educated women are especially likely to support such efforts, either as community volunteers or as social service employees. Their efforts are vital for the new civic America, yet their withdrawal from once-flourishing cross-class federations has surely undercut the clout and attractiveness of interactive, membership-based associations.[23]

POLITICAL OPPORTUNITIES AND ASSOCIATIONAL CHANGE

As much as transformed social realities, fresh political challenges and opportunities encouraged Americans to rechannel their civic energies after the mid-1960s. In an age of upheaval and reform Washington, D.C., suddenly seemed to be where most of the action was, and both associational leaders and politicians learned to contest for national power in innovative, mutually reinforcing ways.

Fresh from grassroots struggles in the Deep South, for example, civil rights lawyer Marian Wright Edelman arrived in Washington in the late 1960s to lobby for Mississippi's Head Start program.[24] She soon realized that arguing on behalf of children might be the best way to influence legis-

lation and sway public and congressional sympathy in favor
of the poor, including African Americans. Between 1968 and
1973 Edelman obtained funding from major foundations and
developed a new advocacy and policy research association,
the Children's Defense Fund. With a skillful staff, a small
national network of individual supporters, ties to social service agencies and foundations, and excellent relationships
with the national media, CDF has been a determined propo-
nent of federal antipoverty programs. The CDF story suggests the lure of Washington, D.C., for activists, including
those who got their start far afield in mass-based social
movements.

New Levers to Pull

Contrary to what many conservatives believe, the post-
1960s U.S. government has not expanded much as a taxer
and spender.[25] No expensive new citizen benefits have been
added since Medicare and Medicaid in 1965. And the ratio
of federal to state and local government spending has
remained remarkably constant. But the range of national
public undertakings has widened, especially those that could
be coerced by federal mandates or encouraged by subsidies,
prompting localities and states to do new things in the public interest—often through contracts with professionally run
local nonprofit agencies.[26] Social movements demanded that
the federal government right old wrongs and address pressing issues of broad public concern, such as environmentalism, consumer rights, and the quest for good government.
Presidents, courts, and the Congress responded, at least to
some degree. Spurred by the upheavals of the long 1960s, the
"age of improvement" arrived.[27]

As the federal government addressed demands for reform—issuing regulations, mandates, and court orders and enacting subsidies—new institutional levers became available to advocates trying to influence public policy. Courts took up new kinds of cases, and federal agencies proliferated. Congressional committees and their staffs subdivided, and more aides were hired to support individual members of Congress.[28] Combined totals of assistants to House and Senate members went from 6,255 in 1960 to 10,739 in 1970, then doubled in 1990 to about 20,000.[29]

All of this meant more people to contact and additional institutional niches through which to attempt influence. Rights-oriented lawyers could make headway in the courts; public interest lobbyists could monitor the federal executive; and media people working for advocacy groups could try to shape public opinion. For all sides on every issue, there were heightened incentives to be right there in the national capital with an expert staff ready to hand. "Washington lobbying is very much a day-to-day activity," Berry explains "[because] influence is achieved through continuous work in the trenches. Simply being in Washington, monitoring what is going on, is important."[30]

Determined to take advantage of new opportunities, staff-heavy research and lobbying associations—the proliferating public affairs and social welfare groups I have already discussed—took much of the action away from more cumbersome popularly based voluntary federations that had previously served as important conduits between the federal government and citizens in the states and districts.[31] Where once it made sense to try to get things done in Washington by first gauging the opinions of grassroots association members and influencing officials and representatives in the localities and states, now it made much more sense for civic activists to aim their efforts at national media and intervene with staffs or agencies in Washington. This was especially true where matters of regulation were at stake—as, increasingly, they were in areas such as environmental protection, civil rights, and consumer or occupational protections. "Since about the time Martin Luther King, Jr., led a 'march on Washington' by thousands of citizens in the civil rights movement in 1963," Walker concludes, "there has been a march to Washington by interest groups as well."[32] Activists have gone where the action is, seeking to harness a more active federal government to their purposes.

During the late 1970s and the 1980s, cycles of advocacy group formation became self-reinforcing, not only because groups arose to counter other groups, but also because groups begot more groups. Civic entrepreneurs in each issue area created more specialized groups to pursue subissues or marshal specific expertise. For example, new legal defense groups or policy research think tanks were formed as partners to existing associations, or added to clusters defined by issue area or ideological outlook.[33] Federal tax laws encourage proliferation by establishing different advantages and penalties for groups more or less directly involved in legislative lobbying.[34] And after a key Supreme Court ruling in 1974 facilitated the flow of electoral contributions through PACs, many advocacy sectors set up groups for this specific purpose.[35] Since then interest group money has poured into electoral campaigns, often playing a crucial role in financing "issue advertisements" on television carefully designed to help specific candidates in key swing states or districts.

Advocates in Electoral Politics

Indeed, the rise of advocacy groups parallels changes in U.S. parties and elections as well as government. Because businesses and citizens use advocacy groups to influence government outside of parties and between elections, it is not surprising that the contemporary group explosion coincides with waning voter loyalty to the two major political parties. But we should not posit a zero-sum trade-off, because advocacy groups and party politicians also maneuver together in transformed routines of electoral politics.[36]

As late as the 1950s U.S. political parties were networks of local and state organizations through which (in many if not all locales) party officials brokered nominations, cooperated with locally rooted membership associations, and sometimes directly mobilized voters.[37] Then demographic shifts, reapportionment struggles, and the social upheavals of the 1960s disrupted old party organizations; and changes in party rules led to nomination elections that favored activists and candidate-centered efforts over backroom brokering by party insiders. Such "reforms" were meant to enhance grassroots participation but in practice have furthered oligarchic ways of running elections. No longer the preserve of party organizations, U.S. election campaigns are now managed by coteries of media consultants, pollsters, direct-mail specialists, and (above all) fund-raisers. Because campaigns depend so much on paid television advertising, they are becoming more and more costly, even as voter turnout declines. Candidates compete to win 51 percent of a contracting electorate, using expert advisers to help them target mailings or media messages on narrow slices of apparently persuadable people who seem highly likely to turn out to vote.[38]

In this revamped electoral arena, advocacy groups have much to offer, hoping to get access to elected officials in return for helping candidates. In low-turnout battles to win party nominations, even groups with modest mailing list constituencies may be able to field enough (paid or unpaid) activists to make a difference. At all stages of the electoral process, advocacy groups with or without members can provide endorsements that may be useful in media or direct-mail efforts. And PACs pushing business interests or public interest causes can help candidates to raise the huge sums of money they need to win.

A NEW MODEL OF ASSOCIATION BUILDING

Of course, attempts to influence politicians and officials are nothing new for American voluntary associations; and groups have established offices in Washington, D.C., his- torically, as well as in recent times. Taken alone, a desire to influence government is hardly sufficient to explain the cur- rent vogue for staff-led advocacy groups. New techniques and models of association building also mattered, and in this respect changes affecting voluntary associations paral- lel those that affected political parties.

Like nineteenth-century party politicians who deployed state and local networks to broadcast the party message and pull as many eligible voters to the polls as possible, classic American association builders took it for granted that the best way to gain national influence, moral or polit- ical, was to knit together national, state, and local groups that met regularly and engaged in a degree of representa- tive governance.[39] Leaders who desired to speak on behalf of masses of Americans found it natural to proceed by recruiting self-renewing mass memberships and creating a network of interactive groups.

There were good reasons why this model came to be taken for granted in classic civic America before the 1960s. After the start-up phase associational budgets usually depended heavily on membership dues and on sales of newsletters or supplies to members and local groups. Supporters had to be continuously recruited through social networks and person-to-person contacts. And if leverage over government was desired, a voluntary federation had to be able influence legislators, citizens, and newspapers across many districts. For all of these reasons, classic civic entrepreneurs with national ambitions moved quickly to recruit activists and members in every state and across as many towns and cities as possible within each state. Like Frances Willard of the Woman's Christian Temperance Union— who visited every U.S. city of five thousand people or more at least once during the 1870s and 1880s and was therefore always on the train and hardly ever "at home" in Evanston, Illinois—leaders traveled around the country, convened face-to-face meetings, and recruited and encouraged intermediate leaders who could carry on the work of member recruitment and retention. "Interact or die" was the watchword for classic American association builders.

Today nationally ambitious civic entrepreneurs proceed in quite different ways.[40] When Edelman got the inspiration to launch a new advocacy research group to lobby for the needs of children and the poor, she turned to private foundations for funding and then recruited an expert staff of researchers and lobbyists. In the early 1970s, when John Gardner launched Common Cause as a national citizens' lobby demanding governmental reforms, he arranged for start-up contributions from several wealthy friends, contacted reporters in the national media, and purchased mailing lists to solicit masses of members to give modest monetary contributions.[41] These examples suggest not just that new routes to civic influence have opened in late twentieth-century America; they also underline the availability of new techniques and resources. Patron grants, direct-mail techniques, and the capacity to convey images and messages through the mass media—all of these have changed the realities of organization building and maintenance.

Follow the Money

Money is important for association building, and new flows of cash apart from membership dues have certainly become available of late. Since the late 1960s tax-exempt private foundations have channeled increasing amounts of money to advocacy groups, policy research think tanks, and other kinds of institutions aiming to influence public policy debates or promote ideological and social transformation.[42] Also of consequence have been a much more narrowly defined set of foundations and grants, those dedicated to what sociologist J. Craig Jenkins calls "social movement philanthropy" supporting collective attempts "to organize or represent the interests of a previously unorganized or politically excluded group."[43] U.S. tax rules encourage foundations, and more and more wealthy people are looking for ways to shape national affairs. During the 1990s, moreover, a booming stock market built the assets of ever more numerous foundations. "As a result," observes social commentator Nicholas Lemann, "foundations have become much bigger and stronger players in the workings of our country."[44]

To be sure, only a tiny fraction of foundation giving goes directly to movement groups advocating social change (just over 1 percent in 1990 by Jenkins's strict definition), but even a little slice of a huge and rising tidal wave of foundation money makes a large difference for many public interest associations, especially in an era when membership dues are much less likely to be used as a prime source of group funding.[45] With the Ford Foundation in the lead, liberal foundations channeled grants to civil rights and public interest advocacy groups starting in the 1950s.[46] From the 1970s on, conservative foundations—such as the Lynde and Harry Bradley Foundation and the John M. Olin Foundation—got into the act too, setting out in a highly self-conscious way to shape public opinion and counter the influence of liberal grant givers. Although avowedly conservative foundations have less aggregate wealth from which to generate grants than do liberal foundations, recent studies suggest that conservatives have been very successful in shifting terms of public debate on economic and social policy.[47]

Across the spectrum, foundation grants have encouraged advocacy groups with expert professional staffs.[48] This often happens deliberately, when foundation grant makers prefer professionally run groups for their expertise and stability. But it can also happen inadvertently, as the availability of foundation largesse encourages informal or membership groups to empower experts able to write and administer grants. What is more, beyond their professionalizing impact on social movements, many civically engaged foundations themselves have become highly professionalized organizations, sites of employment for career-minded men and women who hope to stimulate and supervise civic endeavors executed by others.

In the 1980s Jack Walker and his associates surveyed hundreds of associations with headquarters in Washington, D.C., ranging from trade associations whose "members" were economic organizations to professional associations, nonprofit groups, and citizens' advocacy groups, many of which had individual adherents. What Walker calls "patron grants"—financial aid from wealthy donors, foundations, corporations, government agencies, and previously established associations—figured heavily in the founding of all types of associations. Institutional aid proved especially crucial for citizens' groups. Across all eras of group foundings from the nineteenth century onward, 89 percent of the citizens' groups in Walker's study benefited from some sort of financial start-up help. Before the 1960s grants from individuals or other associations were the typical sources of help; from the 1960s on citizens' associations relied much more heavily on start-up grants from foundations, corporations, and government agencies.[49] And not just start-up grants but continuing support for advocacy groups comes from foundations and other patrons. Again, this is especially true for contemporary citizens' associations that make "purposive" appeals—that is, promises to represent constituents' views in politics and policymaking. Citizens' associations, according to Walker's study, are "very likely to rely heavily upon outside patrons rather than their members for financial support. . . . On average, nearly 40 percent of the budgets of the citizens groups is supplied by patrons—a level of support four times higher than the average received by groups in the profit sector whose memberships are most heavily made up of institutional representatives."[50]

As a partial alternative to continued reliance on foundation grants or government funding, today's advocacy groups can also use various sorts of patron support to get started and then turn to computerized direct-mail solicitations as well as media advertising to develop continuing support from individuals. Pioneered by "new right" groups, direct-mail solicitation spread during the 1970s and 1980s. To name just a few examples, this technique has been effectively used by Common Cause, big environmental groups, the Concord Coalition, and the Mothers Against Drunk Driving.[51] Civic entrepreneurs need generous seed grants to start direct-mail solicitation, because appropriate lists must be purchased and hundreds of thousands of letters sent. For example, "[i]n late March 1970, when [John] Gardner decided to start a new, mass-financed organization, he knew it would cost at least $300,000 for mailings and newspaper ads."[52] Staff expertise is equally necessary, as mailings must be honed and deployed again and again.[53] Only a small portion of people who get a cause letter in the mail actually look at it; and an even smaller fraction send money, with or without a "membership" application.[54]

Communication without Organization

Ready access to national media outlets is the final circumstance allowing today's associations to forgo recurrent contacts among leaders and members. Elite television and news reporters are often recruited directly from universities and operate out of major metropolitan centers.[55] In punditry hubs like Boston, New York, Los Angeles, and Washington, D.C., reporters, politicians, and advocacy spokespersons participate in endless talk shows; and print reporters are constantly on the telephone to advocates as well as politicians.[56] National media outlets want to stage debates among dramatically polarized sets of spokespersons; and advocacy associations need to keep their causes and accomplishments visible. By dramatizing causes through the national media, advocates can enhance their legitimacy and keep contributions flowing from patrons or direct-mail adherents.

The very model of civic effectiveness has, in short, been upended since the 1960s. No longer do civic entrepreneurs think of constructing vast federations and recruiting interactive citizen-members. When a new cause (or tactic) arises, activists envisage opening a national office and managing association building as well as national projects from the center. Contemporary organization-building techniques encourage citizen groups (just like trade and professional associations) to concentrate their efforts in efficiently managed headquarters located close to the federal government and the national media. Even a group aiming to speak for large numbers of Americans does not absolutely need "members" in any meaningful sense of the word.

And even if mass adherents are recruited through the mail, why hold meetings? From a managerial point of view, face-to-face interactions with groups of members may be downright inefficient. In the old-time membership federations, annual elections of leaders and a modicum of representative governance went hand in hand with membership dues and interactive meetings. But for the professional executives of today's advocacy organizations, direct-mail adherents can be more appealing than members attending conventions, because, as Kenneth Godwin and Robert Cameron

Mitchell explain, direct-mail adherents "contribute without 'meddling'" and "do not take part in leadership selection or policy discussions." Contacted individually, "direct-mail members depend for information about the organization on the materials the leadership sends them, and therefore may be more easily manipulated."[57] These adherents are likely to be seen not as fellow citizens but as consumers with policy preferences. While touching base occasionally with adherents' disaggregated "preferences"—through fund-raising appeals and polls—professionals in the central office can keep themselves free to set agendas and maneuver flexibly in the fast-moving worlds of legislation and the media.

CHANGES AT THE TOP

This brings us to what may be the most civicly consequential change in late-twentieth-century America: the rise of a very large, highly educated upper middle class in which "expert" professionals are prominent along with businesspeople and managers. "Since World War II," notes Michael Schudson, "higher education has mushroomed. Of people born from 1911 to 1920, 13.5 percent earned college or graduate degrees; of those born during the next decade, 18.8 percent; but of people born from 1931 to 1950"—who became adults from the mid-1950s through the mid-1970s—"the figure grew to between 26 and 27 percent."[58] With expanded higher education has come a proliferation of "professionals," defined by sociologist Steven Brint as "people who earn at least a middling income from the application of a relatively complex body of knowledge." Brint reports that in "the United States before World War II, only one percent of all employed people were college-educated and classified by the Census Bureau as 'professional, technical, and kindred' workers. Today the comparable group is twelve times as large."[59]

Together with business owners and managers and their families, professional families now constitute the top quarter or so of the American class structure. Since the 1970s such Americans at the top of the educational hierarchy have enjoyed rising incomes, even as less educated salary and wage employees have suffered declining or stagnant incomes.[60] America's managerial and professional families (often headed by a career man and a career woman married to one another) are not just unprecedentedly numerous. They constitute a comfortable and privileged segment of society. David Brooks argues, moreover, that a cultural rapprochement has recently taken place between business and intellectual elites who were once at odds, melding commercial values with emphasis on individual self-expression, social tolerance, and even a whiff of individualistic cultural radicalism.[61] No doubt the primary result of any cultural rapprochement has been a shared emphasis on sophisticated—and expensive—"lifestyles." But an expert-oriented and managerial stance toward politics and community life, not to mention a quiet contempt for "square" traditional values, may also be widely shared by all kinds of contemporary American elites.

From Trustees of Community to Specialized Experts

American professional people and business elites look at their civic responsibilities in new and largely complementary ways. When U.S. professionals and business-people constituted tiny, geographically dispersed strata of the national population, they understood themselves as "trustees of community" in Brint's terminology.[62] Working closely with and for less educated fellow citizens of modest means in thousands of towns and cities, lawyers, doctors, ministers, and teachers once found it quite natural to join—and eventually lead—locally rooted voluntary federations that included broad swatches of their fellow citizens. The same was true of business elites, most of whom retained strong economic and personal ties to regions, states, and localities. Local, state, and regional roots did not come at the expense of national involvements and loyalty, because most locally present membership associations were chapters within representatively governed translocal federations. But notables did have to commence their civic careers through local involvements with many other citizens and then work their way up.

By contrast, in contemporary America professionals as well as business leaders live less rooted lives. Meritorious high school students are recruited into leading universities, often located far from native regions to which they may never return.[63] After many years of education and career development, professionals and managers live and work among themselves, crowded in or near metropolitan centers. They jet around the world to business meetings or conferences and hop on planes again to "escape" for vacations at luxurious retreats or exotic sites. "Community" is much touted by American elites these days but in a slightly romantic and thoroughly disembodied way ("social capital" nicely captures the abstraction and disembeddedness now in vogue). Understandably, just as today's wealthy are likely to see themselves as successful individual entrepreneurs, who can scatter donations here or there to worthy causes, today's professionals see themselves as individually meritorious experts, who can best contribute to national or local well-being by working with other specialists to tackle complex technical or social problems.

Among different kinds of professionals, perhaps the most civicly self-aware are some 18 million people, roughly 8 percent of the labor force, who work as "human service workers, technicians, and staff people who serve their communities in paid positions provided by nonprofit agencies."[64] Nonprofit professionals are likely to see their own work—much of it funded through government and through tax-exempt donations from the wealthy as the very embodiment of community responsibility. "Nonprofit professionals," Wuthnow explains, believe that today's complex social problems "must be addressed by people with special skills who have ample resources at their disposal and who are sufficiently committed to devote themselves to full-time efforts."[65] These same nonprofit professionals manage the institutions that serve as initiators and hosts for many small participatory groups in contemporary America; and they coordinate the efforts of volunteers recruited for ad hoc community projects.

Whether employed primarily in profit-oriented or nonprofit settings, professional men and women have their own membership associations and meetings. Putnam maintains that all sorts of membership associations have declined in tandem since the 1950s and 1960s.[66] But in fact associations of privileged professionals have lost much less ground than membership groups that include citizens from the middling and blue-collar strata. True enough, some peak professional associations have lost "market share" in recent times—that is, a decreasing proportion of all physicians belong to the American Medical Association; a lesser share of all architects belong to the American Institute of Architects; and so forth. Yet as graphed in figure 5.9, Putnam's own detailed data show that, measuring the span from groups' peak memberships in the post–World War II era to 1997, the percentage loss of membership for seven elite professional societies has been less than half as much as the percentage decline for twenty-one cross-class, chapter-based membership federations, and also less than half as much as the percentage decline in unionization rates for five major blue-collar occupations.

Similar patterns appear in nationally representative individual data displayed in figure 5.10. According to the GSS, in just two decades between 1974 and 1994, the gap between college-educated Americans claiming membership in one or more professional groups and non-college-educated Americans claiming union membership grew by more than 50 percent. This is a startling increase, which underlines that we need to take into account not just long-standing elite professions (e.g., lawyers, doctors, engineers) but the recent burgeoning of many other self-styled professional groups. Along with businesspeople, higher-educated Americans who think of themselves as "professionals" are the citizens most likely to pay dues, elect leaders, and regularly attend conventions where sociability and programmatic concerns go hand in hand. Such persistence of long-standing associational forms among the privileged is ironic, of course, because exactly the same kinds of people enjoy disproportionate access to the newer kinds of civic groups—institutions without members, or associations with only mailing list adherents.

FIGURE 5.9

America's Cross-Class Chapter Groups and Blue-Collar Unions Are Losing More Members than Elite Professional Societies

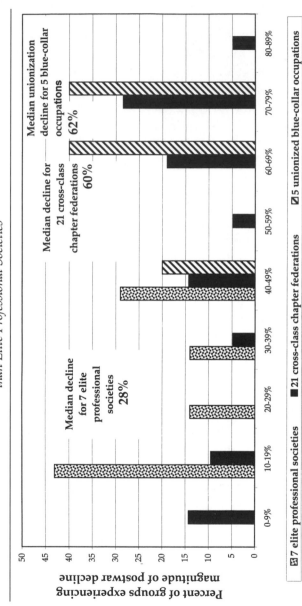

SOURCES: Robert D. Putnam, *Bowling Alone: The Collapse and Revival of American Community*, (New York: Simon and Schuster, 2000), p. 82, for unions; pp. 438–39, for larger cross-class associationa; and additional data on elite professional societies supplied by Putnam.

FIGURE 5.10

The Growing Gap between College-educated Americans Belonging to Professional Societies and Non-college-educated Americans Enrolled in Unions

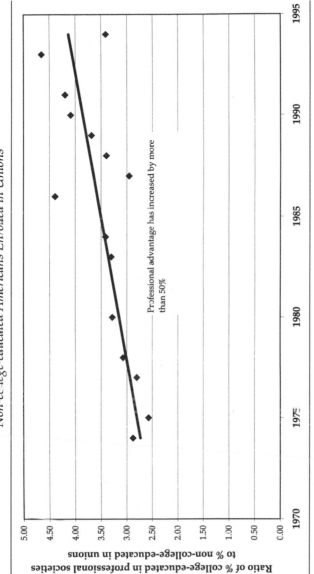

SOURCE: General Social Survey, 1974–94.

Associational Innovations and the New Elites

Refocusing on the big picture, it is clear that America's new civic life—centered not just in still-flourishing business and professional societies but also in advocacy associations and nonprofit institutions—has important affinities with the nation's reconfigured class structure. U.S. managers, businesspeople, and many varieties of professionals have their own advocacy associations in Washington, D.C., and in many state capitals. This certainly includes nonprofit professionals, whose livelihoods typically depend on government funding and tax policies. In addition, the proliferation of staff-led advocacy and service organizations—from citizen groups to trade associations—opens new careers for lawyers, researchers, helping professionals, and assorted white-collar people and activists. But occupational links and careerism are far from the only synergies at work. In more fundamental ways, highly educated and privileged Americans and staff-led civic groups appeal to one another.

Well-educated and well-off elites are exactly the kinds of constituents staff-led civic groups want. Not only are these men and women the Americans most likely to be able to write big checks; they prefer giving money to giving time and thus will be happy to let professional advocates and institutional managers proceed on course. More than that, the highly educated are discerning about matters of public policy. Privileged Americans are an ideal audience, able to appreciate what expert advocates and institutional managers accomplish—and what they need to do their jobs.

At the same time, cause-oriented advocacy groups and professionally managed institutions offer wealthy and well-educated Americans a rich menu of opportunities to, in effect, hire experts to represent their values and interests in public life. Why should highly trained and economically well-off elites spend years working their way up the local-state-national leadership ladders of traditional member-ship federations when they can, instead, simply send checks to advocacy groups, or contribute to service providers, or serve on the boards of their favorite charities? If so inclined, privileged professionals can put in some volunteer time now and then on projects managed by the staffs of charities or social service agencies. Staff-led advocacy groups—along with nonprofit institutions looking for contributions and favorable public policies—are in many ways ideally suited to the aspirations of today's most privileged and confident Americans. Busy career men and women, Amer-ica's professionals and managers are choosy individualists who appreciate the variety and flexibility the vast array of advocacy groups and specialized civic institutions provide. As the chief constituents of the new civic America, the well educated and the well-to-do benefit from professionally run groups—just as much as advocacy groups and civic institutions benefit from their support and attention.

CIVIC LIFE REMADE

Civic life was abruptly and fundamentally reorganized in late-twentieth-century America. Between the 1970s and the 1990s older voluntary membership federations rapidly dwindled, while new social movements and profession-ally managed civic organizations took to the field in huge numbers, redefining the goals and modalities of national civic life.

The most important changes did not happen incrementally; nor did they simply bubble up from below. Government offered new opportunities and obstacles to civic activists. Social ideals changed. And new technologies and sources of funding created fresh opportunities and incentives for civic organizers. Suddenly, mobilizing fellow citizens into dues-paying, interactive associations that met regularly no longer made sense for ambitious elites, who could instead run professionally managed organizations able to gain immediate access to government and the national media. Responding to fresh challenges, resources, and ideals—and determined to get away from the rigidities and prejudices of old-line membership associations—privileged and well-educated citizens led the way in reshaping the associational universe. Leading Americans withdrew from cross-class membership federations and redirected civic energy toward professional advocacy, private foundation grant making, and institutional trusteeship.

The result was a transformed civic America—still a nation of organizers but much less a nation of joiners, because civic leaders were no longer committed to mobilizing vast numbers of fellow citizens into ongoing membership activities.

CHAPTER 6

WHAT WE HAVE LOST

IF AMERICA IN OUR TIME HAS experienced a great civic reorganization from membership federations to professionally managed groups, why should anyone worry? More than a few analysts hold that reorientations of American civic life since the 1960s have been for the best.[1] Our democracy has been enlarged, say the optimists, by social movements and advocacy groups fighting for social rights and fresh understandings of the public interest. Americans are reinventing community too—joining flexible small groups and engaging in ad hoc volunteering while supporting expert advocates who speak for important values on the national stage. Maybe the United States is not so much a nation of joiners as it was half a century ago, but Americans still organize civic ventures of all sorts and in recent times have crossed unprecedented frontiers of social inclusion and open debate.

Many of these points strike me as reasonable responses to pessimistic Cassandras who declare that contemporary civil society is falling apart.[2] In personal lives, at work, and in resourceful neighborhoods, Americans *are* finding new ways to relate to one another personally; and they are devising creative new ways to accomplish specific shared tasks. Fresh perspectives and unprecedented expertise have been injected into our public policy debates, as well as into the delivery of highly valued social services and cultural experiences by nonprofit institutions of many sorts. And who would want to return to the days when most civil associations excluded African Americans, vilified gays, and marginalized women?

But if we look at U.S. democracy in its entirety and bring issues of power and social leverage to the fore, then optimists are surely overlooking the downsides of our recently reorganized civic life. Too many valuable aspects of the old civic America are not being reproduced or reinvented in the new public world run largely by professional trustees and memberless organizations. Although they rarely say it baldly, optimists imply that more of the same is all the United States needs—or, perhaps, what American democracy needs is a revival of "movement activism" in the style of the sixties and seventies. But those days will never return, and optimists fail to appreciate what has been lost as well as gained in their aftermath. Justifiably pleased with advances in social rights and citizen advocacy since the 1960s, optimists have failed to notice that more voices are not the same thing as increased democratic capacity. What is more, optimists do not see—indeed, most are hardly willing to imagine—that gains in some kinds of social equality could be accompanied by erosions of cross-class fellowship and inclusive civic mobilization equally portentous for our democracy.

Despite the multiplicity of voices raised within it, America's new civic universe is remarkably oligarchic. This is true in the world of voluntary associations—those "combinations" that Alexis de Tocqueville posited as central to democratic vitality—and even more true in realms of national

politics and public policymaking that are thoroughly intertwined with associational life. Before we can move on to
discuss what should be done to address civic deficits today,
we need to come face to face with what has been lost as well
as gained from the late-twentieth-century civic watershed.

A TOP-DOWN CIVIC WORLD

Most analysts debating America's current civic health imagine that the 1960s marked a divide between localism and
nationalism in civic life. Pessimists like Robert Putnam
decry the supposed eclipse of local face-to-face groups by
centralized undertakings, while optimists celebrate national
movements and advocacy efforts. "Local communities are
no longer the sine qua non of mobilization," enthuses opti-
mist Debra Minkoff. She is pleased that contemporary
advocacy groups engage in societal conflict, that nationally
focused "identity groups" now "transcend parochial boundaries based on communities of residence."[3]

But to suppose that national projects and identities only
recently emerged is to badly misapprehend America's civic
past. As we have seen, starting in the early 1800s, vast voluntary federations knit American organizers and joiners
together across places and asserted broadly shared values
and identities. Quests for moral influence and political
power were always the rule, not the exception, in American civic life; and conflict and competition have always
been the mother's milk of American democracy. National
associations to lobby government and speak for broadly
shared identities were not invented for the first time in
late-twentieth-century America; they had always existed.
The key change in recent times is less appealing than many

optimists assume. In the advocacy explosions of the 1960s to the 1990s, civic organizers and patrons established an unprecedented number of nationally active associations that lack popular and subnational roots.

Associations with Restricted Reach

Because today's advocacy groups are staff-heavy and focused on lobbying, research, and media projects, they are managed from the top, even when they claim to speak for ordinary people. Even advocacy groups that use canvasses or mailings to recruit large numbers of supporters, tend to gravitate toward upper-middle-class constituencies. An excellent case in point is Common Cause, the quintessential "public interest" advocacy group. Heavily tilted toward liberal Democrats, Common Cause also attracts moderate Republicans. Yet privilege rules across the partisan divide. A 1982 survey showed that an astounding 42.6 percent of Common Cause adherents had completed graduate or professional degrees; 14.5 percent had some graduate or professional education short of degrees; and another 18.7 percent had basic college degrees. In the same survey, the median Common Cause member had a family income 85 percent above the national median at that time.[4] Common Cause has managed to do quite well, thank you, with several hundred thousand of such relatively privileged and sophisticated supporters. The organization really has little need to dig deeper for many times more "members."

There is a certain irony here. Early in the current era, civic entrepreneurs argued that the use of mass media and mailing lists as recruitment devices might reach masses of people left out of traditional associations, thus enlarging the universe of potential recruits to causes and groups and shifting power away from fat cats. Yet evidence beyond the example of Common Cause questions this hopeful expectation. In a 1984 study, Kenneth Godwin and Rondo Cameron Mitchell compared people recruited into the environmental movement through either social networks or direct mail.[5] Overall, the environmental movement disproportionately attracts white, middle-class Americans; but there are an array of associations involved, some chapter based and others more centralized and reliant on direct mail. Direct-mail recruits, Godwin and Mitchell hypothesized, might include more females, shorter-term residents, and either single or elderly people. They set out to explore possibilities that mailing list recruitment could enlarge civic participation.

But Godwin and Mitchell's results suggest otherwise. The study found no gender differences, and the only significant age-related finding went the opposite way from expectations: students were more likely to be drawn into environmental groups through social networks than via direct mail. Overall, direct-mail recruits to environmentalism turned out to be more established types than Godwin and Mitchell had expected. Direct-mail recruits were longer-term residents of larger communities—and perhaps most telling, they reported higher incomes than people recruited to environmental associations through social networks.

Whether we are talking about memberless advocacy groups, advocacy groups with some chapters, mailing list associations, or nonprofit institutions, it is hard to escape the conclusion that the wealthiest and best educated people are more privileged in America's reconfigured civic world than their (less numerous) counterparts were in the pre-1960s civic world centered in cross-class membership federations. Of course, better-educated and wealthier people have always been disproportionately involved in the leadership of U.S. associations apart from labor unions. But pre-1960s membership federations were much more likely to involve less privileged participants along with the privileged. Because they aimed for massive dues-paying memberships as a route to national influence, classic associations had an incentive to espouse broad values and speak to encompassing constituencies. Today, by contrast, professional association leaders have strong incentives to do "niche marketing," to identify specific "hot button" issues that appeal just to well-delineated constituencies, who are likely to be relatively sophisticated and already involved in public life.

Leadership incentives were also very different in classic membership federations—and this is a key contrast with contemporary civic America. In huge membership federations, regional or state plus local chapters were widespread, full of intermediate leaders and members seeking to recruit others. Hundreds of thousands of local and supralocal leaders had to be elected and appointed every year. Including the best educated and wealthiest, all of the men and women who climbed the ladders of vast membership associations had to interact in the process with citizens of humble or middling means and prospects. Classic membership federations built two-way bridges across classes and places and between local and translocal affairs. Now, in a civic America dominated by centralized, staff-driven advocacy associations, such bridges are eroding.

Doing-For instead of Doing-With

The points I have made so far would be granted by many of those who are optimistic about current civic trends, yet they would redirect our gaze toward contemporary interpersonal support groups, community volunteer projects, and "grassroots" movements. We find the true body of contemporary civic life in such undertakings, say optimistic analysts such as Everett Carl Ladd and Robert Wuthnow.[6] But in my view, we cannot safely conclude that either intimate support groups or sporadic volunteer efforts will rebuild the civic bridges that have fallen down.

As Wuthnow acknowledges, most small groups—including twelve-step groups and discussion sessions—are intensely focused on personal concerns. Flexible and intimate, small groups typically focus inward and do not draw individuals into engagements with larger community issues, let alone with state, regional, or national policymaking.[7] Volunteer efforts, meanwhile, are frequently professionally coordinated sporadic or one-shot undertakings.[8] Worthy endeavors, certainly, they involve people in "doing for" others—feeding the needy at a church soup kitchen, tutoring children at an after-school clinic, or guiding visitors at a museum exhibit—rather than in "doing with" fellow citizens as ongoing members of a shared group. Important as ad hoc volunteering may be, it cannot substitute for the central citizenship functions that membership federations performed. Volunteers do not form as many reciprocal ties as members; they are normally not elected to responsible leadership posts; and they are unlikely to experience what millions of members once did, a sense of brotherhood or sisterhood

and fellow American citizenship. Nor is fellowship practiced by the staffs or trustees of the social service agencies
that run civic campaigns or volunteer efforts.

Local groups and grassroots protests are probably not as
plentiful as some analysts suggest (see chap. 4). But whatever their numbers, such efforts can be exceedingly parochial—as "not in my backyard" environmental protests have
frequently proved to be. What is more, disconnected local
parts do not add up to as much as an interconnected
whole. When Ladd argues that proliferating local parent-
teacher organizations are just as good as chapters of the
national PTA, he neglects the important role that state and
national PTA leaders have traditionally played in connecting local school-support groups to state and national legislative campaigns; and he neglects the many bridging ties
that state and national PTA congresses fostered among
parents and teachers from various local communities and
disparate social backgrounds.[9] Unlike the elected representatives and leaders who worked through classic voluntary
federations, purely local small groups or protest efforts may
not learn how problems and solutions are interconnected.
And unless they speak for the most privileged neighborhoods, local activists are unlikely to enjoy sufficient leverage
to make a real difference: to change the behavior of corporations, to persuade city, state, or local governments to act.

Parochialism and lack of leverage are not the only problems. Touted as spontaneous and entirely bottom-up, many
of today's "community organizations" or "grassroots" undertakings are not quite what they seem. Sparked by well-con-
nected leaders, they frequently have—or soon obtain—outside funding from tax-exempt private foundations. There is
nothing wrong with this, but we should not imagine that it

is a fully democratic arrangement. Movements and groups that receive outside funding have to apply and reapply for resources while meeting detailed regulatory guidelines. Professionals often become key unelected leaders, because groups depend on their expertise and connections to the outside funders.

The Role of Foundations

J. Craig Jenkins and Abigail Halcli have done careful empirical research on "social movement" grants given by private foundations from the 1950s to the present. Many social movements have benefited from these grants, including movements launched by grassroots protests, and the results have been both democratizing and demobilizing. Foundation support has institutionalized causes that might have proved ephemeral, and it has enhanced movement capacities to influence public policymaking. But foundation grants have favored professionally run groups—and have gravitated over time toward causes such as environmentalism and world peace favored by middle-class constituencies. Groups oriented to the needs and values of the poor and the working class have received more funding in absolute terms but have also lost relative ground in social movement grant making since the 1970s.

More worrisome, the availability of foundation funding has exempted social movement organizations from organizing broad constituencies. "Social movement philanthropy" by private foundations, Jenkins and Halcli conclude, "has provided needed technical resources and created new organizations that have been vital to securing and implementing movement gains. However, at the same time, it has also reduced the pressure on movement leaders to engage in costly and time-consuming grassroots organizing, thus potentially blunting the impact of these movements."[10]

Considering the big picture, private foundations are dispensing resources subsidized by exemptions from taxation. Shouldn't we Americans wonder about who elects—or in any way holds accountable—institutions controlling vast resources on which so many "grassroots" as well as national associations depend? In the 1960s and 1970s liberal foundations were pioneers in social movement and advocacy funding; now conservative foundations are also very much involved. My question holds for all parts of the ideological spectrum.

In effect, considerable "local" voluntarism as well as national citizen advocacy is tightly connected to translocal institutions and resource flows—just as U.S. associational activity always has been supported by translocal organizations and flows of resources. The difference is that today's supralocal institutions are not accountable, and leaders are not elected. As professional experts and managers, foundation people rarely arrive at their positions by working from within the groups they supervise. And the moneys they dispense come not from membership dues but from wealthy donors who receive indirect tax subsidies from all Americans, subsidies not accompanied by popular oversight or even much understanding of what is at stake. Foundations play a key role in shaping contemporary American civil society, politics, and public debates, but the action happens above the heads and out of sight of most Americans.

Enlarged public discussions and improved public policies have certainly resulted from foundation interventions, which have played an ever greater role in U.S. civil society since the mid-twentieth century. But there is precious little democratic accountability—either in the grantor-grantee relationships or at the level of the polity as a whole. More of the same looms in the U.S. future, as the ranks of the privileged swell, and more wealthy Americans decide to launch tax-exempt foundations to scatter grants to their favorite institutions, think tanks, advocacy groups, and (occasionally) "grassroots" movements. We can celebrate the civic-mindedness of wealthy individuals and families who give so much, yet at the same time realize that their largesse brings attenuated democratic responsiveness—as the public fisc subsidizes ever more top-down civic funding, which in turn exempts increasing numbers of nonprofit and voluntary endeavors from the need to amass widespread popular support.

DIMINISHED DEMOCRACY

The United States today has the most pluralist polity in the world, yet associations claiming to speak for the people lack incentives and capacities to mobilize large numbers of ordinary people through direct personal contacts and ongoing involvement in interactive settings. Yawning gaps have opened between local voluntary efforts and the professional advocates and grant makers who seek national influence. As parallel changes of this sort have unfolded in both electoral and associational life, American public discussions have become polarized in superficial rather than consequential ways. And public policymaking has tilted upward, even in an era of growing social inequality.

The Downside of Impersonal Appeals and
Targeted Activation

Professionally managed, top-down civic endeavors simultaneously limit the mobilization of most citizens into public life and encourage a fragmentation of social identities and trivial polarizations in public debates. To understand why and how, we need to consider the impact on the larger polity of techniques for building influence now employed by most advocacy groups and by aspiring (or already elected) politicians.

Political scientist Steven Schier has written a very insightful book, *By Invitation Only*, describing the transition from relatively broad and inclusive styles of electoral and interest group mobilization through social networks to what he labels "targeted activation"—in which messages are aimed at narrowly defined demographic categories of people. Schier primarily describes the transition in electoral politics, yet acknowledges similar changes in interest group activities. "Old-style mobilization," he explains, "was inclusive because it involved simple . . . messages, communication by personal contact . . . [through] social networks . . . , and adequate time for citizens to absorb the . . . message."[11] By contrast, "activation" involves narrowly crafted messages delivered to narrowly targeted slices of the population in impersonal ways.

Public opinion analysts Lawrence Jacobs and Robert Shapiro describe the new techniques as involving the rise of "crafted talk," which appears responsive to public concerns as measured by endlessly repeated opinion polls but actually allows elites to pursue their own, predetermined policy goals by using data on emotions, words, and phrases to tailor messages designed to push particular categories of people in a desired direction.[12] In contrast to social capital theory, which locates the motor force of change in the erosion of local primary networks, arguments such as those offered by Schier and Jacobs and Shapiro focus our attention on the opportunities and challenges for mobilization faced by ambitious politicians, civic activists, and elected officials hoping to further certain policy goals.

In earlier times ambitious political and associational leaders made broadcast appeals and tried to inspire a cascade of mobilization through many organized intermediaries because they could not be so sure exactly who would respond to appeals for votes, or to appeals to join associations, pay dues, and attend meetings. A by-product of this style of mobilization was to draw more and more folks in, including those not highly motivated by specific issue concerns. Whether or not elites intended it or always knew what they were doing, power and sociability were fused, with the result that huge numbers of voters and lots of citizens from many walks of life were encouraged to get involved in community, state, regional, and national affairs.

In the realm of party politics, this relatively inclusive style of mobilization dominated in the nineteenth century and started to erode when antipartisan "reforms" were enacted in various states during the Progressive Era. In the realm of nonelectoral association building, inclusive styles of membership mobilization persisted much longer. Only in recent decades, since the 1960s, have new approaches to top-down, targeted activation triumphed in associational as well as electoral life. Since the 1970s, as we have seen, many associations use media appeals alone, and others communicate with potential donors through computer-generated mailings, whose messages are carefully crafted to appeal to the worries of carefully delimited audiences.

Recent civic reorganizations have thus created a mutually reinforcing—and deleterious—interlock of professionally managed associational and electoral activities. As Schier explains, "activation arose as a rational response to a political environment characterized by party decline, a proliferation of organized interests, and new efficiencies in communication and campaign technologies."[13] Civic leaders now selectively target carefully delimited slices of the population identified (by expert studies) as already primed to respond to their particular appeals. Large numbers of Americans can easily be ignored if they are parts of groups not seen as likely to give money or turn out to vote for particular causes.

America's new professional consultants and advocacy elites often claim they are engaging in grassroots mobilization, but the overall results of the contemporary politics of expert-directed, impersonal selective activation can be quite demobilizing. Regular folks often do not vote, or join, or attend unless someone they know asks them to get involved. Political scientists Steven Rosenstone and John Mark Hansen have amassed evidence that declining mobilization attempts by elites contributed significantly to dwindling U.S. political participation between the 1960s and the 1980s.[14] And another pair of political scientists, Alan Gerber and Donald Green, have conducted cleverly designed "field experiments" to test the effectiveness of personal contacts versus impersonal mailings and telephone calls in nonpartisan get-out-the-vote drives. Personal contacts are much more effective, their studies show, because "a certain segment of the electorate tends not to vote unless encouraged to do so through face-to-face contact." Unfortunately, "as voter mobilization grows more impersonal, fewer people receive this kind of encouragement," and associational life in general has changed in ways that may make it difficult to revive older forms of either associational or voter mobilization. In the words of Gerber and Green, the "question is whether the long-term decay of civic and political organizations has reached such a point that our society no longer has the infrastructure to conduct face-to-face canvassing on a large scale."[15]

Just as the new techniques used in electoral campaigns and interest group maneuvering can be demobilizing, they can be trivially polarizing. I want to be careful and clear in making this argument. Communitarians often assert that American public life needs to be more "polite," "civil," and antiseptically "nonpartisan." But this could be deadly in my view, because regular people engage in public life only when they think important things are at stake. Hard as it is for educated elites to stomach, emotions matter as much as cognition in group life and politics alike. Conflict, tough argument, and close competition are good for democratic civil society and for electoral democracy. On the other hand, sound and fury about trivial matters can turn citizens off, even educated and astute citizens. And if arguments advanced in public discourse invoke unnecessarily narrow values and identities, they can easily undermine the broadly shared identities and values that nourish majoritarian democratic politics. Unfortunately, there are many factors at work in U.S. advocacy politics today that encourage trivial polarization rather than consequential competition over majority goals.[16]

Professional advocates need visibility for their causes and media outlets look for opposites. In a civic universe crowded with thousands of advocacy groups focused on relatively narrow issues or constituencies, all have an incentive to raise their voices—and push narrowly circumscribed concerns to the fore. Incentives for coalition building are modest; incentives for working out well-calibrated yet bold and far-reaching positions may be absent altogether. Research shows that even associations with substantial mailing list memberships have an incentive to go for drama and controversy. Compared to members recruited through social networks, mailing-list members tend to be, at once, fickle and motivated by intense policy preferences.[17] They will continue to send checks only to advocacy groups visibly speaking for their strong, already formulated policy preferences. So advocacy staffs have every incentive to carve out narrow issues and take dramatic, polarized positions—ideally identifying an immediate threat to which their positions are a response. Although the general public might be genuinely ambivalent about many issues—and share underlying concerns or values—a world of advocacy groups operating in symbiosis with media looking for controversy is not likely to represent the messy middle or search out the underlying possibilities. Shouting and deadlock can easily result, and big problems go unaddressed.

Upward-tilted Public Policymaking

If contemporary America's top-heavy civic world encourages doing-for rather than doing-with, if it limits popular mobilization and promotes trivial polarization in politics, it also skews national politics and public policy making toward the values and interests of the privileged. Interestingly, some of the best evidence for this assertion comes from Jeffrey Berry, an enthusiast for the "new liberalism" propelled by citizen advocacy groups. Berry devised a careful empirical study to explore the impact of citizen advocacy groups versus more traditional, occupationally based interest groups on legislative agendas and media coverage of public issues. Focusing on sessions of Congress in 1963, 1979, and 1991, Berry and his associates traced 205 policy issues "that were the subject of a congressional hearing and received at least minimal coverage in the press."[18] This research design allowed Berry to do something rarely accomplished in social research—trace changes from the early 1960s, when public interest advocacy groups were relatively scarce and not so prominent, through the 1970s and 1980s, when they grew in numbers and importance. Not only did Berry and his associates check which kinds of groups gained a hearing in each year, and thus helped to shape the public agenda, they also traced bills supported by various kinds of interest groups through the end of each respective session of Congress. This additional step generated data on whether advocates got legislative results, in addition to chances to be heard.

Berry's study suggests that late-twentieth-century civic transformations have enhanced the organized clout of the growing U.S. upper middle class, while reducing the influence of groups representing the less educated and affluent majority of ordinary citizens (we must keep in mind that three quarters of Americans do not have college degrees). On the side favoring broader citizen voice, groups speaking for middle-class concerns have gained ground compared to business associations. Citizen advocacy groups not only grew in numbers within the overall Washington, D.C., lobbying community, they gained steadily more disproportionate access, as measured by testimony at congressional hearings and access to the media. As this happened from 1963 to 1979 to 1991, Congress doubled its attention to the "postmaterial" issues pushed by citizen associations—issues defined by Berry as involving value and lifestyle concerns and matters of rights or social welfare *not* directly tied to the occupational self-interest of the groups lobbying on their behalf.

Here was a true triumph of democracy, Berry convincingly maintains. As a higher proportion (though still a minority) of Americans became highly educated and affluent, larger numbers became concerned with postmaterial matters. Citizen advocacy groups responded. Savvy about fund-raising and media relations and willing to speak for genuine public values and concerns, citizen groups gained the capacity to go head to head with traditionally dominant business and economic lobbies and often win. "For citizen groups" and the citizens they represent, Berry writes, "government should be doing more than helping people and corporations to make more money. They see government as having a primary responsibility for enhancing equality, expanding rights, protecting the environment, supporting the traditional nuclear family, and policing corporations so that they are more socially responsible."[19]

But if citizen advocacy groups have enlarged American democracy by bringing widely valued postmaterial concerns to the fore, they have also "concentrated on issues that appeal to their middle-class supporters."[20] As Berry acknowledges, the rise of postmaterial politics pushed by influential citizen lobbies has probably helped to "crowd out" other kinds of domestic concerns, shifting agendas of public discussion and congressional legislation away from the needs and concerns of ordinary working Americans. Assessing "economic equality issues" taken up by Congress, Berry shows that, measured as a proportion of all domestic issues addressed, such issues receded only a little from 1963 to 1991; but the content and fate of legislation changed in ways that paint "a grim picture . . . for those concerned about economic inequality."[21]

Just as new advocacy politics surged between 1963 and 1979, Berry explains, economic legislation taken up in Congress "moved increasingly away from the issues of wages and job training affecting blue-collar workers and . . . toward issues of welfare and pension reform—issues that focus on the poor and the middle class."[22] Still more telling are the bills that actually got enacted. "Although what gets on the congressional agenda is critically important, what ultimately passes may be the truest test of real change," Berry points out. "In 1963, six of ten bills designed to reduce economic inequality passed; in 1979 four of seven, and in 1991 two of seven."[23]

Berry's research not only documents the "rising power of citizen groups" to push middle-class concerns; it also shows that "over time, Congress has come to consider less legislation designed to reduce economic inequality, consider fewer bills designed to raise wages or improve job skills when it does take up such legislation, and pass a smaller proportion of all these economic inequality bills reaching the agenda stage."[24] Other forces have been at work, to be sure, including union decline and social activism on the right. Still, Berry and his associates took one further step that speaks to the broader political context, looking to see whether citizen advocacy groups, most of which are "liberal," had become more likely over time to ally with groups working for economic equality and working-class welfare. Coalitions can be a powerful force in Washington, D.C., legislative maneuvering, so the answer to this question is arguably very important to contemporary liberal politics.

But the answer is no. According to Berry's data, coalitions between advocacy groups focused on lifestyle concerns and associations focused on social equity goals were more common 1963 (when citizen advocacy groups were fewer and less influential) than they are now (when citizen groups could actually add clout to the quest for material equity and social justice).[25] In short, not only are social justice–oriented civic associations, including labor unions and religiously based associations, being crowded out in contemporary advocacy politics, they are increasingly left to their own devices by citizen groups oriented to the values and needs of the upper middle class as well as the very wealthy.

Less Support for Inclusive Social Provision

Possibilities for inclusive and generous public social provision have been greatly diminished by the great civic transition from membership to advocacy and by the concomitant shift from broad, network-based mobilization to targeted talk. Lost chances for inclusive social provision are not simply responses to aggregate shifts in public values and opinion. Although it is true that large numbers of Americans today care about postmaterial lifestyle issues, it is also true that big majorities still want—and have a central stake in—social protections and enhanced opportunities for everyone. In the history of U.S. social policy making, many of the most popular and effective programs simultaneously expressed broadly shared moral values and created greater security and opportunity for many Americans.[26] Examples include public schools, programs for war veterans and their families, farm programs, and Social Security and Medicare. Today, however, civic entrepreneurs are less attuned to majoritarian concerns and more likely to organize and speak for specific issue or identity constituencies. At the same time, politicians often win and hold their offices by raising large amounts of money from special interest groups, to run media campaigns targeted on narrow slices of a shrinking electorate. The waning of voluntary federations leaves relatively few voluntary associations with links to ordinary families and their concerns. And a public sphere crowded with politicians and advocacy groups pursuing narrowly parsed issues acceptable to big funders is not as amenable to government action on broadly shared concerns. The interests and values of the highly educated and the economically privileged get much more attention in this transformed civic America.

Imagine for a moment what might have happened if the G.I. Bill of 1944 had been debated and legislated in a polity configured more like the one that prevailed during the 1993–94 debates about the proposal for national health insurance put forward by the first administration of President Bill Clinton. This is not an entirely fanciful comparison, because goals supported by the vast majority of Americans were at issue in both periods. At issue in the 1940s was how to provide care and opportunity for millions of military veterans returning from World War II—clearly a broadly popular goal. At issue in the early 1990s was how to provide to all Americans a modicum of health insurance coverage—a goal that has always registered majority

support since modern opinion polls started half a century
ago.

Back in the 1940s, moreover, there were elite actors—
university presidents, liberal intellectuals, and conservative congressmen—who left to their own devices might
have produced legislative gridlock, or else fashioned much
less generous veterans' benefits than those ultimately
included in the G.I. Bill.[27] University presidents and liberal
New Dealers initially favored versions of the G.I. Bill that
would have been bureaucratically complicated, niggardly
with public expenditures, and extraordinarily limited—
allowing only a carefully selected minority of veterans to
attend college with full support for more than one year.
Elite ideas about post–World War II veterans' legislation
were not so different from elite proposals for health reforms
in the 1990s. A G.I. bill fashioned in today's advocacy
world would not have extended generous economic and
family benefits to so many Americans and would never
have opened the doors of colleges, universities, and voca-
tional schools to millions of working-class veterans.

But in the actual civic circumstances of the 1940s, managers and professionals did not keep control of public
debates or legislative initiatives. Instead, a vast voluntary
membership federation, the American Legion, stepped in
and drafted a bill to guarantee every one of the returning
veterans the opportunity to receive up to four years of post-
high school education, along with family and employment
benefits, business loans, and home mortgages. The American Legion was not in any way a liberal, pro-welfare state
association! Indeed, many liberals considered the Legion
in the 1940s (and their ideological descendants would consider it now) downright reactionary. But no matter. Because

it was a broad, membership-based organization, hoping to attract the ex-soldiers of World War II to its fold, the Legion had incentives for popular inclusion and responsiveness. And because it was a representatively structured, nation-wide federation, it had the capacity to lobby Congress and mobilize local and state organizations to pressure their representatives. A committee appointed by the national Legion leadership drafted one of the most generous pieces of social legislation in all of U.S. history; and thousands of local Legion posts and dozens of state organizations mounted a massive public education and lobbying campaign to ensure that even conservative congressional representatives would vote for the new legislation.

Half a century later the 1990s health security episode played out in a transformed civic universe dominated by foundation-sponsored advocacy groups, mailing list associations, clashing think tanks, pollsters, and big money media campaigns.[28] Top-heavy advocacy groups did not—indeed could not—mobilize mass support for a sensible reform plan. The drafting of President Clinton's health security legislation was done by a secretive five hundred-person commission full of self-appointed experts, which produced a 1,342-page bill that few could understand, let alone use to mobilize popular support. Hundreds of business and professional groups influenced the Clinton administration's complex policy scheme—only to turn around and use a combination of congressional lobbying and emotional, carefully targeted media campaigns to block enactment of any new health insurance legislation. The American people, especially families of modest means, ended up without the desired extension of health coverage to everyone. And citizens with employer-provided benefits were left to fend for themselves in private markets dominated by cost-cutters.

Since the early 1990s national politicians have been unwilling to resume working for universal health coverage, in significant part because advocacy groups stand ready to mount expensive media attacks, and there are no movements or associations capable of mustering latent public support for some kind of decisive legislation (which might be drafted in one of any number of alternative ways). Of course, politicians and interest groups have not stopped talking about "health care reform," because their pollsters and consultants tell them people care about it. They use dramatic phrases to describe trivial or empty steps—for example, talking only about covering children, who are cheap to cover and in any event are frequently not signed up for insurance by parents who themselves lack coverage. Behind the scenes, congressional committees concentrate on policy measures most appealing to more privileged Americans who already have generous private insurance coverage. On the major unresolved issue—enhanced coverage for the burgeoning millions of the uninsured and barely insured—inaction accompanied by empty rhetoric prevails, even as about one million additional Americans join the ranks of the uninsured with each passing year. The problem gets bigger and bigger, but our top-down politics, mired in well-crafted and targeted sound-bite talk, will not address such a broad, democratic concern.

Waning Faith in Public Life

Before a sudden reversal in the trend following the terrorist attacks on the United States in late summer 2001,

popular distrust of government—and other major institutions—was a topic of great concern among scholars and
pundits, who frequently pointed to Americans' responses
to a regularly repeated survey question: "How much of the
time do you think you can trust the government in Washington to do what is right—just about always, most of the
time . . . only some of the time" or none of the time? Back
in the early 1960s, about three-fourths of Americans said
"always" or "most of the time," but during the 1990s, only
one-fifth to one-third demonstrated this much trust.[29]
Analysts often discussed this precipitous drop in trust as
if it were a reflection of mass irrationality, or a by-product
of societal disintegration. But Americans may have been
reacting to real disappointments with national government and public life. Not only did declines in trust follow
race riots and racially polarized partisan debates about
federal social programs, they coincided with the upheavals
surrounding the war in Vietnam, the Watergate scandals,
and the emergence in the 1970s of uncorrected economic
trends that hit most working families very hard. What is
more, sharp declines in public trust happened along with
the advent of top-down electoral and associational politics
and in tandem with the explosive growth of elite lobbying
in Washington, D.C.

Survey respondents clearly perceived the growing gap
between elites and everyone else. According to political
scientist Gary Orren, between the mid-1960s and the mid-
1990s the proportion of Americans who felt that "the government is run by a few big interests looking out only for
themselves" more than doubled to reach 76 percent; and
the number who believed that "public officials don't care
about what people think" grew from 36 percent to 66

percent.[30] More than six in ten respondents to a 1995 survey, moreover, cited too much influence by special interests as a reason for not trusting government.[31] Top-heavy civic associations, fragmentation and artificial polarization in public debates, and the demobilization and upward tilt of politics make quite understandable these reactions from representative samples of Americans who answered poll questions between the 1960s and the 1990s. Public life as usual was not very engaging for most Americans at the end of the twentieth century—during a time when the nation was at peace, the economy was roaring, politics seemed dispiriting, and most organized civic activity was conducted by professionals maneuvering apart from ordinary citizens.

A CIVIC REVIVAL AFTER SEPTEMBER 11, 2001?

American civic *attitudes*, at least, changed very suddenly in the immediate aftermath of the violent terrorist assaults on U.S. soil on September 11, 2001. As the immediacy of television brought airborne attacks on the World Trade Center and the Pentagon into every living room, the American people responded with an outpouring of patriotism, social solidarity, and renewed hopes for active government. Within a month, more than four out of five Americans were displaying U.S. flags on their homes, clothing, or vehicles.[32] Some 70 percent reported making charitable contributions in response to the events of September 11.[33] Feelings of social solidarity shot up, even across ethnic and racial boundaries where distrust had previously prevailed.[34] And suddenly Americans expressed faith in the national government. By November 2001 "nearly two in three Americans said they trusted the government in Washington to do the right thing either 'just about always' or 'most of the time,' . . . more than double the percentage who expressed similar levels of confidence in . . . April of 2000."[35] The new emphasis, reported political analyst Stanley B. Greenberg, was on "We—Not Me," as people saw the need the adjust priorities. In the words of one focus group participant, "'We need healing and we need each other. . . . Turn your attention to helping our nation.'"[36]

Like the outbreak of earlier wars in U.S. history, September 11 created vast possibilities for civic renewal. Mass outlooks changed, and Americans became eager to cooperate, to reach out, to volunteer. But volunteer for what? Would new attitudes lead to new actions? Would hopes for national solidarity translate into reality, and how sustainable would post-9/11 efforts turn out to be? Worrisome signs soon appeared.

Imbalance in the workings of charity was one of them. Because U.S. charities are now so professionalized and dependent on media coverage, huge popular responses to the human wreckage wrought by the terrorist attacks led to a situation of want amidst plenty. Nearly $2 billion in contributions surged into the coffers of charities promising to help the immediate victims of the 9/11 attacks, while charities providing routine help for the poor and other vulnerable people soon found themselves starved for contributions.[37] An "outpouring for September 11 groups means less for food banks," reported the *New York Times* around Thanksgiving 2001.[38] And as Christmas 2001 approached, the *Chronicle of Philanthropy* described charities as "trimming their holiday hopes," in part because of economic recession, but also because "the flood of support for victims of the September 11 attacks has left some donors feeling tapped out and less likely to write additional checks to charities not connected with those recovery efforts."[39]

In past U.S. wars voluntary federations with an organizational presence in communities all across the nation used a portion of wartime donations to build their coffers and organizational infrastructure, to address broader social needs and build reserves for peacetime as well. Federations could also move resources into various locales, as needed. But nowadays many charities stand organizationally on their own, perhaps serving just one locale. Or national organizations make promises through the national media to use money for very specific purposes. The 2001 crisis prompted Americans everywhere to want to give directly to people damaged by the September 11 attacks in New York City and Washington, D.C. When the Red Cross, still a membership federation as well as a professionalized national bureaucracy, tried to use some of the more than half million dollars contributed to its Liberty Fund for general relief and organization building, popular complaints and media campaigns forced it to change course and promise to channel all the moneys collected to September 11 victims.[40] More generally, national and New York–based charities that focused on the September 11 crisis ended up collecting far more money earmarked for immediate victims than they could usefully spend.[41]

The absence of flourishing membership federations also mattered for Americans who wanted to get personally involved, not just give money. After September 11 people had too few opportunities to channel civic urges into ongoing public projects. In a democracy the outbreak of a war is always a civically propitious moment. Previously in U.S. history, major wars prompted an immediate expansion of government-orchestrated public activities, accompanied by higher taxes and calls for united sacrifice and active mass mobilization—with privileged citizens taking the lead. In some respects, responses to September 11, 2001, proceeded in well-worn grooves, as the administration of President George W. Bush called for national unity, mobilized for military conflict, and proposed new federal expenditures for war and homeland protection. Yet President Bush avoided calling for financial sacrifice by the rich; instead he championed the acceleration of upward-tilting tax cuts that would also substantially reduce the capacities of the federal government over the long run. Even during World War I, when the nation was just emerging from the inegalitarian Gilded Age, taxes were raised, not lowered, on the richest Americans.[42]

As for his overall message to Americans at home, President Bush urged civilians to "get back to normal"—and above all to go to the shopping mall to help revive the sagging economy. Spending money on private consumption was touted as the highest expression of patriotic duty. During the months immediately after September 11, 2001, President Bush's most visible and sustained appeal in the national media took the form of a starring role in a commercial advertisement produced by the U.S. Travel Industry Association. "Americans are asking, 'What can we do?'" the flag-waving advertisement commenced. Express your "courage" by traveling and taking more vacations, was the president's answer. It was unprecedented for a U.S. president to allow his image to be used in a business-sponsored advertisement.[43] And we can be sure that the estimated two-thirds of Americans who eventually saw this ad were far more than the number who ever heard the president's occasional suggestions that people should donate to charities or volunteer for local homeland defense projects.[44]

Beyond the choices made by national leaders, America's "new war" after September 11 also differed from earlier conflicts in ways that may limit its civic impact.[45] Military actions were conducted by small numbers of highly specialized professional military forces, supported by regular military and National Guard units. No national military draft was deemed necessary. Even after anthrax attacks raised public security concerns at home and underlined the need for much more person power in public health and safety agencies, federal leaders remained uncertain about the value of large numbers of new volunteers. In past wars federal agencies could turn to vast, nationwide voluntary membership federations to orchestrate obviously helpful voluntary contributions in areas such as food conservation or liberty bond drives. But in this new antiterrorist struggle, conducted in a transformed civic universe, professionalism seemed more credible—and it was not clear how to recruit or handle or deploy massive numbers of untrained volunteers. "'You just don't put a volunteer out there on the border," explained President Bush's Homeland Security adviser, Tom Ridge. "There are certain levels of law enforcement where you really want professionals involved."[46]

Given all this, it should not surprise us that polls taken during the months after September 11, 2001, documented bifurcations between shifting civic attitudes and largely unchanged behavior. After September 11 Americans told pollsters that religion had become more important, but only those who were already religious or practicing churchgoers started praying or attending services more often. Americans without established connections to religious activities and organizations did not change their behavior.[47] Similarly, Americans in general expressed more social and polit-

ical trust and espoused more charitable feelings. But as figure 6.1 suggests, they did not start actually *doing* more as
members of associations or as volunteers. How could they,
when professionally run agencies were asking for money,
not time, and when national governmental leaders were
touting consumerism over public action?

The horrendous events of September 11, 2001, may not,
therefore, significantly change the nature of American civic
and public life. National elites remain reluctant to expand
government or mobilize mass involvement, and President
Bush's modest expansion of national service programs had
little impact with the American public as late as the middle
of 2002.[48] The profound reorganizations of the late twentieth
century still make it difficult to bridge between national and
local activities and discourage the involvement of large
numbers of citizens in organized, ongoing civic endeavors.
The potential for heightened popular engagement will continue to exist—because riveting events that reinforce patriotism and a sense of national community are conducive to
civic vitality and renewal. Yet as this book has argued, mass
willingness is not enough. Institutions and organizations
must offer opportunities for people to get involved; and citizens must see ways to have sustained clout. If the promise
of civic renewal is to be realized, national leaders, including
federal officials, must reach out to organize and involve the
American citizenry.

Recurrently throughout U.S. history, wartime crises
have triggered eras of civic renewal. But the martial conflicts themselves did not lead to civic revitalization—not
in and of themselves, apart from leaders willing to seize the
opportunity to engage, or create, popularly rooted organizations to undertake important public tasks. As of the

FIGURE 6.1

After Sept. 11, 2001, Civic Attitudes Changed More Than Behavior

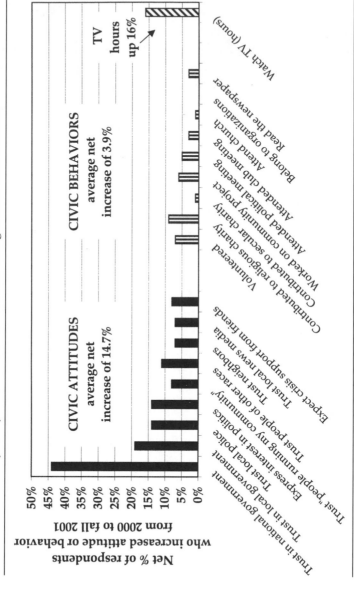

SOURCE: Robert D. Putnam, "Bowling Together," *American Prospect* 13, no. 3 (2002): 22.

early twenty-first century, the United States has too few associations and leaders able and willing to mobilize citizens for shared national undertakings. September 11, 2001, sparked widespread yearning for expanded public undertakings, but the chance for civic revitalization could all too easily dissipate before America's institutions and leaders catch up with America's people.

CHAPTER 7

REINVENTING
AMERICAN CIVIC DEMOCRACY

THE GREAT CIVIC TRANSFORMATION of our time has diminished America's democracy, leaving gaping holes in the fabric of our social and political life. The civic past cannot be revived, of course. Nor should it be. Before the rights revolutions of the late twentieth century, too many people were marginalized and disempowered; and before the recent proliferation of citizen advocacy groups, too many important values were excluded from agendas of public debate. Nevertheless, critical aspects of the classic civic America we have lost need to be reinvented—including shared democratic values, a measure of fellowship across class lines, and opportunities for the many to participate in organized endeavors alongside the elite few.

To strengthen our democracy, we Americans need to reform our civic life, reasserting ourselves as practitioners of the preeminent democratic arts of "combination." But what sorts of reforms should we undertake? Currently fashionable proposals call for shrinking government, concentrating civic energies at the local level, and handing public social services to religious congregations. From the perspective of the history recounted in this book, we can readily grasp why such proposals might do more harm than good.

Then we can move on to consider national-level reforms, including fresh strategies for civic organizing, and measures that could be undertaken to make the national media, elections, and government supportive of renewed democratic vitality in American civil society.

HARMFUL REMEDIES

Every pundit and academic, it sometimes seems, has a prescription for repairing American civil society. The most vocal and visible reformers these days are communitarians of various stripes—along with their cousins, the social capital theorists—who aim to strengthen the roots of U.S. democracy by encouraging more local community and intimate social participation. If neighbors socialize and engage in more community projects, this line of reasoning goes, democratic efficacy will be enhanced. Downright distrustful of government itself, some right-wing communitarians go a step further, urging that we slash taxes and turn the administration of many public social services over to religious congregations, on the grounds that "communities of faith" are more capable than secular bureaucrats of reaching bodies (and souls) in need.[1] But the history of American civic life tells us that such currently fashionable remedies risk worsening the diseases they seek to cure.

The Limits of Local Sociability

From middle-of-the-roaders Robert Putnam, William Galston, and Jean Bethke Elshtain to conservatives Don Eberly and William Schambra, the most eloquent pundits in today's civic engagement debate have converged on amazingly apolitical and locally minded notions of what is wrong with U.S. civic life and how to fix it.[2] The irony is delicious. Here are remarkable movers and shakers—professional men and women who head powerful institutions and are ever to be found traveling on airplanes, speaking at national meetings, and sitting in front of computer screens to peck out manifestos for national reform. Yet they describe the civic past and diagnose the present as if American democratic vitality were primarily local and largely innocent of conflict or aspirations for political power.

This bears little relationship to how it really was, as we have learned. Classic American voluntary groups were built by and for the citizens of a nation on the move. These associations expressed broadly shared identities and values, engaged in raucous conflict with one another, and linked local people to state, regional, and national centers of power. Voluntary federations also sought to influence government and in many cases worked closely with it. You would never know this, however, from today's civic communitarians, who are urging Americans to turn toward local endeavors detached from politics.

"Activist government" and political movements are not the answer, declares the National Commission on Civic Renewal, because the real drive for civic renewal is happening "within the neighborhoods, the towns, the local communities of America."[3] In the conclusion to *Bowling Alone*, Putnam offers a similar "Agenda for Social Capitalists."[4] Workplaces must be made "friendly" to families and communities—a worthy goal, yet an objective Putnam implies can be achieved by mere exhortation of private employers. Democracy is ideally local; thus elections and government should be "decentralized as far as possible to bring decisions to smaller, local jurisdictions." Schools should provide more civic education to the young; and communities should be designed to "encourage more casual socializing with friends and neighbors." In Putnam's view, Americans need to participate much more actively in spiritual communities and cultural activities ranging from "group dancing to songfests to community theater to rap festivals." Above all, we should "spend less time traveling and more time connecting with our neighbors."

Such prescriptions evoke warm and fuzzy feelings in all of us caught in increasingly frenzied worlds of demanding work and hard-pressed family life. But as strategies for the revitalization of U.S. democracy, recommendations so preoccupied with local social life—remedies that ignore issues of economic inequality, power disparity, and political demobilization—are simply not plausible. Can we imagine rates of voter participation and organized public activity sharply improving if people heed the call to hold more picnics and songfests? If managers and professionals schmooze more with their neighbors, will American elites stop being enamored of upward-tilting tax cuts and conspicuously luxurious private consumption—and otherwise start behaving in more democratically responsive ways? If localism prevails, will ordinary American citizens be able to make a difference on things that count?

We live in a nation marked by growing gaps between the rich and the upper middle class versus everyone else—in a country experiencing the withdrawal of privileged people into gated communities, Potemkin village vacation spots, separate schools, and expensive box seats at sporting events. America's civic life has shifted from membership-mobilization to advocacy and management and from stress on shared values and goals to the pursuit of specialized interests. In an era when the highly educated and the well-to-do are cocooning within separate and privileged arrangements of all kinds, at a time when money and top-heavy initiatives count for more and more in organized politics and associational life, how could our national democracy possibly be revitalized through indiscriminate increases in any and all kinds of local sociability and neighborly charity? The people most likely to take local community and "social capitalism" to heart—to benefit from them and feel self-satisfied—are, I fear, the same folks already flourishing, in increasingly privatized ways, in America's ever more lightly governed version of just plain old capitalism.[5] Improving local communities, and social life more generally, will not create sufficient democratic leverage to tackle problems that can only be addressed with concerted national commitment.

The state of Maine, for example, is a wonderfully civic place, scoring near the top of Putnam's cross-state index of social capital.[6] No surprise, for Maine has strong civic traditions, a progressive Clean Elections Law, and relatively high voting rates. The state boasts remarkably neighborly towns; active nonprofits and citizens' groups; elected officials readily available for personal contact; public radio and television stations plus the *Bangor Daily News* practicing civic journalism at its best; and native wealthy citizens (above all novelist Stephen King and his wife, Tabitha) who give generously and wisely to community undertakings everywhere in Maine. All of the good things prescribed by communitarians and social capital theorists are already happening in Maine.[7] But Mainers still need to be part of a broader national community and democratic politics with real clout. Over the decade of the 1990s, four-fifths of Maine families have experienced a steady deterioration in real incomes.[8] What is more, the erosion of health insurance marches forward inexorably, as more and more Maine businesses and middle-class as well as poor people suffer from the rate-setting practices of nationally powerful insurance companies.[9] Despite local civic vitality, in other words, many Maine communities and people have been badly hurt by the erosion of active democratic government in the United States.

Much the same may be true across the United States. A recent Pew Foundation study found that 77 percent of Americans "feel connected to their communities, and say the quality of life there is excellent or good."[10] Detailed results debunk "the popular myth that Americans are isolated in their homes and offices." They document that "people have a profound sense of connectivity to their communities and their neighbors, are volunteering in record numbers, are helping neighbors to solve problems, and are optimistic about the future."[11] Yet "Americans still have many concerns," concluded Suzanne W. Morse, executive director of the Pew Partnership for Civic Change, who directed the study. Respondents were asked to rank order various concerns, and the "top problems . . . facing communities across the country" turned out to be "the lack of jobs that pay a living wage" and "access to affordable health care."[12] These, of course, are widespread problems that must be addressed by active democratic government. They cannot be solved by scattered local action, neighborly interactions, or occasional volunteering orchestrated by church congregations or nonprofit agencies. The Pew results suggest that many pundits in the current civic engagement debate have misdiagnosed the problem.

The Civic Perils of Faith-based Services

Another fashionable remedy that could hurt more than help is government subsidy of faith-based social services. Democrat Al Gore and Republican George W. Bush agreed on little during the 2000 presidential campaign, but they concurred that "faith-based communities" should be encouraged to apply for public funding to implement social services for the needy and for troubled segments of the population such as drug users, teenage mothers, and families of prisoners. Shortly after assuming office, President Bush established the White House Office of Faith-based and Community Initiatives to carry out his vision of "compassionate conservatism." "When we see social needs in America," the president declared, "my administration will look first to faith-based programs and community groups, which have proven their power to save and change lives."[13] As the president later elaborated, "[F]ederal policy should reject the failed formula of towering, distant bureaucracies that too often prize process over performance. . . . We must heed the growing consensus across America that successful government programs work in fruitful partnership with community-serving and faith-based organizations."[14]

In a way, nothing new is being proposed here. From the Salvation Army and Lutheran Social Services to Jewish Family Services and Catholic Charities, religiously connected agencies have long played a prominent role, along with secular nonprofits, in administering publicly funded social services across the United States. Current faith-based reforms would, however, go considerably further toward fragmenting and decentralizing publicly funded programs. They would encourage tens of thousands of local religious congregations to compete for public grants and set aside or relax many of the federal and state legal rules that have heretofore required religiously connected agencies to meet the same nondiscriminatory employment norms and standards of safety, efficiency, and fiscal probity that apply to public agencies and secular nonprofit groups. Faith-based procedures could put programs sponsored by thousands of religious congregations on the public dole—or at least raise the hopes of their clergy that they could tap into taxpayer funds for congregational charities.

Liberals have denounced proposed faith-based reforms on constitutional and legal grounds.[15] And social analysts point out that there is no hard empirical evidence for the proposition that faith-based social programs are more effective than governmental or secular programs in reaching and helping the needy, the disabled, and the troubled. Relevant as such criticisms may be, they seem to me to miss the chief danger of faith-based proposals—that they could further erode membership-based associational life in America. After President Bush took office and declared his intention to push faith-based social provision farther than the preceding Democratic administration had done, an article in the *New York Times* explained that states and localities were making "unprecedented efforts to encourage religious charities to apply for government money." States and localities, after all, are always strapped for money to pay for social services, and they will jump on any bandwagon that promises more resources. Thus authorities all over the country convened conferences and encouraged "new collaborations between clergy members and state social service departments." At a typical state-sponsored seminar in Virginia, "a roomful of ministers and grant writers scribbled notes" as an official explained that there would not be any extra, earmarked funds for churches, but they could now "compete with other community agencies for the same limited funds. . . . Many at this conference said they were prepared to jump through the hoops because the financing amounted to more than they could raise passing the plate. Most had already started programs and were looking to professionalize and expand."[16]

Under a "faith-based" regime of social provision, the United States might well spend even less public money on social programs for the poor and the vulnerable. Without additional resources to help the poor and troubled, leaders of religious congregations will be encouraged to compete with public agencies and established secular and religious nonprofits for modest grants to administer hard-pressed social services.[17] One civic downside of this likely scenario is that governments might lay off their unionized public employees as they contract out social services to religious congregations, whose low-paid employees and volunteers promise to do more with less funding. Given that public employee unions are about the only ones growing inside the AFL-CIO these days, this possible side effect of faith-based social services clearly delights Republicans and perturbs many Democrats. But regardless of partisan considerations, all Americans who care about the vitality of our civic life should worry that religiously administered social services could increase professional management and "civic entrepreneurship" in the one major sector of American civil society that, as of now, still relies heavily on membership, fellowship, and voluntary dues.

Historically, American religion, like U.S. voluntarism in general, flourished in a governmental matrix that facilitated competitive organization and offered groups access to the public arena while limiting official sponsorship and patronage. Rights to organize and speak out were established, however tenuously, by the Constitution and the Bill of Rights. Federalism and representative democracy created multiple points of access for voluntary associations, religious and secular alike. These forms of public facilitation nourished a raucous variety of American voluntary groups and movements, each of which had to compete for popular support. On occasion, to be sure, public officials jump-started voluntary associations such as veterans' or farm groups. What is more, federal and state authorities often conducted campaigns or implemented legislation in cooperation with well-established associations. Nevertheless, ongoing public funding was rarely available to classic U.S. voluntary membership associations. Like leaders of other types of membership groups, American religious leaders had to rely on dues-paying members—who could, if they chose, take both their time and their monetary contributions elsewhere. If association leaders or religious clerics wanted to launch pet projects or sustain professional staffs, they had to do so with significant ongoing support from dues-paying memberships.

Clerical reliance on voluntary lay support mobilized in a free and competitive environment has been highly propitious for American religion. All over the world in the modern era, government-patronized churches have lost élan and popular support; yet American religion has remained vital—and always on the move, with new religious movements periodically rising to challenge and bypass older, more routinized and bureaucratized denominations.[18] If U.S. national, state, and local governments now begin to

offload social service programs onto local congregations, subsidizing professional projects managed by the clergy and their
staff employees, the vitality of American religion could easily
be threatened. Ironically, the greatest harm might be done to
congregations of poor people, whose ministers already spend
energy and resources chasing grants from private foundations.[19] Religious leaders heading agencies rather than shepherding congregations will be bad for American civil society.
Clergy will become less oriented to their flocks—and organized religion will head down much the same road toward
management rather than membership that the rest of contemporary civil society has already traversed.

In short, faith-based "reforms," as well as efforts to focus
civic renewal at the local level, could actually hurt rather
than help American civic democracy. The end result could
simply be more sociability and solidarity among the privileged, more management rather than membership, and
dribbles of charity for those among the needy who happen
to catch the attention of privileged do-gooders, with everyone else left to their own devices in an unforgiving economy barely buffered by dwindling public supports. The
localists, the social capitalists, and the faith-based reformers
have missed some fundamental points. Democracy is about
more than sociability and trust, and it certainly requires
much more than charitable ties between the privileged and
other citizens. Effective democracy requires powerful representative government and strong, encompassing associations that afford collective leverage by and for the majority.

To correct for recent civic losses and revitalize American
democracy, we must find ways to nurture national solidarity as well as local community. And we need national-level
reforms with bite, targeted on powerful institutions and

nationally ambitious activists. No more than anyone else who has studied civic trends in the United States do I have a magic wand to produce immediate civic revitalization. That acknowledged, let me make some bold, even speculative recommendations—most of which run very much against the grain of currently fashionable civic reforms.

NEW MODELS OF CIVIC DEMOCRACY

As we learned in chapters 4 and 5, civic transformations happened abruptly in late-twentieth-century America, driven by youthful activists who bypassed older membership federations, launched new social movements, and ended up fashioning new models of professional advocacy to press rights for the disadvantaged and fresh understandings of the public interest. Social, political, and technological factors converged to facilitate the civic transformation of the 1970s to 1990, yet new ideas about the value of professional association building were also crucial. Now that the downsides of earlier changes are becoming apparent, there is, once again, room for fresh understandings of what it will take to enhance American civic democracy. Leaders who understand the democratic deficits of our overly professionalized and elitist contemporary civic life can devise new models of association building, blending the best of the old and the new civic America.

Innovation need not proceed in a vacuum, because promising reinventions are already under way. From a broad brush perspective, the substitution of professional management and advocacy for mass-mobilizing politics and membership-based associational activities has been the dominant trend since the 1960s. But organizers in certain

social movements have more or less self-consciously combined classic and innovative styles of civic organizing—
using the most up-to-date communications tactics for fund-
raising and lobbying while at the same time drawing large
numbers of Americans into associational networks and
organized shared endeavors. Many of these same movements and associations have also rediscovered the efficacy
of using social contacts to draw members and their friends
and neighbors into political campaigns. The latest political
science research reveals that when it comes to drawing people to the polls on election day, person-to-person contact
works better than repeated mailings or anonymous telephone canvasses, let alone impersonal television advertising.[20] Strengthening participatory associations may thus be
the key to political as well as civic revitalization. During the
1990s, a number of real-world associations and movements
discovered, and practiced, this truth for themselves.

Unionists, Environmentalists, and Conservative Christians

Since 1995, for example, a reenergized American Federation of Labor and Congress of Industrial Organizations
(AFL-CIO), under the presidency of John Sweeney, has
combined staff-led lobbying with grassroots organizing in
workplaces and during election campaigns. Along with
some (though not all) of its member internationals, the AFL-
CIO now welcomes and nurtures unconventional activists,
devoted to organizing new workplaces and activating
minority and women workers who historically were marginalized in union bureaucracies. Some of these new organ-
izer-recruits come from blue-collar and professional workplaces; others come from college campuses, from other social

movements, and from religious seminaries. AFL-CIO training efforts include innovative efforts such as "Union Summer" and "Seminary Summer."[21]

The AFL-CIO's organizing drives have paid off by drawing in new sets of public employees, service workers, and
professionals—and turning some cities, like Los Angeles,
into hotbeds of "new unionism," with Latino immigrants
in the vanguard.[22] Reversing union membership losses
since the 1950s remains an uphill struggle, given an often-
unfriendly regulatory environment plus ongoing shifts in
the U.S. economy that batter older enclaves of unionized
blue-collar employees. Nevertheless, as it revitalizes workplace organizing, the new AFL-CIO has also learned to
build coalitions with churches and community groups, and
it has taken to blending network-based and modern media
strategies to magnify its impact on electoral candidates and
legislative policymaking.[23] The AFL-CIO has become a formidable player in election campaigns, not simply (as conservatives assert) by using membership dues to help pay
for well-crafted television advertising, but also by devising
workplace and community-based campaigns of voter education and mobilization and making innovative use of the
Internet to support these network-based efforts.

The AFL-CIO is far from the only site of innovative associational and political practices that seek to involve large
numbers of nonelite Americans. In different but equally
notable ways, the modern environmental movement and
contemporary American Christian conservatism combine
advocacy strategies with membership recruitment and
democratic leadership training for public purposes. Like
the renovated modern U.S. union movement, these other
movements all share the fundamental ingredients of vital

civic democracy. In its own way, each movement invokes a moral worldview and asserts a broadly shared social identity; each combines local roots with much broader reach; and each synthesizes social fellowship with public clout.

As we learned in chapter 4, many of the new environmental organizations launched since the 1970s are staff organizations or professionally run associations with mailing list constituencies. Still, the contemporary environmental movement as a whole includes a mix of partially competing but mostly cooperating groups ranging from think tanks and advocacy associations to chapter-based membership federations and small groups situated in particular communities or workplaces.[24] Many Americans who belong to none of the above are also informed about environmental issues and sympathetic to the efforts of environmental associations.

Although environmentalism is not embodied in one big, nation-spanning, chapter-based membership federation, interactions among the full range of organizations and constituencies that make up the movement as a whole in some sense represent the functional equivalent of classic forms of civic associationalism, with a similar blend of national and local, political and social undertakings. The environmental movement includes leaders and experts devoted to doing research, making public arguments, and lobbying Congress, state legislatures, and public agencies. It also includes grassroots groups that pursue specific projects (such as auditing an environmental site or clearing trails in a national park) or just get together for recreational activities (like cycling, hiking, or bird-watching). Disparate environmentalist activities sometimes proceed largely detached from one another. But at times groups of recreational environmentalists who gather, say, on weekends for bird-watching expeditions, also follow state, regional, and national policy debates. What is more, some environmental associations, such as the Sierra Club, deliberately maintain networks of representatively governed chapters capable of influencing, as well as supporting, public policy campaigns.

Even more successful at blending membership-based activities with expensive and expert national advocacy have been new right conservatives in contemporary America. As Putnam argues, political activists on the right have been able to connect to previously existing networks grounded in membership-based institutions—namely, church congregations and intercongregational ties among clergy and church members.[25] But dense religious social capital did not in and of itself generate broader civic engagement on the right. Evangelical Christians have risen in numbers over recent decades, yet the numbers of Americans holding conservative political views have not changed much. Before the mid-1970s religious conservatives were considered a relatively politically quiescent population. That they have subsequently increased their levels of civic and political engagement is due as much to leadership strategies and the construction of Christian right associations beyond churches as such as it is attributable to the simple existence of grassroots church networks. Antiabortion activists, for example, have dramatized threats from Supreme Court decisions and legislative enactments to build issue-focused but locally rooted associations that may well feed off of evangelical Protestant and Catholic churches but are not directly run by them. A similar story unfolded on the broader political right.[26]

The original new right groups of the early 1970s were professionally run advocacy operations, which actually

pioneered direct-mail tactics for raising money and influencing opinion among well-targeted potential constituencies. But these tactics soon reached a plateau of effectiveness;
and even during the apparently propitious 1980s, with
conservative president Ronald Reagan in power, the so-
called Christian right was not making much new headway.
A lot of money as well as organizing efforts went into the
campaign of Christian right candidate Pat Robertson for
the 1988 Republican presidential nomination. The campaign flopped, but afterward Robertson gave the go-ahead
to a new mobilizing approach led by Ralph Reed. Lists of
names from old petitions and mailings lists were deployed
not just to ask people for more money through the mail but
to build up a federated association, the Christian Coalition,
devoted to group mobilization and leadership training in
local communities, every congressional district, and each
state, as well as at the national level. Christian right activists
were recruited and messages disseminated through churches,
yet the clergy were somewhat bypassed—much as the
nineteenth-century WCTU bypassed them. What is more,
Christian right participants were given a chance to develop
the group resources and leadership clout to penetrate state-
level Republican parties and local congressional campaigns.
As federated association building proceeded, conservative
foundations used grants to build up new ideas for right-
wing groups to popularize; and expert-led think tanks and
advocacy groups worked away in Washington, D.C. Much
as in the environmental movement but with more concerted
and organized efforts in the states and localities, the new
conservatives coordinated and blended top-down policy
advocacy with updated membership organizing.

Notice that contemporary movements successfully blending old and new associational approaches have been openly politically ambitious. Looking for roads to power, strategically minded leaders could not find easier ways, so they turned to popular engagement not just out of civic goodness but for *political* reasons—indeed often in response to perceived political threats. People-oriented strategies were not usually the first choice. Only after decades of dwindling returns from insider lobbying did the AFL-CIO finally move toward new workplace campaigns, community outreach, and a combination of media politics and network contacting during elections. Only after diminishing returns from direct-mail efforts and a failed presidential campaign did Christian right politicos invest in local and state organizing—tactics themselves encouraged by the need and opportunity to build Republican influence in Congress.

The Industrial Areas Foundation

Less nationally visible than the AFL-CIO, environmentalists, and the Christian right is another movement that has proved innovative and effective in the civic arena, a movement consisting of the interlinked regional organizing efforts led by the Industrial Areas Foundation (IAF). As described by its best-known spokesperson, Ernesto Cortes, the IAF is "the center of a national network of broad based, multiethnic, interfaith organizations in primarily poor and moderate-income communities. . . . The central role of IAF organizations is to build the competence and confidence of ordinary citizens and taxpayers so that they can reorganize relationships of power and politics in their communities."[77]

IAF organizations exist in various regions of the United States, including a new one in the greater Boston metropolitan area, the Greater Boston Interfaith Organization, which is forging links between the inner city and the suburbs and includes committed participants from Catholic and Protestant churches, Jewish synagogues, congregations of other faiths, and also some labor organizations.

Perhaps the best-known IAF network consists of interrelated organizations in Texas and other southwestern cities.[28] These community organizations draw considerable support from church congregations prepared to pay dues and commit people to community organizing. IAF organizers help to train community leaders, and the leaders in turn recruit expanding networks of additional leaders and participants, who, when ready, identify important public issues around which to make demands of government or powerful private institutions. IAF organizing is both locally rooted and federated. It uses biblical and other religious stories to express shared moral concerns. And it melds professional training for organizers with a long-term commitment to "relational organizing" through person-to-person contacts. The results have been impressive, for IAF city and regional organizations have successfully tackled issues of school reform, neighborhood improvement, and the establishment of job training programs that lead to positions with wages and benefits sufficient to sustain families.

Unlike most other "people mobilizing" movements in the United States today, IAF organizations maintain a nonpartisan political stance, so that they can make demands of politicians and officeholders from both parties. What is more, IAF organizations rarely seek media publicity, for fear of privileging individual "stars" in their organizations.

Instead, IAF organizations quietly develop popular leaders and group capacities, drawing local movements together on occasion for metropolitan, state, or regional campaigns on issues carefully selected to express concerns shared across ethnic and racial lines. A careful student of the Texas efforts, sociologist Mark Warren, concludes that the " IAF combines authority with participation to create a dynamic form of intervention in democratic politics. . . . Many well-grounded community groups remain weak and isolated in their localities. Most advocacy groups, on the other hand, are top-heavy, lobbying in Washington without an organized base. The IAF has found a way to balance the two sides, placing a relentless concentration on local organizing while leveraging power at higher levels."[29]

Further Possibilities for Civic Innovation

Taking heart from such already existing models of popular civic mobilization, as well as from America's long civic history, contemporary activists have various strategies open to them as they launch new associations, reorient existing ones, or take part in multigroup movements for social and political change.

Civic activists (and the patrons who help them to get started) can consider building networks of chapters, holding recurrent representative meetings, and raising ongoing resources through dues from members—or affiliated groups. Since the 1960s America's "civic entrepreneurs" have rarely proceeded in these ways, because it seems so much easier to open central offices with media people, lobbyists, and computerized mailing lists. But as the IAF experience shows, taking longer and asking for a greater commitment may result in a greater payoff. Sustained infrastructure building—provided it is not just local but translocal—can generate greater influence than centralized efforts focused on Washington, D.C., or ephemeral plays for attention in the national media. It takes time to connect leaders and members to one another across places or institutions, yet this is the only way to draw large numbers of people into a movement and the best way to generate sustained leverage to make a difference beyond one issue battle or election.

Interestingly, there are signs that some Washington, D.C.-based advocacy groups are becoming more interested in federated chapter building. In recent years, the AARP has hired organizers to work full time at developing new state and local chapters. And Jonah Edelman, son of the leader of the professionally run Children's Defense Fund, has been working for some time now to develop networks of dues-paying chapters in an associated organization called Stand for Children.[30] The hallmark of such approaches is leadership training and steady recruitment through an outward-radiating network of contacts. In turn, leader-organizers have to be given an ongoing stake in the associational effort through shared and representative decision making.

Old-style representative federations grounded in specific localities are one model, but they are not the only one. Future U.S. voluntary federations might weave ties among units situated in workplaces or religious congregations or other nongeographically defined settings. Leadership training, network building across sites; and transparent procedures for representative decision making are what count. Patrons who fund associational start-ups should consider directing their resources to support leadership training and membership-based organizing rather than just handing out grants to fund mass mailings or sustain professionally run offices. And civic activists should let their imaginations roam and look for ways to reinvent membership organizing along new lines suited to today's constituencies and technologies.

Professionally run advocacy groups and research institutes can also learn to form persistent partnerships with membership associations. Not every civic association, old or new, needs to become a full-fledged membership network. Advocacy groups, research institutes, and other memberless kinds of civic organizations can continue to do the professional tasks they do best, simultaneously forming partnerships with membership groups or institutions. Planned synergy of this sort fueled many of the most successful social movements and legislative drives in American history, and there is no reason why Washington, D.C.-based advocacy groups cannot seek out unlike (as well as like) partners in contemporary coalitions. "Inside the Beltway" ought to become an outdated phrase for advocates—especially for those who care about causes not favored by the most powerful established interests. Of course, people who want democratic changes should continue to work for and with Washington, D.C.-based groups. But citizen advocacy groups should always be looking for ways to cooperate with—and stimulate and learn from—organizations that themselves have widespread, interactive memberships.

It is not incidental that religious institutions and congregants have become key participants in some of the most influential democratic movements in our time—ranging from the Christian Coalition on the right, to the IAF's urban and regional interfaith alliances on the center-left. Churches are the one sector remaining where it is appropriate for people to come together across occupational lines, where family life and ongoing membership activities intersect, and where it seems normal for people to invoke values and moral judgments. All of these are essential ingredients for popularly inspiring democratic politics. There is no necessary reason, however, why churches should be the only membership-based institutions involved in interorganizational alliances for change. Many other possibilities await imaginative coalition building by leaders who realize the value of blending professionalism with groups grounded in fellowship or ongoing daily activities.

THE MEDIA AND DEMOCRATIC REVITALIZATION

Reinventing American civic democracy must start with new strategies on the part of Americans who build and sustain civic associations. But national institutions also matter, because they create rules of influence and power that provide opportunities and incentives to civic organizers and social movements. Shortly, I will consider the impact of electoral politics and government, but first let me comment on the national media.

Because social communication is critical to a healthy civil society, the practices of leading newspapers and opinion magazines and the choices made by television producers have a substantial impact on the kinds of civic and political activities that are advantaged and disadvantaged. Without necessarily intending to do so, national media outlets have adopted strategies for portraying and gathering information that encourage unrepresentative leadership, ridicule organized group activities, and ignore or disparage representative politics. Recently, media professionals have tried to become more self-conscious about their civic impact and responsibilities. Leading outlets have joined the "civic journalism" movement, which in practice encourages the use of in-depth polling and focus-group techniques to figure out issues many citizens care about, in order to focus reasonable coverage on such matters.[31] This may be helpful as far as it goes, but it leaves in place practices that promote elitism and undermine associational efforts.

In all realms of public life, polling techniques have displaced consultations with popularly rooted organizations and representative leaders as strategies for measuring "public opinion." Presumably, we should all celebrate this fact, for it arguably produces more comprehensive and representative measurements. Maybe so, but exclusive use of polling furthers an ever more total bifurcation between "public opinion" and democratic capacity. Polling is a top-down procedure in which experts devise and pose the questions, and respondents, contacted individually, give answers detached from context. Polls, moreover, tell us what aggregates of people think—for the moment—but not much about what organized groups can or will do.

Polls will not go away, any more than television will, but they need not be overused. During the protracted 2000 presidential election season, for example, national media outlets spent the many-months interval between the primaries and the national Republican and Democratic Conventions worrying about every little twist in the national polls—at a time when most Americans were not paying much attention to the presidential contest. Countless stories were written and broadcast about why Bush was up and Gore was losing, and about how campaigns were doing this or that in response to polls. This was not just a waste of resources and attention. It was a lost opportunity. In this period of the presidential election, why not focus media attention on the doings of popularly rooted movements and associations? How were their members framing and thinking about the issues? What were they doing to get ready for the fall elections?

From time to time, media do cover such matters, yet almost always in a disparaging tone. Groups active in politics are portrayed as "special interests"—even if, like the AFL-CIO or the Christian Coalition, they have millions of supporters. As is the case with the doings of Congress, political arguments inside associations or movements are recounted as personality clashes or dispiriting faction fights. Rarely do we see informative or respectful coverage of democratic decisions about leaderships or issue positions. National media have done much to build up expert advocates, giving them respectful visibility and voice, but apart from a few star politicians, elected representative leaders rarely appear. *The Newshour with Jim Lehrer*, for example, has professional advocates and pundits galore— plus, of late, increasing numbers of media people and experts commenting on other media people. But how often do viewers of even this very civic-minded television news program see elected leaders of major unions or civic associations, not to mention leaders of the fast-growing evangelical religious denominations? Civic leaders who organize or represent others are rarely visible in American national life.

It does not have to be this way. The media are not just portraying what is out there; their current practices help to push things in an undemocratic direction. These practices can be modified. To make news coverage more complete and avoid unintended disparagement of democratic practices, media people could take a series of small steps in new directions. They could, for one thing, regularly invite representatively chosen associational leaders to give opinions on major public issues. Both television and newspapers can nudge away from so much reliance on "experts" from memberless think tanks, advocacy groups, and academia as their chief commentators on politics and public policy issues. Look instead for leaders—ideally, representatively chosen leaders—who can legitimately speak for many others. Fewer "talking heads" and more "talking representatives" should be the watchword. This recommendation runs against my self-interest as an academic talking head. But so be it. In a democracy, those chosen for visibility on television and in the print media should prominently include people who have organized, led, and represented their fellow citizens.

Media outlets could also portray representative decision-making processes in more informative and respectful ways. This applies to everything from platform discussions in the major parties to elections for associational presidencies to associational discussions of what issues and strategies to emphasize. Newspaper and television reporters could do American democracy a big favor by promoting greater understanding of the meaning and value of vigorous political arguments, competition, and mobilization around pivotal decisions within associations and institutions, as well as within the polity as a whole. Do not just portray these as breakdowns of managerial discipline. Tell us which groups care, why, and how they are engaging others to win contests or work out compromises. That is what democracy is all about.

Perhaps my most controversial suggestion is that television and newspapers should rely less exclusively on polling and artificially assembled focus groups. Of course media institutions are going to make continued use of in-depth polling to assess overall trends in public opinion, but reporters could simultaneously track developments in naturally occurring institutions, organizations, and associations. How do Americans who regularly interact with one another (not just people who meet once in a focus group!) puzzle through an issue, disagree about it, and evolve from one set of positions to another? What do people think, and do, when they see a gap between their values and the choices offered by politicians or other institutional elites? Associational leaders could even be asked to speculate about what might be done. This would be more informative than the endless guesses about what will happen that media pundits are now asked to make. Given the great communicative power of national media outlets, providing additional visibility to membership groups and movements and more respectful coverage of representative leadership and honest political debate could go a long way toward encouraging democratic revitalization in the United States.

REFORMING NATIONAL POLITICS

Finally, we come to the need for reforms in government and politics. It may seem perverse to wind up a book about civic transformation by talking about changes in government and electoral politics, but this historical tour has taught us that representative government and politics serve as both *models* and *opportunity structures* for associational activities. Americans became a civic people in the first place by building voluntary associations that imitated the routines of representative government—and voluntary federations often, in turn, sought to influence and work with government. Not incidentally, recent shifts toward management rather than membership have coincided with a turn toward regulatory politics in Washington, D.C. And recent civic changes have unfolded in parallel with shifts toward professionally managed and television-oriented electoral campaigns. As long as centralized and professionally managed institutions and advocacy groups retain special access to government and the media and as long as advocacy groups and pollsters have more to offer office-seeking politicians than other kinds of actors, American civic democracy will not become much more inclusive—and local voluntary efforts will remain detached from national centers of power.

To achieve civic revitalization, therefore, we must also modify the workings of politics and government. Yet currently touted approaches to "political reform" may not be what we need. Too many liberal reformers have gravitated to the notion that getting big money out of electoral politics is *the* master key to civic improvement. Elections are currently as much about raising money as about mobilizing voters. Candidates and public officials spend high proportions of their time talking to rich people at fund-raisers. And a horde of money-dispensing special interests swarm around every congressional legislative battle in Washington, D.C. So it is easy to see why Common Cause and other "good government" groups obsess about money in politics. But the problem is that good-government reform strategies, while unlikely in practice to succeed at reducing the political advantages of the wealthy, could easily undermine what remains of organized, popularly rooted political mobilization.[32] In the name of limiting big money, a number of current good-government reforms would limit the ability of unions and popular groups to raise issues during elections; and some may greatly weaken political party efforts to mobilize new voters.

Long traditions of American political reform stretch back to the Mugwumps and the elite Progressives around 1900. These reformers hated nineteenth-century political party machines, which they saw as promoting corruption. So the reformers worked for measures that would emphasize an unemotional, educational style of politics—and measures that would, ideally, give every individual citizen equal voice.[33] However, the highly competitive, well-organized party networks so hated by the Mugwumps were also very adept at organizing and inspiring voters and turning them out on election days. Voter participation in the United States has never been so high—as a proportion of all those legally eligible to vote—as it was when the party machines held sway.[34]

The United States has now had more than a century of experience with what I will call "neo-Mugwump" reforms, which promise to revitalize democracy by elevating the thinking individual over all kinds of group mobilization— and the results are not happy. With renewed vigor in recent times, Americans keep passing laws designed to get money out of politics, only to see each new round of "reforms" quickly circumvented. Of late, we have also passed tax laws to keep civic associations and institutions from engaging in "partisan" activities. In practice, such laws merely encourage professionally managed groups to proliferate, especially groups that can claim to be involved in "research" and "educational" lobbying while eschewing direct popular political mobilization.[35] Intentionally or not, late-twentieth-century neo-Mugwump reforms have pushed our polity away from true popular mobilization in politics—and probably in other associational realms, as well. If twenty-first-century Americans continue down the neo-Mugwump reform road, by passing laws that make it still harder for all kinds of groups to draw people into politics, the results will further the tilt toward the rich and those with advanced degrees.[36] Instead we need to envision and enact reforms designed to *get broadly organized groups of people into politics.*

After the 2000 presidential election culminated in a series of tawdry legal and judicial maneuvers, there was an understandable resurgence of interest in how U.S. elections are conducted. Reforms have been proposed by various groups, including the National Commission on Federal Election Reform co-chaired by former presidents Jimmy Carter and Gerald Ford.[37] National discussion is certainly healthy, but arguments are overly focused on how to count votes already cast rather than on ways to draw many more Americans into politics. After all, only about half of eligible American adults bother to vote at all, even in closely contested national contests. Unfortunately, the reform ideas getting the most attention are technical or regulatory fixes, while too little attention has been paid to one of the most promising recommendations of the National Commission on Federal Election Reform the proposal to make federal election day a national holiday.

National elections enhance civic engagement, researchers have shown, because they encourage popular involvement and build national solidarity.[38] We should take note of this fact and do all we can to build drama, group efforts, and collective effervescence into National Election Day. Interestingly, Puerto Rico is the one part of the greater United States where contemporary voting turnout is unusually high—averaging 83 percent in presidential election years, and 70 percent on "off years," up to 35 percentage points above turnouts on the mainland. Economist Richard Freeman has investigated the Puerto Rican phenomenon. He argues that institutional rather than personal factors must be involved, because when Puerto Ricans migrate to the mainland, they vote at a depressed rate like other Americans. In Puerto Rico itself, off-year elections are held on Sundays, and presidential-year elections occur on holiday Tuesdays, when the highest turnouts are recorded. "By reducing the cost of voting and making voting day a dedicated event," Puerto Rico has increased turnout significantly, Freeman suggests. "Citizens with time constraints find it easier to vote on the Tuesday holiday or Sunday off-day," and "citizens who would otherwise not vote are induced to vote by making the voting day a special event, which galvanizes political parties and their activities."[39] In effect, with its voting holiday, Puerto Rico has reinvented some of the entertainment, drama, and collective solidarity characteristic of nineteenth-century U.S. elections.[40]

Like Puerto Rico's Tuesday holiday every presidential election year, a new U.S. Election Day should not just be "time off"—for experience has taught us that removing obstacles to individual registration and voting is not enough to raise turnout. We need "motivated voters," as Marshall Ganz explains, and much of the motivation must come from social example and organized mobilization.[41] Twenty-first-century Americans should aim to make elections fun and compelling. The increased visibility of a holiday election day could, in itself, encourage more individual citizens to vote. But the holiday should also be an occasion for group involvement by unions, churches, institutions, civic associations, and all manner of other organizations. Politically active groups could use the holiday time to deploy poll watchers and get-out-the-vote activists, yet there might be additional ways to make Election Day an occasion. States, for instance, could declare contests, so that the localities doing the best job of raising their voting rates would get bonus grants for locally designated public projects. Workplaces and associations could also stage contests, to see which units or chapters can achieve high turnouts. Institutions and associations can encourage people to go to the polls and throw after-the-vote parties to celebrate. Anything that enhances the social side of citizenship would help turnout— and an important side effect would be to strengthen associational bonds for groups that get involved.

Unfettering Associations in Politics

Just as important as election reforms are measures to encourage political organizing and associational involvements in politics. "Reform" in the neo-Mugwump tradition often treats politics as if it were something dirty and implicitly holds up the ideal of an educated elite safely above and outside of politics. Ironically, although liberal advocacy politics grew out of the popular movements of the 1960s and 1970s, much of it has ended up reinforcing the Mugwump disdain for popular involvement in politics. Expertise and "public education" are often favored by advocacy leaders—which is understandable, because these reflect their special capacities as professionals. U.S. tax rules also push associations toward reliance on expertise and educational strategies. But it is not clear that this style of politics has the passion, heft, or social reach to pull regular people in, let alone to enable majorities of citizens to exert true political leverage.

As matters now stand, many associations in America have to go through convoluted and legally risky maneuvers to engage in politics. Election regulations and tax rules erect barriers between "partisan" and "nonpartisan" activities, and both liberals and conservatives use these rules (and advocate new ones) to demobilize their opponents. When conservative Republican Newt Gingrich was Speaker of the House, he was investigated and reprimanded for running a political education operation designed to train and mobilize conservatives to (horror of horrors!) win elections. Liberals applauded this reprimand and were equally pleased when the Internal Revenue Service investigated the mass distribution of voter guides by the Christian Coalition (on the grounds that it violated rules preventing tax-exempt religious associations from engaging in partisan politics). At the other end of the partisan spectrum, right-wingers are constantly agitating against political expenditures by the AFL-CIO and the American Federation of Teachers, calling on Congress to pass so-called paycheck protection legislation that would prevent union expenditures on politically relevant activities without first asking each union member if he or she wants a portion of individual dues spent in these ways.

All of these measures are equally perverse. As small-*d* democrats, all Americans should be happy when politicians engage in training other leaders and mobilizing voter bases—that he did this so effectively was one of Gingrich's enduring contributions to U.S. public life. We should also be delighted when civil associations get involved in politics, especially groups such as the Christian Coalition and the AFL-CIO with large memberships that enjoy some representation in associational governance. Whatever one may think of any given group or its issue positions, political education and mobilization by popularly rooted federations enhance leadership capabilities and prospects for organized democratic leverage in America. And organized group efforts also make it much more likely that individual citizens will be personally contacted, actively invited into political and civic participation.

I conclude that the United States should repeal or modify all kinds of rules designed to create fire walls between partisan and nonpartisan activities. This does not mean that campaign finance reforms cannot proceed. In fact, the best reforms have been enacted at the state level and involve voluntary adherence to rules of the game by candidates who, in return, gain access to public funding.[42] Election reforms in the future can follow the example of the Maine Clean Elections Law, which limits fund-raising and expenditures on advertisements by candidates who accept to run under its rules *but* allows associations to use their internal newsletters and communication mechanisms to distribute materials to voters. Such intraassociational expenditures do not count against the legal spending limits—and this, of course, can have the effect of strengthening membership-based electoral contacting on right, center, and left alike.

At the national level, reformers should work for both election reforms and tax incentives that would deliver the biggest advantages to associations that derive relatively high proportions of their funding from membership contributions and actually have interactive members who enjoy rights to participate in associational decision making. Some degree of tax exemption can still go to nonprofits and professionally run advocacy groups engaged in research and education. But more could go to groups with members who enjoy rights to participate in decision making, including the selection of associational leaders. Old-style chapter-based associations are not the only ones that could qualify if such rules were properly designed. Tomorrow's associations will figure out ways to use new technologies to encourage membership participation, contributions, and interaction. Why shouldn't our electoral rules and our tax systems encourage exactly that?

Governing in Partnership with Membership Associations

The way politicians govern after their election also has a profound impact on civic life. Elected officials and political party leaders often feel beleaguered by clamoring interest groups and overwhelmed by the need to court wealthy donors. They easily forget that political leaders have considerable ability to influence the mix of groups in their environment and some ability to shape the strategies used by actors who want to influence them. When public officials hold hearings or bring groups together to advise them about policy agendas and options, they understandably include experts and advocates with established track records in a given policy area. But when they want to know what constituents think, they often turn to pollsters—or to the expert staffs of nonprofit institutions or professionally run advocacy groups. Devising policies becomes bifurcated from selling them. Associations and movements with large numbers of popular supporters—but few lobbyists or experts stationed in Washington, D.C., or the state capitol—

get the message that they don't count for much in setting agendas or choosing policy options.

Institutions, movements, and associations with large memberships could be assigned more prominent roles in congressional hearings and consultations by congressional staffs—not just symbolically, but in ways that could build public understanding and involvement in legislative decision making. This could happen when party leaderships in Congress are deciding how to frame agendas for entire legislative sessions; it could also happen when decisions must be made about how to approach a major policy concern, such as reforming health care. What I have in mind is more than just asking associational leaders to come to a hearing one day and take a position on a policy question. Associational leaders could be asked to pose questions to their memberships and gather a range of responses from state or regional meetings, from local chapter discussions, or maybe through Internet sessions with members. Congressional committees and staffers could make it clear they would value learning about the full range of responses and the reasons people give for them. At a later point, when actual legislation is being debated, elected representatives might return to groups that favor the options in question and ask for their help in explaining legislation and mobilizing broader public support.

Involving membership-based associations more directly in setting policy agendas and developing policy designs could produce better legislation—in closer touch with citizens' everyday concerns and more likely to be successfully implemented. Experts are not the only ones who have useful things to say about, for example, the kind of health insurance patients and doctors need, or the sort of Patients'

Bill of Rights that Americans really prefer. If broader consultations with popularly rooted groups had occurred during the 1993–94 national debates about health insurance reform, not only would reform legislation have been more likely to pass Congress, the proposals at issue would probably have been much better designed and more widely understood than the arcane plan designed by the advocates and experts who dominated the official planning process.[43] Involving membership associations in the effort could only have produced better results—just as it did back in 1944 with the G.I. Bill.

Better policies would not be the only result of involving membership networks in governmental policy deliberations. When the word gets around that discussions at the PTA, or the union hall, or the local environmental club will formulate ideas to be fed into a report to Congress (or the city council or state legislature), people will find it more worthwhile to join the discussion. If public officials raise the visibility and clout of popularly rooted associations—putting them at least on a par in policy planning with business lobbies, pollsters, and expert-dominated think tanks and advocacy groups—then the popular associations will seem more relevant to the very people those associations hope to attract and involve. If membership associations are obviously part of the action as authoritative governmental decisions are made on issues of broad popular concern, they will quickly become more attractive to potential joiners.

REVITALIZING AMERICA'S DIMINISHED DEMOCRACY

I have argued that Americans must find ways to strengthen the links between democratic governance and representatively governed civic associations capable of involving large numbers of citizens. The specific strategies I have outlined in this chapter may, or may not, be fruitful. In all likelihood, other thinkers and popular movements can come up with much better ideas. The process of civic revitalization must proceed by trial and error—and the more experimenters, the better. However, if I am not totally confident of the answers to our present dilemmas I have briefly outlined, I am much more certain of the diagnosis I have offered, inspired by a richer understanding of America's civic past and a clear-eyed view of the startling civic changes of our time.

From the nineteenth through the mid-twentieth century, American democracy flourished within a unique matrix of state and society. Not only was the United States the world's first manhood democracy and the first nation in the world to establish mass public education. It also had a uniquely balanced civic life, in which markets expanded but could not subsume civil society, in which governments at multiple levels deliberately and indirectly encouraged federated voluntary associations. Federated membership associations linked people across places and classes in a vast nation and infused American citizenship with shared meaning and organized clout. In classic civic America, millions of ordinary men and women could interact with one another, participate in groups side by side with the more privileged, and exercise influence in both community and national affairs. The poorest were left out, but many others were included. National elites had to pay attention to the values and interests of millions of ordinary Americans.

Over the past third of a century, the old civic America has been bypassed and shoved to the side by a gaggle of professionally dominated advocacy groups and nonprofit institutions rarely attached to memberships worthy of the name. Ideals of shared citizenship and possibilities for democratic leverage have been compromised in the process. Since the 1960s many good things have happened in America. New voices are heard, and there have been invaluable gains in equality and liberty. But vital links in the nation's associational life have frayed, and we need to find creative ways to repair those links if America is to avoid becoming a country of managers and manipulated spectators rather than a national community of fellow democratic citizens.

There cannot be any going back to the civic world we have lost, but we Americans can and should look for ways to re-create the best of our civic past in new forms suited to a renewed democratic future. To accomplish this, we will need to go beyond moral exhortation and local do-goodism; and we certainly should avoid extending professional tendencies and patronage-based funding to our religious institutions, which have heretofore flourished through congregational fellowship and membership contributions. New strategies for translocal association building must be devised. And we must reform our national institutions to encourage and unfetter civic leaders who organize large numbers of their fellow citizens.

America has gained in important ways as professional management has displaced membership in our recently refashioned and enlarged civic life. But we need to be clear about the good things we have lost—about the diminished democracy and losses in fellowship across class lines that contemporary tranformations have, often inadvertently, wrought. Taking lessons and inspiration from our nation's rich civic history, we must find ways to fashion again for our own times the sorts of great voluntary combinations that long ago impressed Alexis de Tocqueville with the extraordinary capacity of Americans for the vigorous practice of civil and political democracy.

NOTES

CHAPTER 1

1. Durgin's occupations are listed on his "Soldier's Claim for Pension" of July 14, 1890, a copy of which was obtained from the Union veterans' records held in the U.S. National Archives.

2. These words are quoted from the 1865 "Special Order" appointing Durgin, as reproduced in the *Lewiston Journal*, February 11, 1933, Maine Section, page A1.

3. Extensive quotes from that interview were later published in "Lovell was Home of Last Surviving Pall-Bearer," *Lewiston Journal*, February 11, 1933, Maine Section, p. A1. According to that article, the original interviewer was "Don Seitz, well-known newspaper man, who, for many years, had a summer home in Norway, Maine."

4. My chief source of reminiscences about Warren Durgin was his then eighty-seven-year-old grandniece, Mrs. Hester McKeen Mann, of South Paris, Maine, a former schoolteacher with whom I spoke several times by telephone in July 1998. After inquiring about Durgin—who lived as a Civil War pensioner in the household of Hester's mother during the final decades of his life and the first decades of hers—I asked Hester about her own associational activities, which turned out to be equally extensive. Hester had participated in groups and events at the Lovell community church.

She was also an active member of her local grange and county (pomona) grange, attaining the highest, seventh, degree in the Patrons of Husbandry, which accepts both men and women as equal members. For a time, Hester was also a member of the Pythian Sisters (her husband was in the Knights of Pythias); and she was devoted enough to the Eastern Star to become a Vice Matron. Along with other local ladies, Hester took the lead in founding the Lovell auxiliary to the Veterans of Foreign Wars. All in all, she was a very civically involved woman who participated in cross-class associations analogous to those in which her uncle Warren was involved.

5. Bill was driving through North Lovell and stopped to talk with an old man sitting on the porch of his home across from an abandoned store. In the course of recounting local stories, the man mentioned Durgin's gravestone and told Bill how to find it on a backroad.

6. See, for example, the biannual series of *Biographical Sketches of the Members of the Senate and House of Representatives of Maine*, available at the Maine State Archives in Augusta.

7. Biographical portraits including civic affiliations are often available for public officials and other elites. An unusually detailed set of profiles was compiled every year from the 1890s in the state of Massachusetts, under various titles over the years. For the years around 1900, the best series are *A Souvenir of Massachusetts Legislators*, published annually by A. M. Bridgman of Brockton, Massachusetts; and then *Public Officials of Massachusetts*, published yearly under state auspices by various commercial printers. Both are available at the Massachusetts State Library.

8. Christopher Beem, *The Necessity of Politics: Reclaiming American Public Life* (Chicago: University of Chicago Press, 1999), p. 197.

9. Robert D. Putnam, *Making Democracy Work: Civic Traditions in Modern Italy* (Princeton: Princeton University Press, 1993) and

Bowling Alone: The Collapse and Revival of American Community (New York: Simon and Schuster, 2000).

10. Putnam's *Making Democracy Work* uses social capital theory to explain economic development and administrative efficiency in different regions of contemporary Italy. Chapters 17–20 of *Bowling Alone* stress the impact of social capital on health, education, and happiness.

11. Michael Sandel, *Democracy's Discontent: America in Search of a Public Philosophy* (Cambridge, Mass.: Harvard University Press, 1996).

12. Council on Civil Society, *A Call to Civil Society: Why Democracy Needs Moral Truths* (New York: Institute for American Values, 1998).

13. National Commission on Civic Renewal, *A Nation of Spectators: How Civic Disengagement Weakens America and What We Can Do about It* (College Park: National Commission on Civic Renewal, University of Maryland, 1998).

14. Michael S. Joyce and William A. Schambra, "A New Civic Life," in *To Empower People: From State to Civil Society*, 2d ed., edited by Michael Novak (Washington, D.C.: AEI Press, 1996), pp. 15, 25.

15. Peter F. Drucker, *The Ecological Vision: Reflections on the American Condition* (New Brunswick, N.J.: Rutgers University Press, 1993), p. 9; and George Will, "Look at All the Lonely Bowlers," Washington Post, January 5, 1995, p. A29.

16. Polls by the National Election Survey, the Kaiser Family Foundation / Harvard Kennedy School, and the *Washington Post* have repeatedly asked Americans whether they "trust the federal government to do the right thing." In 1964, 76 percent trusted the federal government "always" or "most of the time," but that percentage declined to 36 percent by 1974 and to 29 percent by the year 2000. After September 11, 2001, however, a sharp reversal occurred, as, suddenly, 64 percent of Americans reported trusting the federal government always or most of the time. Pre- and

post-September 11 surveys by Robert D. Putnam also record a comparable doubling of Americans' faith in national government. For more in-depth analysis, see Stanley B. Greenberg, "'We'— Not 'Me,'" *American Prospect*, December 17, 2001; and Richard Morin and Claudia Deane, "Poll: Americans' Trust in Government Grows," dateline September 28, 2001, available at http://www.washingtonpost.com.

17. Charles Moskos and Paul Glastris, "Now Do You Believe We Need a Draft?" *Washington Monthly*, November, 2001, pp. 9–11; and Richard Just, "Suddenly Serviceable: Is This the Moment for National Service?" *American Prospect*, 13, no. 1 (2002): 15–17.

18. For the proposed expansion of AmeriCorps, see President Bush's 2002 State of the Union Address.

19. See "Excerpts From President's Speech 'We Will Prevail' in War on Terrorism," delivered in Atlanta, Georgia, on November 8, 2001, as published in the *New York Times*, November 9, 2001, p. B6. A few weeks later Bush called on Americans simply to give money to local charities. See "President Urges Support for America's Charities," released by the Office of the White House Press Secretary, November 20, 2001. Bush gave this speech when he learned that many local nonprofits faced a drop in fund-raising after millions of Americans diverted charitable contributions to the September 11 relief funds.

20. Information on the Initiative is available at the White House website: http://www.whitehouse.gov. Further discussion and a critique of the Faith-based Initiative appear below in chapter 7.

21. Alexis de Tocqueville, *Democracy in America*, edited by J. P. Mayer, translated by George Lawrence (New York: Harper-Collins, [1835–40] 1988), pp. 244, 522.

22. For relatively optimistic accounts of recent civic developments, see Jeffrey M. Berry, *The New Liberalism: The Rising Power of Citizen Groups* (Washington, D.C.: Brookings Institution Press,

1999); Debra C. Minkoff, *Organizing for Equality: The Evolution of Women's and Racial-Ethnic Organizations in America, 1955–1985* (New Brunswick, N.J.: Rutgers University Press, 1995); Debra C. Minkoff, "Producing Social Capital: National Social Movements and Civil Society," *American Behavioral Scientist* 40, no. 5 (March–April 1997): 606–19; Michael Schudson, *The Good Citizen: A History of American Civic Life* (Cambridge, Mass.: Harvard University Press, 1998), chap. 6; Robert Wuthnow, *Loose Connections: Joining Together in America's Fragmented Communities* (Cambridge, Mass.: Harvard University Press, 1998); and Everett Carll Ladd, *The Ladd Report* (New York: Free Press, 1999).

23. Michael Schudson is an exception, but his book *The Good Citizen* is an interpretive look at selected aspects of the meaning and practice of citizenship throughout American history; it does not pretend to offer systematic data analyses. Among the data analysts, Wuthnow relies on social surveys and field observations of present-day American communities; Minkoff and Berry use impressive new data sets that nevertheless include only civic associations created since the 1950s; and Putnam exhaustively mines social surveys that record comparable attitudes and self-reported behaviors since the 1970s. To be sure, Putnam also traces longer-term trends in associational memberships but only for a nonrandom subset of local chapter–based associations he has selected because they seem to have been prominent in the post–World War II era. If Putnam had included a broader and more typical array of associations from the past, his conclusions would necessarily have changed.

24. Gabriel A. Almond and Sidney Verba, *The Civic Culture: Political Attitudes and Democracy in Five Nations* (Princeton: Princeton University Press, 1963).

25. See especially Sidney Verba, Kay Lehman Schlozman, and Henry E. Brady, *Voice and Equality: Civic Voluntarism in American Politics* (Cambridge, Mass.: Harvard University Press, 1995).

26. For more on the research approach I am using here, see Paul Pierson and Theda Skocpol, "Historical Institutionalism in Contemporary Political Science," in *Political Science: The State of the Discipline*, edited by Ira Katznelson and Helen Milner (New York: W. W. Norton, 2002).

CHAPTER 2

1. The quote comes, of course, from Alexis de Tocqueville, *Democracy in America*, edited by J. P. Mayer, translated by George Lawrence (New York: HarperCollins, [1835–40] 1988), p. 513.

2. Arthur Schlesinger, "Biography of a Nation of Joiners," *American Historical Review* 50, no. 1 (October 1944): 24.

3. Council on Civil Society, "A Call to Civil Society: Why Democracy Needs Moral Truths" (New York: Institute for American Values, 1998), p. 9.

4. Michael S. Joyce and William A. Schambra, "A New Civic Life," in *To Empower People: From State to Civil Society*, 2nd ed., edited by Michael Novak (Washington, D.C.: AEI Press, 1996), pp. 11–12. Joyce and Schambra are conservatives, but similar views about America's past are held by liberals involved in the current civic engagement debate. Debra Minkoff, for example, assumes that national associations espousing goals and articulating symbolic identities are new to post-1950s civic life, because "traditional bases of collective identity" were rooted in "the local community." See her "Producing Social Capital: National Social Movements and Civil Society," *American Behavioral Scientist* 40, no. 5 (March–April 1997): 613.

5. Tocqueville, *Democracy in America*, p. 516. This is the key specific example in Tocqueville's constantly quoted chapter, "On the Use Which Americans Make of Associations in Civil Life."

6. James Bryce, *The American Commonwealth* (New York: Macmillan, 1895), vol. 2, p. 278.

7. Schlesinger, "Nation of Joiners," pp. 2, 19, 25.

8. Ibid., p. 5

9. Ibid., p. 11.

10. Ibid., p. 16.

11. Local studies include Stuart M. Blumin, *The Emergence of the Middle Class: Social Experience in the American City, 1760–1900* (Cambridge: Cambridge University Press, 1989); Don H. Doyle, "The Social Functions of Voluntary Associations in a Nineteenth-Century American Town," *Social Science History* 1, no. 3 (1977): 333–55; and Mary P. Ryan, *Cradle of the Middle Class: The Family in Oneida County, New York, 1790–1865* (Cambridge: Cambridge University Press, 1981). Exemplary studies of prominent voluntary associations include Christopher J. Kaufman, *Faith and Fraternalism: The History of the Knights of Columbus, 1882–1982* (New York: Harper and Row, 1982); David I. Macleod, *Building Character in the American Boy: The Boy Scouts, YMCA, and Their Forerunners, 1870–1920* (Madison: University of Wisconsin Press, 1983); Stuart McConnell, *Glorious Contentment: The Grand Army of the Republic, 1865–1900* (Chapel Hill: University of North Carolina Press, 1992). And excellent studies of types of associations include Mary Ann Clawson, *Constructing Brotherhood: Gender, Class, and Fraternalism* (Princeton: Princeton University Press, 1989); Jed Dannenbaum, *Drink and Disorder: Temperance Reform from the Washingtonian Revival to the WCTU* (Urbana: University of Illinois Press, 1984); Wallace Evan Davies, *Patriotism on Parade: The Story of the Veterans' Hereditary Organizations in America, 1783–1900* (Cambridge, Mass.: Harvard University Press, 1955); Anne Firor Scott, *Natural Allies: Women's Associations in American History* (Urbana: University of Illinois Press, 1991).

12. See notes 18 and 20 below for citations of articles by Richard Brown and Gerald Gamm and Robert D. Putnam.

13. I stress *membership* associations, because many people use the term "voluntary groups" to refer to contemporary nonprofit social service delivery agencies or, historically, to groups

devoted to providing charity to the needy. In this chapter and in the civic engagement project, I focus on voluntary associations of citizens, groups in which people did things together as fellow members, even if they also engaged in some delivery of charitable aid to others or delivery of services to the broader community.

14. We believe this list is nearly complete. A small number of additional very large membership associations may eventually be found and documented. But any additions are unlikely to change the overall patterns reported here.

15. Especially useful sources of lists of groups have been Sophinisba P. Breckinridge, *Women in the Twentieth Century: A Study of Their Political, Social, and Economic Activities* (New York: McGraw-Hill, 1933), pt. 1; Arthur R. Preuss, *A Dictionary of Secret and Other Societies* (St. Louis: Herder, 1924); Alvin J. Schmidt, *Fraternal Organizations* (Westport, Conn.: Greenwood, 1980); and Albert C. Stevens, *Cyclopedia of Fraternities* (New York: Hamilton, 1899).

16. In addition to Schmidt, *Fraternal Organizations*, Appendix 3, pp. 487–89, we have developed lists of associations from Edward Nelson Palmer, "Negro Secret Societies," *Social Forces* 23 (December 1944): 207-12, and from the dozens of articles on individual ethnic groups in Stephan Thernstrom, Ann Orlov, and Oscar Handlin, eds., *Harvard Encyclopedia of American Ethnic Groups* (Cambridge: The Belknap Press of Harvard University Press, 1980).

17. Between the mid-1800s and mid-1900s, directories for cities of all sizes often listed churches and voluntary groups in addition to businesses and individual citizens. Formats of such listings were not always standardized, because local or regional businesses produced them. With some attention to issues of consistency, however, they are a very useful source. We have also used *Maine Registers*, statewide directories that listed associations for every local community between the 1870s and 1920s.

18. Gerald Gamm and Robert D. Putnam, "The Growth of Voluntary Associations in America, 1840–1940," *Journal of Interdisciplinary History* 29, no. 4 (Spring 1999): 511–57.

19. For the full presentation of our analysis, see Theda Skocpol, Marshall Ganz, and Ziad Munson, "A Nation of Organizers: The Institutional Origins of Civic Voluntarism in the United States," *American Political Science Review* 94, no. 3 (September 2000): 527–46, esp. tables 3 and 4.

20. Richard D. Brown, "The Emergence of Urban Society in Rural Massachusetts, 1760–1830," *Journal of American History* 6, no. 1 (1974): 47.

21. Based on data from Brown, "Emergence of Urban Society," pp. 40-41, table 1. Most associational proliferation occurred between 1790 and 1830, when the population of Massachusetts and Maine slightly more than doubled.

22. Brown, "Emergence of Urban Society," p. 31.

23. Ibid., p. 43.

24. Scott, *Natural Allies*, chap. 1.

25. Carroll Smith-Rosenberg, *Disorderly Conduct: Visions of Gender in Victorian America* (New York: Knopf, 1985), p. 120.

26. Carl Bode, *The American Lyceum: Town Meeting of the Mind* (Chicago: University of Chicago Press, 1968); John A. Monroe, "The Lyceum in America before the Civil War," *Delaware Notes: Bulletin of the University of Delaware* 37, no. 3 (1942): 65–75. Holbrook also called for a federated organization of lyceums, with state and national bodies consisting of representatives sent from below. See his "American Lyceum," *American Annals of Education* 6 (1836): 474–76; 7 (1837): 183–84.

27. Dannenbaum, *Drink and Disorder*; John Allen Krout, *The Origins of Prohibition* (New York: Knopf, 1925).

28. Milton Maxwell, "The Washingtonian Movement," *Quarterly Journal Studies on Alcohol* 11, no. 3 (1950): 410–51; A. B. Grosh, *Washingtonian Pocket Companion*, 2d ed. (Utica, N.Y.: R.W. Roberts, 1842).

29. Samuel W. Hodges, "Sons of Temperance—Historical Record of the Order," in *Centennial Temperance Volume* (New York: National Temperance Society and Publication House, 1877), 544–98.

30. William W. Turnbull, *The Good Templars: A History of the Rise and Progress of the Independent Order of Good Templars* (n.p., 1901).

31. Kathleen Smith Kutolowski, "Freemasonry and Community in the Early Republic: The Case for Antimasonic Anxieties," *American Quarterly* 34 (1982): 543–61; Lorman Ratner, *Antimasonry: The Crusade and the Party* (Englewood Cliffs, N.J.: Prentice-Hall, 1969).

32. Dorothy Ann Lipson, *Freemasonry in Federalist Connecticut, 1789–1835* (Princeton: Princeton University Press, 1977); Steven C. Bullock, *Revolutionary Brotherhood: Freemasonry and the Transformation of the American Social Order, 1730–1840* (Chapel Hill: University of North Carolina Press, 1996). The Masonic grand lodges corresponded to the U.S. states after the Revolution, and they remained sovereign, because the (basic, blue lodge) Masons never agreed to institute a national institutional center.

33. Theodore A. Ross, *Odd Fellowship: Its History and Manual* (New York: M. W. Hazen, 1888), chaps. 1–3.

34. Ibid., chap. 14.

35. Paschal Donaldson, *The Odd Fellows' Text Book*, 6th ed. (Philadelphia: Moss and Brother, 1852), p. 9. Interestingly, on p. 14 Donaldson argues that the Odd Fellows were an excellent example of the kind of association Tocqueville celebrated in *Democracy in America*.

36. Charles H. Lichtman, ed., *Official History of the Improved Order of Red Men*, rev. ed. (Boston: Fraternity, 1901), pp. 314–15.

37. John T. Ridge, *Erin's Sons in America: The Ancient Order of Hibernians* (New York: AOH Publications, 1986).

38. Stevens, *Cyclopedia of Fraternities*, pp. 234–35, 282–84.

39. Joseph Martinek, *One Hundred Years of the CSA: The History of the Czechoslovak Society of America*, translated by R. A. Gorman (Cicero, Ill.: Executive Committee of CSA, 1985), p. 22.

40. William Alan Muraskin, *Middle-Class Blacks in a White Society: Prince Hall Freemasonry in America* (Berkeley: University of California Press, 1975).

41. Edward Nelson Palmer, "Negro Secret Societies," *Social Forces* 23, no. 2 (1944): 208. Palmer adds that the "three years following the end of the Civil War saw the inclusion of every southern state in the Negro Masonic ranks" after the slaves were freed.

42. Stevens, *Cyclopedia of Fraternities*, pp. 236–37. See also Charles H. Brooks, *The Official History and Manual of the Grand United Order of Odd Fellows in America* (Freeport, N.Y.: Books for Libraries Press, [1902] 1971), p. 91.

43. John H. Aldrich, *Why Parties? The Origin and Transformation of Political Parties in America* (Chicago: University of Chicago Press, 1995), pt. 2; and Martin Shefter, *Political Parties and the State: The American Historical Experience* (Princeton: Princeton University Press, 1994), pp. 61–71.

44. Kathryn Kish Sklar, "The 'Quickened Conscience': Women's Voluntarism and the State, 1890–1920," *Report from the Institute for Philosophy and Public Policy* 18, no. 3 (1998): 27.

45. Roger Finke and Rodney Stark, *The Churching of America, 1776–1990* (New Brunswick, N.J.: Rutgers University Press, 1992).

46. Donald G. Mathews, "The Second Great Awakening as an Organizing Process, 1780–1830: An Hypothesis," *American Quarterly* 21, no. 1 (1969): 23–43; Nathan O. Hatch, *The Democratization of American Christianity* (New Haven: Yale University Press, 1989).

47. For an overview of American women's civic empowerment, see Paula Baker, "The Domestication of Politics: Women and American Political Society, 1780–1920," *American Historical Review* 89, no. 3 (1984): 620–47; Scott, *Natural Allies*; Theda

Skocpol, *Protecting Soldiers and Mothers: The Political Origins of Social Policy in the United States* (Cambridge, Mass.: Harvard University Press, 1992), chap. 6.

48. Sklar, "'Quickened Conscience,'" p. 27. On women in the temperance movements, see Dannenbaum, *Drink and Disorder*; Barbara Leslie Epstein, *The Politics of Domesticity: Women, Evangelism, and Temperance in Nineteenth-Century America* (Middletown, Conn.: Wesleyan University Press, 1981).

49. Patricia Kelley Hall and Steven Ruggles, "Moving through Time: Internal Migration Patterns of Americans, 1850–1990," paper presented at the annual meeting of the Social Science History Association, Fort Worth, Texas, November 1999. See also Edward Kopf, "Untarnishing the Dream: Mobility, Opportunity, and Order in Modern America," *Journal of Social History* 11 (Winter 1977): 202–27; Howard Chudacoff, *Mobile Americans: Residential and Social Mobility in Omaha, 1880–1920* (New York: Oxford University Press, 1972).

50. Roland Berthoff, *An Unsettled People: Social Order and Disorder in American History* (New York: Harper and Row, 1971), chap. 27.

51. Richard John, *Spreading the News: The American Postal System from Franklin to Morse* (Cambridge, Mass.: Harvard University Press, 1995), p. 31.

52. Ibid., p. 5.

53. Ibid., p. 3.

54. Ibid., chap. 5.

55. Ibid., chaps. 6–7.

56. Across all of U.S. history, nearly three-fourths of all ultimately very large membership associations adopted national-state-local federal organizational arrangements, and most of the rest instituted alternative kinds of three-tiered structures (for example, with regional rather than state-level intermediate tiers). Two groups, the Masons and the Washingtonians, had no national organizational centers; and of course the Masons had

strong state-level grand lodges. Only six out of fifty-eight very large associations were permanently institutionalized as center-local organizations. Representative intermediate organizations have been typical for large U.S. membership federations.

57. See: Herbert P. Kitschelt, "Political Opportunity Structures and Political Protest: Anti-Nuclear Movements in Four Democracies," *British Journal of Political Science* 16 (January 1986): 57–85; Sidney Tarrow, "States and Opportunities: The Political Structuring of Social Movements," in *Comparative Perspectives on Social Movements*, edited by Doug McAdam, John D. McCarthy, and Mayer N. Zald (Cambridge: Cambridge University Press, 1996), 41–61.

58. As quoted in Turnbull, *The Good Templars*, pp. 88–89.

59. Walter W. Powell and Paul J. DiMaggio, eds., *The New Institutionalism in Historical Analysis* (Chicago: University of Chicago Press, 1991).

60. Elisabeth S. Clemens, *The People's Lobby: Organizational Innovation and the Rise of Interest Group Politics in the United States, 1890–1925* (Chicago: University of Chicago Press, 1997).

61. Henry Leonard Stillson, *The History and Literature of Odd Fellowship* (Boston: Fraternity, 1897), p. 214.

62. Independent Order of Odd Fellows, *Journal of Proceedings of the Right Worthy Grand Lodge of the Independent Order of Odd Fellows . . . to the Close of the Annual Session, 1843 . . .* (New York: McGowan and Treadwell, 1844), p. xv.

63. See, for example, the international disputes discussed in Ralph J. Pollard, *Freemasonry in Maine, 1762–1945* (Portland: Grand Lodge of Maine, 1945), pp. 67–68. Residence requirements for membership are spelled out in the constitutions of fraternal groups, dozens of which I have reviewed.

64. Robert H. Wiebe, *The Search for Order, 1877–1920* (New York: Hill and Wang, 1967).

65. Gamm and Putnam, "Growth of Voluntary Associations in America," fig. 2, pp. 526–27.

66. Jeffrey A. Charles, *Service Clubs in American Society* (Urbana: University of Illinois Press, 1993).

67. Ibid.; and Clifford Putney, "Service over Secrecy: How Lodge-style Fraternalism Yielded Popularity to Men's Service Clubs," *Journal of Popular Culture* 27 (1993): 664–83.

68. Gamm and Putnam, "Growth of Voluntary Associations in America," fig. 2, pp. 526–27.

69. Based on quantitative analysis of entries in directories cited above in note 16.

70. The war itself disrupted many groups because leading citizens and many men marched off to war from so many communities. In contrast, women flooded into war-support groups and into leading temperance associations. And fraternals like the Masons and Odd Fellows attracted many young men headed into or already in military service. These brotherhoods had well-established methods for aiding members away from home; and some Masonic grand masters allowed the establishment of special "military lodges" in the armed forces. Immediately after the war's end, moreover, divided U.S. membership federations quickly reunited. According to Ross, *Odd Fellowship*, pp. 158–79, the Odd Fellows left chairs for Southern grand lodge representatives sitting symbolically empty at each of their wartime national conventions, calling the names of those states and mailing reports to them. Within months of Appomattox, southern grand lodge representatives returned to their waiting seats in Odd Fellows' conventions. But the U.S government and political party system would take years longer to put back together.

71. This point is developed empirically and discussed theoretically in Skocpol, Ganz, and Munson, "A Nation of Organizers." A further statistical analysis demonstrates the continuing impact of the Union Civil War victory on associational formation through the 1920s; see Jocelyn Elise Crowley and Theda Skocpol, "The Rush to Organize: Explaining Associational Formation in the

United States, 1860s–1920s," *American Journal of Political Science* 45, no. 4 (October 2001): 813–29.

72. See Tocqueville, *Democracy in America*, pp. 395, 646–50.

73. Linus Pierpont Brockett, *The Philanthropic Results of the War in America. Collected from Official and Authentic Sources from an American Citizen* (New York: Sheldon, 1864).

74. James M. McPherson, *Battle Cry of Freedom: The Civil War Era* (New York: Ballantine Books, 1988), p. 313.

75. Ibid., p. 330. Because most Civil War officers led from the front rather than directed from behind, they also died in staggering numbers.

76. James W. Geary, *We Need Men: The Union Draft in the Civil War* (DeKalb: University of Northern Illinois Press, 1991), pp. 173–74, passim.

77. McPherson, *Battle Cry of Freedom*, p. 480.

78. For more detail on particular groups, see Skocpol, Ganz, and Munson, "A Nation of Organizers," p. 530, table 1.

79. The New York Sorosis Club called together some five dozen women's clubs from across the United States to found the General Federation. See Mildred White Wells, *Unity in Diversity: The History of the General Federation of Women's Clubs* (Washington, D.C.: General Federation of Women's Clubs, 1953), chap. 2.

80. J. J. Upchurch, *The Life, Labors, and Travels of Father J. J. Upchurch, Founder of the Ancient Order of United Workmen*, edited by Sam Booth (San Francisco: A. T. Dewey, 1887).

81. James R. Carnahan, *Pythian Knighthood: Its History and Literature* (Cincinnati: Pettibone Manufacturing Company, 1890), chaps. 5–6.

82. Sven D. Nordin, *Rich Harvest: A History of the Grange, 1867–1900* (Jackson: University of Mississippi Press, 1974), chap. 1.

83. For a thorough and important argument to this effect, see Judith Ann Giesberg, *Civil War Sisterhood: The U.S. Sanitary Commission and Women's Politics in Transition* (Boston: Northeastern University Press, 2000).

84. Ibid., p. 5.

85. Walter J. Davidson, *History of the American National Red Cross*, vol. 39, *General Organization* (Washington, D.C.: American National Red Cross, 1950).

86. Norton Mezvinsky, "The White-Ribbon Reform: 1874–1920" (Ph.D. dissertation, University of Wisconsin, 1959).

87. Reprinted in Helen E. Tyler, *Where Prayer and Purpose Meet: The WCTU Story, 1874–1949* (Evanston, IL: Signal, 1949), p. 18.

88. It would be wrong to suppose, however, that southern whites confined themselves to local voluntary groups. Instead, they tended to form congregations within southern church denominations, and they swelled the ranks of Masonic bodies governed by state-level sovereign grand lodges and Scottish Rite higher Masonic orders governed by the powerful Southern Jurisdiction. After 1860, in short, the former Confederates formed or joined federations with a regional or states' rights governing structure at a higher per capita rate than they joined associations with national governing centers headquartered in the North.

89. References and an overview of available data on African American fraternal and mutual aid groups appear in Theda Skocpol and Jennifer Oser, "Organization despite Diversity: The Origins and Development of African American Fraternal and Mutual Aid Associations," paper presented at the annual meeting of the Social Science History Association, Chicago, Illinois, November 2001. For some official histories of lesser-known groups, see W. H. Gibson Sr., *History of the United Brothers of Friendship and Sisters of the Mysterious Ten* (Louisville, Ken.: Bradley & Gilbert, 1897); Wendell P. Dabney, *Maggie L. Walker and the I.O. of Saint Luke* (Cincinnati: Dabney, 1927); A. E. Bush and P. L. Dorman, *History of the Mosaic Templars of America: Its Founders and Officials* (Little Rock, Ark.: Central Publishing Company, 1924).

90. For overviews and additional references, see Scott, *Natural Allies*; Breckinridge, *Women in the Twentieth Century*, pt. 1; Elisabeth S. Clemens, *The People's Lobby: Organizational Innovation*

and the Rise of Interest Group Politics in the United States, 1890–1925 (Chicago: University of Chicago Press, 1997); Elisabeth Clemens, "Securing Political Returns to Social Capital: Women's Associations in the United States, 1880s-1920s," *Journal of Interdisciplinary History* 29, no. 3 (1999): 613–38; Skocpol, *Protecting Soldiers and Mothers*, pt. 3.

91. Clawson, *Constructing Brotherhood*, chap. 6.

92. Seymour Martin Lipset and Earl Raab, *The Politics of Unreason: Right-Wing Extremism in America, 1790–1970* (New York: Harper and Row, 1970), pp. 81–104.

93. This is based on the analysis of founding dates for various types of fraternals listed in Schmidt, *Fraternal Organizations*, Appendix 3, pp. 387–89.

94. On the heights reached by group proliferation around 1910, see the data in table 2.1 (above) and in Skocpol, Ganz, and Munson, "A Nation of Organizers." After the early twentieth century chapters of cross-class voluntary groups probably ceased to proliferate overall, but we should not interpret this as a decline of cross-class associations so much as a consolidation, for all of the reasons outlined in this paragraph. For example, Gamm and Putnam, "Growth of Voluntary Associations in America," stresses the decline in group proliferation after 1910, especially for fraternal groups. But they fail to take into account the rise of much larger urban lodges in consolidated fraternal groups such as the Elks, Moose, Eagles, and Knights of Columbus. Gamm and Putnam's method of simply counting local groups in relation to population can prove quite misleading when the rules of associational formation change while memberships remain constant or continue to grow.

95. For excellent overviews, see David M. Kennedy, *Over Here: The First World War and American Society* (New York: Oxford University Press, 1980); Ronald Schaffer, *America in the Great War: The Rise of the War Welfare State* (New York: Oxford University Press, 1991); Ellis W. Hawley, *The Great War and the Search for*

Modern Order: A History of the American People and Their Institutions, 1917–1933 (New York: St. Martin's Press, 1979). However, none of these syntheses pays adequate attention to the major role of cross-class voluntary federations in the wartime mobilizations. All are written from a managerial perspective and stress business-government cooperation.

96. On foundings of business and professional associations, see W. Lloyd Warner, editor, *The Emergent American Society, Volume 1: Large-Scale Organizations* (New Haven: Yale University Press, 1967), pp. 317–25; W. Lloyd Warner, *National Trade and Professional Associations of the United States, 1966* (Washington, D.C.: Potomac Books, 1966), pp. v–vii; Joseph F. Bradley, *The Role of Trade Associations and Professional Business Societies in America* (University Park: Pennsylvania State University Press, 1965), chap. 2.

97. For discussion of wartime foundings of nationally federated business and professional women's groups, see *A History of the Oklahoma Federation of Business and Professional Women, 1919–1993* (Oklahoma Federation of Business and Professional Women, n.d.), pp. 11–12.

98. William Pencak, *For God and Country: The American Legion, 1919–1941*, (Boston: Northeastern University Press, 1989), chaps. 2–4; Thomas A. Rumer, *The American Legion: An Official History, 1919–1989* (New York: M. Evans, 1990), pp. 5–56.

99. Orville Merton Kile, *The Farm Bureau Movement* (New York: Macmillan, 1921).

100. Walton Rawls, *Wake Up, America! World War I and the American Poster*, with foreword by Maurice Rickards (New York: Abbeville Press, 1988).

101. Charles Howard Hopkins, *History of the Y.M.C.A. in North America* (New York: Association Press, 1951), pp. 485–504; Henry P. Davison, *The American Red Cross in the Great War* (New York: Macmillan, 1920); Kaufman, *Faith and Fraternalism*, chaps. 4, 6–9; National Jewish Welfare Board, *Final Report of War Emergency Activities* (New York: National Jewish Welfare Board, 1920). For

background, see also Benjamin Rabinowitz, *The Young Men's Hebrew Associations (1854–1913)* (New York: National Jewish Welfare Board, 1948).

102. Mitch Reis, *The Boy Scouts of America during World War I & II* (private publ., 1984), chap. 1.

103. William C. Mullendore, *History of the United States Food Administration, 1917–1919* (Stanford: Stanford University Press, 1941); Ida Clyde Clarke, *American Women and the World War* (New York: D. Appleton, 1918), pp. 61–73; James R. Nicholson, Lee A. Donaldson, and Raymond C. Dobson, *History of the Order of Elks, 1868–1978*, rev. ed. (Chicago: Grand Secretary's Office, 1978), pp. 246–47.

104. Kennedy, *Over Here*, pp. 27–29, 258–59.

105. This argument is developed and further documented in Theda Skocpol, Ziad Munson, Andrew Karch, and Bayliss Camp, "Patriotic Partnerships: Why Great Wars Nourished American Civic Voluntarism," in *Shaped by War and Trade: International Influences on American Political Development*, edited by Ira Katznelson and Martin Shefter (Princeton: Princeton University Press, 2002), 134–80.

106. William Preston Jr., *Aliens and Dissenters: Federal Suppression of Radicals, 1903–1933*, 2d ed. (Urbana: University of Illinois Press, [1963] 1994), chap. 4.

107. Ridge, *Erin's Sons*, pt. 2 (passim) on the development of the order in various regions and states.

108. Frederick C. Luebke, *Bonds of Loyalty. German-Americans and World War I* (DeKalb: Northern Illinois University Press, 1974), chaps. 9–10.

109. Ibid., pp. 269–70; Committee on the Judiciary, U.S. Senate, "National German-American Alliance Hearings Before the Subcommittee of the Committee on the Judiciary United States Senate, Sixty-Fifth Congress, Second Session on S. 3529 . . . , February 23–April 13, 1918 (Washington, D.C.: Government Printing Office).

110. This story is especially well told by Michael E. McGerr, *The Decline of Popular Politics* (New York: Oxford University Press, 1986), and by Michael Schudson, *The Good Citizen: A History of American Civic Life* (New York: Free Press, 1998).

111. See the graphs for a selected set of twentieth-century chapter-based groups in Putnam, *Bowling Alone*, Appendix 3.

112. An argument to this effect appears in David T. Beito, *From Mutual Aid to the Welfare State: Fraternal Societies and Social Services, 1890–1967* (Chapel Hill: University of North Carolina Press, 2000). Although I do not think the displacement argument Beito makes holds up, his book offers rich case studies of important social service institutions run by a variety of fraternal federations.

113. See J. C. Herbert Emery's excellent review of Beito, *From Mutual Aid to the Welfare State*, posted on H-URBAN@H-NET.MSU.EDU in August 2000.

114. McConnell, *Glorious Contentment*; Skocpol, *Protecting Soldiers and Mothers*, chap. 2.

115. Nordin, *Rich Harvest*; John Mark Hansen, *Gaining Access: Congress and the Farm Lobby, 1919–1981* (Chicago: University of Chicago Press, 1991).

116. Skocpol, *Protecting Soldiers and Mothers*, pt. 3.

117. Henry J. Pratt, *The Gray Lobby* (Chicago: University of Chicago Press, 1976).

118. For a self-congratulatory overview of Eagle activities on behalf of "new hope and security to many millions of plain Americans—and a new kind of fellowship," see Richard S. Davis, "Fifty Years of Service," *Eagle* 36, no. 2 (February 1948): 7–9.

119. Michael J. Bennett, *When Dreams Came True: The G.I. Bill and the Making of Modern America* (Washington, D.C.: Brassey's, 1996); Davis R. B. Ross, *Preparing for Ulysses: Politics and Veterans during World War II* (New York: Columbia University Press, 1969); Theda Skocpol, "The G.I. Bill and U.S. Social Pol-

icy, Past and Future," *Social Philosophy and Policy* 14, no. 2 (1997): 95–115.

120. Schlesinger, "Nation of Joiners," p. 2.

CHAPTER 3

1. Jason Kaufman and David Weintraub, "How 'Local' Were Late 19th Century Fraternal Organizations? A Spatial Analysis of the Knights of Pythias Membership Rolls of Buffalo, New York (1894)" (unpublished paper, Department of Sociology, Harvard University, 2001).

2. Calculated from information in Shirley Donnelly, *History of Oddfellowship in Oak Hill, W. Va.* (locally published pamphlet, 1952).

3. David M. Fahey, *Temperance and Racism: John Bull, Johnny Reb, and the Good Templars* (Lexington: University of Kentucky Press, 1996), pp. 19–20.

4. *Ritual of a Rebekah Lodge under the Jurisdiction of the Sovereign Grand Lodge of the Independent Order of Odd Fellows* (Sovereign Grand Lodge of the I.O.O.F., 1928), p. 50, passim. I hope Rebekahs will excuse me for quoting, briefly, from an old copy of their secret ritual.

5. See the discussion in Theda Skocpol, *Protecting Soldiers and Mothers: The Political Origins of Social Policy in the United States* (Cambridge, Mass.: Belknap Press of Harvard University Press, 1992), pp. 323–40.

6. *Ritual Veterans of Foreign Wars of the United States* (Kansas City, Mo.: National Headquarters, Veterans of Foreign Wars, 1942), pp. 52–53.

7. Based on membership ribbon badges for this group in the author's personal collection. When the Knights and Ladies of Security became the Security Benefit Association in the 1920s, it changed its badge to represent both the man and the woman in modern dress.

8. Guy H. Fuller, ed., *Loyal Order of Moose and Mooseheart* (Loyal Order of Moose, 1918); Robert W. Wells, *Mooseheart: The City of Children* (Loyal Order of Moose, 1965).

9. This framed certificate was purchased by the author in October 1999 from an antique store in Guthrie, Oklahoma.

10. From "The Maccabees: A Service Organization for the Entire Family," an undated pamphlet in the author's personal collection.

11. From the author's personal collection of association ephemera. Purchased in an antique store in Machias, Maine.

12. Data on this point appear in Theda Skocpol, Marshall Ganz, and Ziad Munson, "A Nation of Organizers: The Institutional Origins of Civic Voluntarism in the United States," *American Political Science Review* 94, no. 3 (September 2000): 536–37.

13. Postcard in the author's personal collection, purchased from an antique dealer in Maine.

14. Reverand F. E. Clark, "The United Society of Christian Endeavor: State and Local Unions," (United Society of Christian Endeavor, Boston, 1892), p. 4; emphasis in original. Purchased at an antique store in Ellsworth, Maine, this pamphlet is part of the author's collection of association ephemera.

15. See Skocpol, Ganz, and Munson, "A Nation of Organizers," p. 540, including fig. 5.

16. The classic "Tenth Federalist Paper" is reproduced in James Madison, *The Federalist Papers* (New York: Doubleday, 1966). See also Theodore Lowi, *The End of Liberalism*, 2d ed. (New York: Norton, 1979).

17. Reported in Henry Leonard Stillson, *The History and Literature of Odd Fellowship* (Boston: Fraternity, 1897), p. 355.

18. David Royal, "Introduction of the Order of Knights of Pythias in the Grand Domain of Minnesota," handwritten document, no date [1890s], Knights of Pythias Archives, Quincy, Mass.

19. Maurice Francis Egan and John B. Kennedy, *The Knights of Columbus in Peace and War*, vol. 1 (New Haven: Knights of Columbus, 1920), p. 72.

20. Reported in Jennie June Croly, *The History of the Women's Club Movement in America* (New York: Henry G. Allen, 1898), p. 779.

21. Skocpol, Ganz, and Munson, "A Nation of Organizers," pp. 534–36, including table 3.

22. W. A. Northcott, *The Woodman's Hand Book* (Davenport, Iowa: Egbert, Fidlar, & Chambers, 1894), p. 83, in a discussion of "The Lodge a School."

23. Ibid.

24. Pledge card, found in a Maine antique mall, in author's personal collection of association ephemera.

25. I could have quoted similar rules from many groups' constitutions. This quote comes from *Constitution and General Laws of the Ancient Order Knights of the Mystic Chain of Pennsylvania* (Pittsburgh: Herald Printing Co., 1899), p. 52.

26. Northcott, *Woodman's Hand Book*, p. 83.

27. Frederick A. Fickardt, "The Order of the Sons of Temperance of North America, as a School for Popular Debate and Eloquence," in *The National Temperance Offering, and Sons and Daughters of Temperance Gift*, edited by S. F. Cary (New York: R. Vandien, 1850), pp. 168–69. Emphasis in original.

28. Ibid., pp. 169–70. Emphasis in original.

29. This point is stressed and documented in Sidney Verba, Kay Lehman Schlozman, and Henry E. Brady, *Voice and Equality: Civic Voluntarism in American Politics* (Cambridge, Mass.: Harvard University Press, 1995).

30. *Ritual of the Household of Ruth G.U.O. of O.F.* (Philadelphia: Subcommittee of Management, Grand United Order of Odd Fellows, 1902), pp. 37–38 in the "Charge" part of the Obligation and Installation ceremony. I hope the members of the Household of

Ruth will forgive me for quoting briefly from an old version of their secret ritual.

31. Ibid., p. 37.

32. All quotes are from Walter B. Hill, "The Great American Safety-Valve," *Century Magazine* 44, n.s. 22 (May–October 1892): 383–84.

33. This paragraph and the next draw on pp. 24–28 of a typescript of chapter 5, "Civic Density," from Douglas Rae, "The End of Urbanism: Changing Geographies of Growth, Leadership, and Civic Density in New Haven, 1910–2000" (unpublished manuscript, Yale University, 2000). All quotes come from these pages.

34. For scholarly studies that document class backgrounds at the chapter level, see Kaufman and Weintraub, "How 'Local' Were Late 19th Century Fraternal Organizations?"; Stuart McConnell, "Who Joined the Grand Army? Three Case Studies in the Construction of Union Veteranhood, 1866–1900," in *Toward a Social History of the American Civil War*, edited by Maris A. Vinovskis (Cambridge: Cambridge University Press, 1990), pp. 139–70; and Mary Ann Clawson, *Constructing Brotherhood: Gender, Class, and Fraternalism* (Princeton: Princeton University Press, 1989), chap. 3. Within the fraternal world, some orders such as the Masons and the Elks recruited more from the elite down to the upper-blue-collar ranks, while other groups such as the Odd Fellows and the Moose were centered more in the blue-collar and lower-white-collar ranks. And the same variety existed among lodges of a given order. But it would be rare to find a fraternal lodge that did not combine at least some men from elite, white-collar, and blue-collar statuses. Many chapters of federated women's clubs were probably somewhat tilted toward the top of the social order but, again, almost invariably included a fair number of wives of lower-white-collar employees, skilled blue-collar workers, and (in rural areas) farmers.

35. Guy H. Fuller, ed., *Loyal Order of Moose and Mooseheart* (Mooseheart, Ill.: Mooseheart Press, 1918), p. 166.

36. Quoted from a widely distributed pamphlet (n.d.) apparently published by the Modern Woodmen of America called "W. J. Bryan's Speech at the M.W.A. Class Adoption in Lincoln, Nebraska, on May 6, 1903."

37. During the 1920s, the National Farm News published the *Religious & Fraternal Directory of Your National Government,* "showing religious, fraternal, and political affiliations of Congress and the executive and judicial branches of your national government." Affiliation with the Masons was proclaimed by 70 percent of the 435 members of the House of Representatives and two-thirds of the 100 U.S. senators. Many other fraternal groups were also frequently listed, so that fraternals easily surpassed listings of religious affiliations.

38. Warner Olivier, *Back of the Dream: The Story of the Loyal Order of Moose* (New York: E. P. Dutton, 1952), p. 69.

39. James Michael Curley, *I'd Do It Again* (Englewood Cliffs, N.J.: Prentice-Hall, 1957), pp. 57–60; see also pp. 45, 78, 85, 334. Curley also benefited from his participation in the Foresters of America, the Young Men's Catholic Association, the St. Patrick's Total Abstinence and Literary Society of Boston, the Roxbury Tammany Club, and other Irish political groups.

40. Royce D. Delmatier, *Rumble of California Politics, 1848–1970* (New York: Wiley, 1970), p. 241.

41. Janann Sherman, *No Place for a Woman: A Life of Senator Margaret Chase Smith* (New Brunswick, N.J.: Rutgers University Press, 2000), pp. 46–47, 82–83.

42. Paschal Donaldson, *The Odd-Fellows Textbook*, 6th ed. (Philadelphia: Moss and Brother, 1852), p. 232.

43. "W. J. Bryan's Speech at the M.W.A. Class Adoption in Lincoln, Nebraska, on May 6, 1903."

44. "Address by Col. Paul V. McNutt, National Commander of the American Legion, before the 84th Legislature, January 24th, 1929" (undated pamphlet), p. 11.

45. Minutes book and set-in memo in author's personal collection.

46. As listed in the *Girls' High School Parent-Teacher Program of Meetings 1933–1934* (pamphlet with no date or publisher). From the author's personal ephemera collection, purchased via the Internet.

47. One of the columns in table 2.1 indicates whether very large U.S. voluntary associations were or are "involved in politics." The tally reported here does not include four major associations (indicated in table 2.1) that repeatedly entered into national partnerships to help fight great wars. Nor does the tally include all groups that supported official wartime mobilizations, or fraternal groups like the Masons whose members often ran for or held elective office. If I had considered all facets of involvement, virtually all major groups would have been classified as "involved in politics."

48. "Shall This Iowa Boy Become President?" (pamphlet, Woman's Christian Temperance Union of Iowa, n.d.), p. 4. From the author's personal collection of association ephemera.

49. Skocpol, *Protecting Soldiers and Mothers*, pt. 3.

50. Elisabeth S. Clemens, *The People's Lobby* (Chicago: University of Chicago Press, 1997), makes this case powerfully.

51. Gabriel A. Almond and Sidney Verba, *The Civic Culture: Political Attitudes and Democracy in Five Nations* (Princeton: Princeton University Press, 1963).

CHAPTER 4

1. The list of large membership associations presented here comes from the research of the Civic Engagement Project that I described in chapter 2. Obviously, voluntary associations vary considerably in what they mean by "membership." Our research allows each group to use its own definition, and the Red Cross and the March of Dimes indicate some of the outer limits of what

groups may mean. "Members" of the Red Cross are all persons who donate even a small amount of money in a given year; and "members" of the March of Dimes include those who volunteer during the annual fund drive. As explained by David Sills, *The Volunteers: Means and Ends in a National Organization* (New York: Free Press, 1957), the National March of Dimes Foundation also has local chapter-based members, far fewer in number than the participants in the annual drives. On such national health associations in general, see Richard Carter, *The Gentle Legions: National Voluntary Health Organizations in America*, rev. ed. (New Brunswick, N.J.: Transaction Books, 1992).

2. Calculated in a slightly different way, post–World War II membership trends for various associations appear in Robert D. Putnam, *Bowling Alone: The Collapse and Revival of American Community* (New York: Simon and Schuster, 2000), Appendix 3.

3. Putnam, *Bowling Alone*; Jeffrey A. Charles, *Service Clubs in American Society: Rotary, Kiwanis, and Lions* (Urbana: University of Illinois Press, 1993), chap. 7; Louise M. Young, *In the Public Interest: The League of Women Voters, 1920–1970* (Westport, Conn.: Greenwood Press, 1989), chaps. 13–15.

4. For ethnic fraternals, see the yearly listings for the late 1950s and early 1960s in Gale Research Company, *The Encyclopedia of Associations*, vol. 1 (Detroit: Gale Research Company, 1955 and after). On the twentieth-century expansion of the African American Elks, see Charles H. Wesley, *History of the Improved Benevolent and Protective Order of Elks of the World, 1898–1954* (Washington, D.C.: Association for the Study of Negro History, 1955).

5. Gabriel A. Almond and Sidney Verba, *The Civic Culture: Political Attitudes and Democracy in Five Nations* (Princeton: Princeton University Press, 1963), p. 302, table 2. Interestingly, the "fraternal" category in this table appears only for the United States and includes one of the highest proportions of citizens claiming a type of membership.

6. Ibid., p. 302, table 1, on overall membership levels; p. 303, table 3, on males and females; and p. 304, table 4, on educational levels. The ratios of citizens with "some university" education to those with "primary or less" schooling claiming membership in "some organization" were as follows (where a higher ratio indicates more class differential): USA, 1.45; Great Britain, 2.24; Germany, 1.51; Italy, 1;84; and Mexico, 3.23. That the United States did as well as it did on this measure is a powerful indicator of the prevalence of associations that drew less-educated Americans in to a considerable degree, because, after all, the United Sates lagged behind Germany and (especially) Britain in union memberships (see table 2, p. 302).

7. Ibid., p. 306, table 5. Overall, 24 percent of Americans claimed a group they were affiliated with was involved in politics, compared to 19 percent of Britons, 18 percent of Germans, 6 percent of Italians, and 11 percent of Mexicans. Of course, political parties may have borne more of the weight of organizing mass involvement in politics in some or all of the other nations. Nevertheless, these data show that voluntary associations mediated a significant amount of political engagement in 1960.

8. Thomas A. Rumer, *The American Legion: An Official History, 1919–1989* (New York: M. Evans, 1990), pp. 211–393, passim; Bill Bottoms, *The VFW: An Illustrated History of the Veterans of Foreign Wars of the United States* (Rockville, Md.: Woodbine House, 1991), chaps. 5, 6, passim.

9. Richard S. Davis, "Fifty Years of Service: What the Eagle Record Has Meant to Everyone," *Eagle* 36, no. 2 (February 1948): 7–9; Lloyd Gladfelter, "Your Social Security," *Eagle* 39, no. 3 (March 1951): 7–9. One side of a medallion issued in 1948 to celebrate the fiftieth anniversary of the Fraternal Order of Eagles portrayed a tableau of people helped by the public social programs the Eagles had championed in state and national politics: mothers' pensions, old-age pensions, workmen's compensation, and social security.

10. John Mark Hansen, *Gaining Access: Congress and the Farm Lobby, 1919–1981* (Chicago: University of Chicago Press, 1991), chaps. 3, 5.

11. Mildred White Wells, *Unity in Diversity: The History of the General Federation of Women's Clubs* (Washington, D.C.: General Federation of Women's Clubs, 1953), pp. 168–69, 210–11. For an overview of PTA involvements with public policy issues, see the "Historical Information" on the organization's website at http://www.pta.org.

12. Theda Skocpol, "The G.I. Bill and U.S. Social Policy, Past and Future," *Social Philosophy and Policy* 14, no. 2 (1997): 106–9; Michael J. Bennett, *When Dreams Came True: The G.I. Bill and the Making of Modern America* (Washington, D.C.: Brassey's, 1996), chaps. 2, 3.

13. Doug McAdam, *Political Process and the Development of Black Insurgency* (Chicago: University of Chicago Press, 1982); Aldon D. Morris, *The Origins of the Civil Rights Movement: Black Communities Organizing for Change* (New York: Free Press,1984).

14. Todd Gitlin, *The Sixties: Days of Hope, Days of Rage* (New York: Bantam, 1989); J. Craig Jenkins and Charles Perrow, "Insurgency of the Powerless," *American Sociological Review* 42 (1977): 249–68; Debra C. Minkoff, *Organizing for Equality: The Evolution of Women's and Racial-Ethnic Organizations in America, 1955–1985* (Philadelphia: Temple University Press, 1995), chap. 2.

15. See the useful discussion in Elisabeth S. Clemens, *The People's Lobby: Organizational Innovation and the Rise of Interest Group Politics in the United States, 1890–1925* (Chicago: University of Chicago Press, 1997), chap. 2.

16. See especially Morris, *Origins of the Civil Rights Movement*.

17. Ibid., chaps. 1, 2.

18. Joyce Gelb and Marian Lief Palley, *Women and Public Policies* (Princeton: Princeton University Press, 1982), chap. 2. My discussion of organizations involved in the new feminism draws on Gelb and Palley's study.

19. Jo Freeman, "The Origins of the Women's Liberation Movement," *American Journal of Sociology* 78 (1973): 792–811.

20. Gelb and Palley, *Women and Public Policies*, pp. 14–15.

21. Rachel Carson, *Silent Spring* (Boston: Houghton Mifflin, 1962).

22. Robert Cameron Mitchell, Angela E. Mertig, and Riley E. Dunlap, "Twenty Years of Environmental Mobilization: Trends among National Environmental Organizations," in *American Environmentalism: The U.S. Environmental Movement, 1970–1990*, edited by Riley E. Dunlap and Angela E. Mertig (New York: Taylor and Francis, 1992), pp. 13–14. Greenpeace USA was established in 1988 as a distinctly institutionalized part of the transnational movement launched earlier.

23. Ibid., pp. 12–14. Before the 1960s all of those groups were relatively small membership associations.

24. See the discussion of this issue and some empirical tests, in Frank R. Baumgartner and Bryan D. Jones, *Agendas and Instability in American Politics* (Chicago: University of Chicago Press, 1993), p. 186.

25. For the per capita trend, see Putnam, *Bowling Alone*, p. 50, fig. 7.

26. Jeffrey M. Berry, *The Interest Group Society*, 3d ed. (New York: Longman, 1997), chap. 2. See also Jack L. Walker Jr., *Mobilizing Interest Groups in America: Patrons, Professions, and Social Movements* (Ann Arbor: University of Michigan Press, 1991.

27. Minkoff, *Organizing for Equality*, p. 17.

28. Ibid., p. 61.

29. Ibid., p. 62, fig. 3.1.

30. Ibid., p. 17.

31. Ibid., p. 62, fig. 3.2.

32. Ibid., p. 63.

33. Kay Lehman Schlozman, "Representing Women in Washington: Sisterhood and Pressure Politics," in *Women, Politics, and*

Change, edited by Louise A. Tilly and Patricia Gurin (New York: Russell Sage Foundation, 1990), 339–82.

34. Gelb and Palley, *Women and Public Policies*, p. 14. See also Ann N. Costain, "Representing Women: The Transition from Social Movement to Interest Group," *Western Political Quarterly* 34 (March 1981): 100–13.

35. Gelb and Palley, *Women and Public Policies*, p. 25.

36. The best studies of these associations are: Jeffrey M. Berry, *Lobbying for the People: The Political Behavior of Public Interest Groups* (Princeton: Princeton University Press, 1977); Jeffrey M. Berry, *The New Liberalism: The Rising Power of Citizen Groups* (Washington, D.C.: Brookings Institution Press, 1999); Andrew S. McFarland, *Common Cause: Lobbying in the Public Interest* (Chatham, N.J.: Chatham House, 1984); Walker, *Mobilizing Interest Groups*, pp. 33–35.

37. Berry, Lobbying for the People, chap. 2. See also Putnam, *Bowling Alone*, p. 51.

38. Berry, *Lobbying for the People*, p. 34.

39. Kay Lehman Schlozman and John C. Tierney, *Organized Interests and American Democracy* (New York: Harper and Row, 1986), pp. 75–76.

40. Walker, *Mobilizing Interest Groups*, chap. 4.

41. Berry, *Interest Group Society*, pp. 31–37.

42. Jeffrey M. Berry, "The Rise of Citizen Groups," in *Civic Engagement in American Democracy*, edited by Theda Skocpol and Morris P. Fiorina (Washington, D.C.: Brookings Institution Press; and New York: Russell Sage Foundation, 1999), pp. 368–69.

43. Baumgartner and Jones, *Agendas and Instability*, pp. 186–87.

44. Findings of previous studies are well summarized in Frank R. Baumgartner and Beth L. Leech, *Basic Interests* (Princeton: Princeton University Press, 1998), esp. pp. 100–101, 105–6.

45. Walker, *Mobilizing Interest Groups*, chap. 4; Berry, *Interest Group Society*, pp. 37–42; Kevin Phillips, *Arrogant Capital:*

Washington, Wall Street, and the Frustration of American Politics (Boston: Little, Brown, 1994), p. 32. See also John B. Judis, "The Pressure Elite: Inside the Narrow World of Advocacy Group Politics," *American Prospect*, no. 9 (Spring 1992): 15–29.

46. Baumgartner and Jones, *Agendas and Instability*, p. 183.

47. Ibid., p. 184.

48. Jeffrey Berry, "Building an Effective Lobby," paper presented at the annual meeting of the American Political Science Association, San Francisco, California, August 30–September 1, 2001, p. 27. This paragraph and the next draw on the arguments and research presented in this article.

49. Ibid., pp. 2–3.

50. Two groups listed in table 4.1, the Red Cross and the March of Dimes, are not included here. These associations base their "membership" claims on general counts of yearly contributors or volunteers, and in recent years the claims have become vague and repetitive.

51. Among fraternal groups, the Fraternal Order of Moose has done better than others in recent decades. I do not have any definitive explanation for this. But it may be that the Moose, all along, had proportionately more working-class members than the Elks or Masons or Eagles. As I argue in the next chapter, contemporary fraternal groups have experienced especially great losses at the top of the class structure. To the extent that this is true, it follows that groups with a higher elite component in the first place would have experienced greater relative losses in the 1960s and 1970s.

52. Berry, *Interest Group Society*, p. 27, fig. 2.4.

53. Burdett A. Loomis and Allan J. Cigler, "Introduction: The Changing Nature of Interest Group Politics," in *Interest Group Politics*, edited by Allan J. Cigler and Burdett A. Loomis, 5th ed. (Washington, D.C.: CQ Press, 1998), p. 12. My account of the AARP also draws on Charles R. Morris, *The AARP: America's Most Powerful Lobby and the Clash of Generations* (New York: Times Books, 1996).

54. Loomis and Cigler, "Introduction," p. 12.

55. Allen M. West, *The National Education Association: The Power Base for Education* (New York: Free Press, 1980).

56. Kelly Patterson, "The Political Firepower of the National Rifle Association," in *Interest Group Politics*, 5th ed., edited by Allan J. Cigler and Burdett A. Loomis (Washington, D.C.: CQ Press, 1998), 119–42.

57. For these figures, I have dropped the practice of listing all associations that exceeded 1 percent of men or women or all adults, in favor of tracing very large groups by absolute size. This is done to maintain a consistent metric during an era when gender-segregated groups became increasingly scarce.

58. These numbers are pieced together from the *Encyclopedia of Associations* and from Mitchell, Mertig, and Dunlap, "Environmental Mobilization," p. 13.

59. Gelb and Palley, *Women and Public Policies*, p. 29; *Encyclopedia of Associations*.

60. Data for the General Federation come from directly from the association's records. Data for NOW come from the 1993 volume of the *Encyclopedia of Associations*.

61. Putnam, *Bowling Alone*, p. 51 (including references), summarizes these studies and adds findings and calculations of his own.

62. Calculated by the author from 1998 CD-rom data provided by Gale Research Company, corresponding to data in the 34th edition of the *Encyclopedia of Associations*. There can be a problem using retrospective data on founding dates, but in this case I think it is entirely appropriate, because surviving groups from those founded in the 1960s through the 1980s have had a chance to build up their memberships to the degree that they have aimed to do so. Some groups say nothing at all about memberships, and a few of these may actually have members. But they are unlikely to have many members; and the names and statements of purpose of most such groups

indicate that they are usually memberless or based on organizational constituencies.

63. Everett Carl Ladd, *The Ladd Report* (New York: Free Press), p. 50.

64. Putnam, *Bowling Alone*, pp. 61–62.

65. Ibid., pp. 31–43. Emphasis in original. All quotes in this paragraph come from these pages.

66. Putnam, *Bowling Alone*, pp. 57, 451 (n. 20). See also Susan Crawford and Peggy Levitt, "Social Change and Civic Engagement: The Case of the PTA," in *Civic Engagement in American Democracy*, edited by Theda Skocpol and Morris P. Fiorina (Washington, D.C.: Brookings Institution Press; New York: Russell Sage Foundation, 1999), pp. 253, 273–75.

67. Crawford and Levitt, "The Case of the PTA," pp. 276–77.

68. Ibid., pp. 275–76; Laura M. Litvan, "Is the PTA Now a Teacher's Pet? Close Ties to Unions Spur Some to Break Away," *Investor's Business Daily*, October 20, 1997, pp. A1, A40.

69. Ladd, *The Ladd Report*, p. 33

70. Ibid, p. 49.

71. Michael W. Foley and Bob Edwards, "The Paradox of Civil Society," *Journal of Democracy* 7, no. 3 (July 1996): 44.

72. Nicholas Freudenberg and Carol Steinsapir, "Not in Our Backyards: The Grassroots Environmental Movement," in *American Environmentalism*, edited by Riley E. Dunlap and Angela G. Mertig (New York: Taylor and Francis, 1992); Bob Edwards, "With Liberty and Justice for All: The Emergence and Challenge of Grassroots Environmentalism in the United States," in *Ecological Resistance Movements*, edited by Bron Raymond Taylor (Albany: State University of New York Press, 1995), 35–55.

73. Foley and Edwards, "Paradox," p. 44.

74. Bob Edwards, "Semiformal Organizational Structure among Social Movement Organizations: An Analysis of the U.S. Peace Movement," *Nonprofit and Voluntary Sector Quarterly* 23,

no. 4 (Winter 1994): 309–33, using data from the *Grassroots Peace Directory* (Pomfort, Conn.: Topsfield Foundation, 1987).

75. Edwards, "U.S. Peace Movement," p. 327.

76. See esp. Edwards, "U.S. Peace Movement," p. 314, table 1, on the various types of peace organizations and constituencies. I have calculated overall percentages using this table and the proportions Edwards gives for large-budget groups overall (7%) and smaller-budget groups overall (93%).

77. Edwards, "U.S. Peace Movements," pp. 328, 327.

78. Robert Wuthnow, *Sharing the Journey: Support Groups and America's New Quest for Community* (New York: Free Press, 1994). This study chiefly rests on a representative national survey conducted at one point in time, November 1991 (see Appendix A). But Wuthnow also uses in-depth interviews and evidence about national institutional trends.

79. Ibid., p. 23, chap. 2.

80. Ibid., p. 76.

81. Charles Trueheart, "Welcome to the Next Church," *Atlantic Monthly* 278, no. 2 (August 1996): 37–58.

82. This point is developed in Robert Wuthnow, "Mobilizing Civic Engagement: The Changing Impact of Religious Involvement," in *Civic Engagement in American Democracy*, edited by Theda Skocpol and Morris P. Fiorina (Washington, D.C.: Brookings Institution Press, and New York: Russell Sage Foundation, 1999), pp. 361–62.

83. Wuthnow, *Sharing the Journey*, p. 76, table 3.2. See also p. 65, table 3.1.

84. Ibid., pp. 70–75.

85. Ibid., p. 76, table 3.2.

86. Wuthnow reports that 26 percent of small-group members say their group has a "membership fee." Ibid., p. 135, table 5.1.

87. On the development of the contemporary New Right, see Lisa McGirr, *Suburban Warriors: The Origins of the New American Right* (Princeton: Princeton University Press, 2001).

88. Evangelical Christians are also the people most likely to attend religious services regularly rather than sporadically. See Putnam, *Bowling Alone*, pp. 75–78, 161–62.

CHAPTER 5

1. Robert D. Putnam, *Bowling Alone: The Collapse and Revival of American Community* (New York: Simon and Schuster, 2000).

2. For an elaboration of this perspective, see Steven J. Rosenstone and John Mark Hansen, *Mobilization, Participation, and Democracy in America* (New York: Macmillan, 1993). I am developing an argument about civic life analogous to the one Rosenstone and Hansen developed for electoral politics.

3. There are some exceptions to note. Among white-dominated associations, the Knights of Labor and some trade unions accepted women, as did the major farm federations and certain temperance federations (above all the Independent Order of Good Templars). What is more, African American fraternal and mutual aid groups were much more likely than similar white groups to include both men and women. Indeed, some mixed-gender African American groups, such as the Independent Order of Saint Luke, were founded and led by women. About the Order of St. Luke, see Wendell P. Dabney, *Maggie L. Walker and the I. O. of Saint Luke: The Woman and Her Work* (Cincinnati: Dabney Publishing Company, 1927).

4. On female fraternalists, see Mary Ann Clawson, *Constructing Brotherhood: Gender, Class, and Fraternalism* (Princeton: Princeton University Press, 1989), chap. 6; David T. Beito, *From Mutual Aid to the Welfare State: Fraternal Societies and Social Services, 1890–1967* (Chapel Hill: University of North Carolina Press, 2000), pp. 31–36 passim; and Elizabeth B. McGowan, "The Scope of Woman's Influence and Its Greatest Avenue for Good in Fraternal Organizations," *Ladies Review* 7 (January 1, 1901).

5. Independent women's federations were more likely than white male fraternals to try to work out some sort of sisterhood across racial lines. The Young Women's Christian Association made strong efforts to promote interracial groups and programs. The WCTU included some integrated groups outside the South and institutionalized parallel African American unions in various southern states, allowing white and black women to attend national conventions together. Perhaps because they were founded later in the nineteenth century, when racial segregation was in full force in the South, the General Federation of Women's Clubs and the PTA did not go this far. After arguments at the national level accompanied by threats to withdraw by southern white women, both federations decided to exclude blacks from full participation. Yet national PTA and GFWC leaders, and leaders of some state units in each federation, made some attempts to coordinate programs with counterpart membership federations for African American women. In general, white women saw parallel associations among African Americans as partners in pursuing such shared goals as fighting alcohol, helping children and families, and improving public education.

6. *What It Means to Be an Elk: Information Relating to the Order Collected and Published Specially for the Instruction of Initiates* (no date or publisher, probably 1950s), p. 8. This is a paperback pamphlet from the author's personal collection of association ephemera.

7. Many whites were not even willing to share names and symbols with African Americans committed to the same universally framed ideals of fraternal brotherhood. Although the courts ultimately rebuffed such efforts, many white fraternals agitated for state laws that would prevent African American counterparts from using similar labels like "Elks" or "Knights of Pythias."

8. A full analysis appears in Susan Crawford and Peggy Levitt, "Social Change and Civic Engagement: The Case of the PTA," in *Civic Engagement in American Democracy*, edited by Theda

Skocpol and Morris P. Fiorina (Washington, D.C.: Brookings Institution Press; New York: Russell Sage Foundation, 1999), pp. 249–96.

9. Robert Wuthnow, *Loose Connections: Joining Together in America's Fragmented Communities* (Cambridge, Mass.: Harvard University Press, 1998), p. 253, n. 51.

10. Putnam, *Bowling Alone*, p. 268; plus figure provided by Putnam to the author.

11. Loyal Order of Moose, *Moose Facts*, 4th rev. ed. (Mooseheart, Ill.: Supreme Lodge Supply Department, 1944), p. 29. Each page in this little pamphlet in the author's ephemera collection has an inspirational heading, and this one is called "FATHER-AND-SON."

12. See, e.g., James R. Nicholson, Lee A. Donaldson, and Raymond C. Dobson, *History of the Order of Elks, 1868–1978*, rev. ed. (Chicago: Grand Secretary's Office of the Benevolent and Protective Order of Elks of America, 1978), sections K and L.

13. Trends among Americans with some years of college are omitted from the figures to make them readable, but fraternal and veterans' memberships also declined for these respondents.

14. The Massachusetts State Library has a continuous run of these directories, formerly called *Public Officials of Massachusetts* and currently titled *Public Officers of the Commonwealth of Massachusetts*.

15. Figure 5.3 understates the decline of fraternal memberships over the decades, because many Massachusetts senators used to list multiple fraternal groups, whereas those who continued to indicate any fraternal ties in the 1980s and 1990s usually mentioned just one group—typically of Catholic or ethnic origin (such as the Knights of Columbus, the Sons of Italy, or the Ancient Order of Hibernians).

16. Mabel Newcomer, *A Century of Higher Education for American Women* (New York: Harper, 1959), p. 46, table 2. See Theda Skocpol, *Protecting Soldiers and Mothers: The Political Origins of*

Social Policy in the United States (Cambridge, Mass.: Harvard University Press, 1992), pp. 340–43, for more discussion and references.

17. See Robert D. Mare, "Changes in Educational Attainment and School Enrollment," in *State of the Union: America in the 1990s*, vol. 1: *Economic Trends*, edited by Reynolds Farley (New York: Russell Sage Foundation, 1995), pp. 164–67.

18. Ibid., p. 167; Suzanne M. Bianchi, "Changing Economic Roles of Women and Men," in *State of the Union: American in the 1990s*, vol. 1: *Economic Trends*, edited by Reynolds Farley (New York: Russell Sage Foundation, 1995), pp. 124–25, tables 3.6 and 3.7.

19. Figure from the U.S. Bureau of the Census, cited in Wuthnow, *Loose Connections*, p. 241, n. 5.

20. Wuthnow, *Loose Connections*, p. 76. See also Kay Lehman Schlozman, "Did Working Women Kill the PTA?" *American Prospect* 11, no. 20 (September 11, 2000): 14–15. This article has a misleading title. The facts it presents have to do with aggregate levels of political involvement by employed versus nonemployed women. All kinds of political involvement are counted, including giving money.

21. Dora L. Costa and Matthew E. Kahn, "Understanding the Decline in Social Capital, 1952–1998" (unpublished paper prepared with support from the National Bureau of Economic Research and presented to the Economic History Workshop, Harvard University, 2001).

22. Wuthnow, *Loose Connections*, pp. 78–79.

23. Putnam ends up attributing only a small fraction of decline in traditional civic activities to changing gender roles in homes, communities, and workplaces. But this conclusion is too rigidly defined by a narrow use of statistical methodology. Putnam sorts women into categories, full-time employees, part-time, and stay-at-home, and then considers only differences in levels of participation across those categories. He does not delve

into the kinds of groups the most educated women have joined and led over time. And more to the point, he does not consider interaction effects. When highly educated women shift group affiliations and styles of participation, that affects other women, and men, too. And when divisions of labor between home and paid work change, that affects everyone's cultural ideals and everyone's time schedules. Time squeeze alone is not the problem. Equally pertinent are possibilities for people to *coordinate* blocks of time for non-wage-work activities. Highly educated women today, like highly educated men, may remain very civically involved, but they do different types of things. And it is virtually impossible to schedule regular meetings to accommodate them!

24. See the account of the CDF in David Walls, *The Activist Almanac* (New York: Fireside, 1993), p. 279; and also Marian Wright Edelman, *Families in Peril: An Agenda for Social Change* (Cambridge, Mass.: Harvard University Press, 1987).

25. Putnam, *Bowling Alone*, p. 281.

26. Allan J. Cigler and Burdett A. Loomis, "Introduction: The Changing Nature of Interest Group Politics" in *Interest Group Politics*, edited by Allan J. Cigler and Burdett A. Loomis (Washington, D.C.: CQ Press, 1983), pp. 11–12; and Steven Rathgeb Smith and Michael Lipsky, *Nonprofits for Hire: The Welfare State in the Age of Contracting* (Cambridge, MA: Harvard University Press, 1993).

27. This phrase comes from Hugh Heclo, "Issue Networks and the Executive Establishment," in *The New American Political System*, edited by Anthony King (Washington, D.C.: American Enterprise Institute, 1978), p. 89.

28. Morris P. Fiorina and Paul E. Peterson, *The New American Democracy* (Boston: Allyn and Bacon, 1998), p. 352, chap. 12.

29. Kevin Phillips, *Arrogant Capital: Washington, Wall Street, and the Frustration of American Politics* (Boston: Little, Brown, 1994), pp. 25, 32. According to Fiorina and Peterson, *New American Democracy*, p. 352, congressional staffs are currently split about 60/40 between aides working in Washington and aides serving in district offices.

30. Jeffrey M. Berry, *The Interest Group Society*, 3d ed. (New York: Longman, 1997), p. 220.

31. For one instance of this transition, see John Mark Hansen, *Gaining Access: Congress and the Farm Lobby, 1919–1981* (Chicago: University of Chicago Press, 1991), pt. 2.

32. Jack L. Walker, *Mobilizing Interest Groups in America: Patrons, Professions, and Social Movements* (Ann Arbor: University of Michigan Press, 1991), p. 72.

33. Phillips, *Arrogant Capital*, chap. 2; David M. Ricci, *The Transformation of American Politics: The New Washington and the Rise of Think Tanks* (New Haven: Yale University Press, 1993); Andrew Rich and R. Kent Weaver, "Advocates and Analysts: Think Tanks and the Politicization of Expertise," in *Interest Group Politics*, 5th ed., edited by Allan J. Cigler and Burdett A. Loomis (Washington, D.C.: CQ Press, 1998), 235–53.

34. Karen Paget, "Citizen Organizing: Many Movements, No Majority," *American Prospect*, no. 2 (Summer 1990): 115–28.

35. On PACs, see Berry, *Interest Group Society*, pp. 55–58, chap. 7; and M. Margaret Conway and Joanne Connor Green, "Political Action Committees and Campaign Finance," in *Interest Group Politics*, 5th ed., edited by Allan J. Cigler and Burdett A. Loomis (Washington DC: CQ Press, 1998), pp. 193–214.

36. Berry, *Interest Group Society*, chap. 3.

37. This paragraph draws especially on Walker, *Mobilizing Interest Groups*, pp. 23–27. Transformations in party politics inside and outside of government are also analyzed by John H. Aldrich, *Why Parties? The Origin and Transformation of Political Parties in America* (Chicago: University of Chicago Press, 1995), pt. 3.

38. Marshall Ganz, "Voters in the Crosshairs: How Technology and the Market are Destroying Politics," *American Prospect*, no. 16 (Winter 1994): 100–109.

39. For an excellent discussion of the broad styles of popular mobilization used by nineteenth-century U.S. political parties, see Steven E. Schier, *By Invitation Only: The Rise of Exclusive*

Politics in the United States (Pittsburgh: University of Pittsburgh Press, 2000), esp. chap. 2.

40. For a good overview, see Michael T. Hayes, "The New Group Universe," in *Interest Group Politics*, 2d ed., edited by Allan J. Cigler and Burdett A. Loomis (Washington, D.C.: CQ Press, 1986), 133–45.

41. Andrew S. McFarland, *Common Cause: Lobbying in the Public Interest* (Chatham, N.J.: Chatham House, 1984), pp. 1–2, 75–76.

42. For an overview of U.S. foundations, see Joseph C. Kiger and Sara L. Engelhardt, *Philanthropic Foundations of the Twentieth Century* (Westport, Conn.: Greenwood Press, 2000); and Teresa Odendahl, *America's Wealthy and the Future of Foundations* (New York: Foundation Center, 1987). Recent trends in grant expenditures and the creation of new foundations are documented by the Foundation Center, at http://fdncenter.org.

43. J. Craig Jenkins and Abigail Halcli, "Grassrooting the System? The Development and Impact of Social Movement Philanthropy, 1953–1990," in *Philanthropic Foundations: New Scholarship, New Possibilities* (Bloomington: Indiana University Press, 1999), p. 230, table 10.1.

44. Nicholas Lemann, "Citizen 501(c)(3)," *Atlantic Monthly* (February 1997): 19.

45. Jenkins and Halcli, "Grassrooting the System." On the dwindling importance of membership dues, see Putnam, *Bowling Alone*, 63.

46. See J. Craig Jenkins, "Channeling Social Protest: Foundation Patronage of Contemporary Social Movements," in *Private Action and the Public Good*, edited by Walter W. Powell and Elisabeth S. Clemens (New Haven: Yale University Press, 1998), pp. 206–16; Joyce Gelb and Marian Leif Palley, *Women and Public Policies* (Princeton: Princeton University Press, 1982), pp. 42–50; and Berry, *Lobbying for the People*, pp. 71–76. Berry studied eighty-three public interest associations in 1972–73 and found that nearly half got significant funding from foundations. Unfor-

tunately, he does not report variations within funding categories by founding dates of associations.

47. Robert Lerner, Althea K. Nagai, and Stanley Rothman, *Giving for Social Change: Foundations, Public Policy, and the American Political Agenda* (Westport, Conn.: Praeger, 1994), chap. 8, "Foundations and Their Public Policy Grants"; Sally Covington, *Moving a Public Agenda: The Strategic Philanthropy of Conservative Foundations* (Washington, D.C.: National Committee for Responsive Philanthropy, 1997). Liberal foundations, influenced by ideas about multiculturalism and worried about being attacked as overtly partisan, channel some of their resources to avowedly "nonpartisan" recipients, whereas conservative foundations almost never do. More important, liberal foundations have moved in recent decades toward giving large numbers of modest, short-term grants to community organizing efforts or issue-specific advocacy groups. They scatter their largesse and keep recipient groups jumping through hoops to make applications, host site visits, and write reports. Conservative foundations, in contrast, use larger and longer-term grants to build research and media capacities aimed at reinforcing political mobilization on the Right.

48. On trends in foundation grants and their impact, see especially Jenkins and Halcli, "Grassrooting the System," and Jenkins, "Channeling Social Protest." On the impact on African American movements in particular, see J. Craig Jenkins and Craig M. Eckert, "Channeling Black Insurgency: Elite Patronage and Professional Social Movement Organizations in the Development of the Black Movement," *American Sociological Review* 51 (December 1986): 812–29.

49. Walker, *Mobilizing Interest Groups*, chap. 5, esp. tables 5-1, 5-2.

50. Walker, *Mobilizing Interest Groups*, pp. 93–94.

51. On the shifting funding strategies of environmental groups, see Christopher J. Bosso, "The Color of Money: Environmental Groups and the Pathologies of Fund Raising," in *Interest*

Group Politics, 4th ed., edited by Allan J. Cigler and Burdett A. Loomis (Washington, D.C.: CQ Press, 1995), pp. 101–30; Paul E. Johnson, "Interest Group Recruiting: Finding Members and Keeping Them," in *Interest Group Politics*, 5th ed., edited by Allan J. Cigler and Burdett A. Loomis (Washington, D.C.: CQ Press, 1998), pp. 35–62.

52. McFarland, *Common Cause*, p. 76.

53. For good overviews of direct-mail techniques, see Berry, *Interest Group Society*, pp. 77–80; R. Kenneth Godwin and Rondo Cameron Mitchell, "The Implication of Direct Mail for Political Organizations," *Social Science Quarterly* 65, no. 3 (1984): 829–39.

54. Johnson, "Interest Group Recruiting."

55. This transition is described in James M. Fallows, *Breaking the News: How the Media Undermine American Democracy* (New York: Pantheon, 1996).

56. Howard Kurtz, *Hot Air: All Talk, All the Time* (New York: Times Books, 1996).

57. Godwin and Mitchell, "Implications of Direct Mail," p. 836.

58. Michael Schudson, "What If Civic Life Didn't Die?" *American Prospect*, no. 25 (March–April 1996): 19. See also Mare, "Changes in Educational Attainment," pp. 166–67.

59. Steven Brint, *In an Age of Experts: The Changing Role of Professionals in Politics and Public Life* (Princeton: Princeton University Press, 1994), p. 3.

60. Sheldon Danziger and Peter Gottschalk, *America Unequal* (New York: Russell Sage Foundation; Cambridge, Mass.: Harvard University Press, 1995); Mare, "Changes in Educational Attainment," pp. 203–7.

61. David Brooks, *Bobos in Paradise: The New Upper Class and How They Got There* (New York: Simon and Schuster, 2000).

62. Brint, *Age of Experts*.

63. Robert H. Frank and Philip J. Cook, *The Winner-Take-All Society* (New York: Free Press, 1995), p. 12, chap. 8.

64. Wuthnow, *Loose Connections*, p. 47.

65. Ibid., p. 46.

66. Putnam, *Bowling Alone*, chaps. 3–5.

CHAPTER 6

1. For citations of relevant works by analysts who are optimistic about current civic trends, see chapter 1, note 22.

2. For citations of works and reports by pessimists, see chapter 1, notes 9 and 11–13.

3. Debra C. Minkoff, "Producing Social Capital: National Movements and Civil Society," *American Behavioral Scientist* 40 (March–April 1997): 606–7.

4. Andrew S. McFarland, *Common Cause: Lobbying in the Public Interest* (Chatham, N.J.: Chatham House, 1984), pp. 48–49.

5. R. Kenneth Godwin and Robert Cameron Mitchell, "The Implications of Direct Mail for Political Organizations," *Social Science Quarterly* 65, no. 3 (1984): 829–39.

6. Everett Carl Ladd, *The Ladd Report* (New York: Free Press, 1999), chaps. 1–3; Robert Wuthnow, *Sharing the Journey* (New York: Free Press, 1994).

7. Wuthnow, *Sharing the Journey*, pp. 3–6, 358–60.

8. Robert Wuthnow, *Loose Connections: Joining together in America's Fragmented Communities* (Cambridge, Mass.: Harvard University Press, 1998), pp. 77–78.

9. Ladd's arguments were presented in chapter 4.

10. J. Craig Jenkins and Abigail Halch, "Grassrooting the System? The Development and Impact of Social Movement Philanthropy, 1953–1990," in *Philanthropic Foundations: New Scholarship, New Possibilities*, edited by Ellen Condliff Lagemann (Bloomington: Indiana University Press, 1999), p. 253.

11. Steven E. Schier, *By Invitation Only: The Rise of Exclusive Politics in the United States* (Pittsburgh: University of Pittsburgh Press, 2000), p. 3.

12. Lawrence R. Jacobs and Robert Y. Shapiro, *Politicians Don't Pander: Political Manipulation and the Loss of Democratic Responsiveness* (Chicago: University of Chicago Press, 2000).

13. Schier, *By Invitation Only*, p. 3.

14. Steven J. Rosenstone and John Mark Hansen, *Mobilization, Participation, and Democracy in America* (New York: Macmillan, 1993).

15. Alan S. Gerber and Donald P. Green, "The Effects of Canvassing, Telephone Calls, and Direct Mail on Voter Turnout: A Field Experiment," *American Political Science Review* 94, no. 3 (September 2000): 662.

16. Morris P. Fiorina has developed arguments to help explain this phenomenon. See his "Extreme Voices: The Dark Side of Civic Engagement," in *Civic Engagement in American Democracy*, edited by Theda Skocpol and Morris P. Fiorina (Washington, D.C.: Brookings Institution Press; New York: Russell Sage Foundation, 1999), pp. 395–425; and "Parties, Participation, and Representation in America: Old Theories Face New Realities" (unpublished paper presented at the annual meeting of the American Political Science Association, Washington, D.C., August 31–September 3, 2000).

17. Godwin and Mitchell, "Implications of Direct Mail."

18. Jeffrey M. Berry, *The New Liberalism: The Rising Power of Citizen Groups* (Washington, D.C.: Brookings Institution Press, 1999), p. 9.

19. Ibid., pp. 34–35.

20. Ibid., p.57.

21. Ibid., pp. 55–56.

22. Ibid.

23. Ibid., p. 56.

24. Ibid.

25. Ibid., pp. 56–57.

26. For the full development of this argument, see Theda Skocpol, *The Missing Middle: Working Families and the Future of*

American Social Policy (New York: Norton and the Century Foundation, 2000).

27. My account of the G.I. Bill draws especially on Michael J. Bennett, *When Dreams Came True: The G.I. Bill and the Making of Modern America* (Washington, D.C.: Brassey's, 1996); Davis R. B. Ross, *Preparing for Ulysses* (New York: Columbia University Press, 1969); and Theda Skocpol, "The G.I. Bill and U.S. Social Policy, Past and Future," *Social Philosophy and Policy* 14, no. 2 (1997): 95–115.

28. For a full analysis and references, see Theda Skocpol, *Boomerang: Health Care Reform and the Turn against Government* (New York: Norton, 1997). On public opinion and polling in this episode, see Jacobs and Shapiro, *Politicians Don't Pander*, pt. 2.

29. Gary Orren, "Fall from Grace: The Public's Loss of Faith in Government," in *Why People Don't Trust Government*, edited by Joseph S. Nye Jr., Philip D. Zelikow, and David C. King (Cambridge, Mass.: Harvard University Press, 1997), pp. 80–81, including fig. 3-1 graphing responses to this question in American National Election Studies, University of Michigan, 1958–96.

30. Ibid., p. 81.

31. Robert J. Blendon, John M. Benson, Richard Morin, Drew E. Altman, Mollyann Brodie, Mario Brossard, and Matt James, "Changing Attitudes in America," in *Why People Don't Trust Government*, edited by Joseph S. Nye Jr., Philip D. Zelikow, and David C. King (Cambridge, Mass.: Harvard University Press, 1997), p. 210.

32. "USA Today Snapshots: Stars and Stripes Are Flying High," *USA Today*, October 19–21, 2001, p. 1.

33. "A Survey of Charitable Giving after September 11, 2001," prepared for Independent Sector by Wirthlin Worldwide, October 23, 2001. For an overview, see http://www.independentsector.org/sept11/survey.html.

34. E-mail communication from Robert D. Putnam about results of a post-9/11 polling of respondents who had answered

an earlier survey of his. It is worth noting, however, that while reports of new levels of trust in African Americans and Hispanics did not preclude the eruption of public controversy when sponsors of a memorial to New York firefighers proposed a symbolic modification of a picture of three white firefighers raising the U.S. flag on the rubble of the World Trade Center. The sponsors wanted the statue to portray one white, one African American, and one Hispanic firefighter, but backed off in the face of public criticism.

35. Richard Morin and Claudia Deane, "Poll: Americans' Trust in Government Grows," *Washington Post Online*, September 28, 2001.

36. Stanley B. Greenberg, "'We'—Not 'Me,'" *American Prospect* 12, no. 22 (December 17, 2001): 26.

37. Fred Kaplan, "Charity Chief Says Giving Far Exceeds Sept. 11 Goal," *Boston Sunday Globe*, January 27, 2002, pp. 1, A24.

38. Winnie Hu, "Outpouring for Sept. 11 Groups Means Less for Food Banks," *New York Times*, November 21, 2001, p. B8.

39. Stephen G. Greene et. al., "Trimming Holiday Hopes," *Chronicle of Philanthropy*, December 13, 2001.

40. See "The American Red Cross Hears America," an advertisement in the *New York Times*, November 27, 2001, p. B10. The Red Cross also dissolved into a bitter internal leadership struggle, which was ongoing yet exacerbated by the strains following September 11. See Deborah Sontag, "Who Brought Bernadine Healy Down?" *New York Times Magazine*, December 23, 2001, pp. 32–40, 52–55.

41. Kaplan, "Charity Chief."

42. David M. Kennedy, *Over Here: The First World War and American Society* (New York: Oxford University Press, 1980), pp. 106–13.

43. "Bush's Star Role in TV Travel Ad May Shine On," in the "Washington Wire" column of the *Wall Street Journal*, November 21, 2001, p. 1.

44. On Monday, January 14, 2002, the Travel Industry Association of America proclaimed on its website (http://www.tia.org) that "an incredible 70 percent of American consumers say they saw the industry TV ads featuring President Bush. And more than half the adult population of the U.S. can accurately describe the ads."

45. Although he overstates the case, useful contrasts of this war on terrorism to World War II appear in Michael Barone, "Not a Victory for Big Government," *Wall Street Journal*, January 15, 2002, p. A16.

46. Alison Mitchell, "After Asking for Volunteers, Government Tries to Determine What They Will Do," *New York Times*, November 10, 2001, p. B7.

47. "Post 9-11 Attitudes: Religion More Prominent, Muslim-Americans More Accepted," Pew Research Center for the People and the Press, December 6, 2001.

48. Albert R. Hurt, "Waiting for the Call," *Wall Street Journal*, May 30, 2002, p. A15.

CHAPTER 7

1. The most articulate exposition of this position appears in Marvin Olasky, *Compassionate Conservatism: What It Is, What It Does, and How It Can Transform America* (New York: Free Press, 2000), with a foreword by George W. Bush.

2. For Schambra's localist views, see Michael S. Joyce and William A. Schambra, "A New Civic Life," in *To Empower People: From State to Civil Society*, 2d ed., edited by Michael Novak (Washington, D.C.: AEI Press, 1996). Galston and Elshtain played leading roles in the national civic reform commissions described in chapter 1; and Don E. Eberly is a key adviser to President George W. Bush. For his views, see his *America's Promise: Civil Society and the Renewal of American Culture* (Lanham, Md.: Rowman & Littlefield, 1998).

3. National Commission on Civic Renewal, "A Nation of Spectators: How Civic Disengagement Weakens America and What We Can Do About It" (College Park, Md.: National Commisson on Civic Renewal, 1998), p. 9, and recommendations on pp. 9–20.

4. Robert D. Putnam, *Bowling Alone: The Collapse and Revival of American Community* (New York: Simon and Schuster, 2000), chap. 24. All references and quotes in this paragraph come from reform recommendations highlighted in this chapter.

5. Enhanced social connectedness might make many individuals happier and healthier and might help schools, workplaces, and public agencies run more smoothly, as Putnam documents in *Bowling Alone*, pt. 4. The only consequences Putnam assesses for democracy as such (see chap. 21) rest on the dubious proposition that more local face-to-face interaction is the motor of democratic participation.

6. Putnam, *Bowling Alone*, chap. 16.

7. Putnam's favorite example of a supremely social capital-rich state is New Hampshire. As summarized in Tamar Lewin, "One State Finds Secret to Strong Civic Bonds," *New York Times*, August 26, 2001, pp. 1, 14, data recently collected by Putnam show that New Hampshire citizens participate in community activities relatively equally across class lines. Their participation is overwhelmingly locally focused, however, and this raises big questions about how civicly healthy New Hampshire really is. State government capacities are weak, for the state has no income tax or sales tax. Less privileged New Hampshire citizens suffer from many of the same problems but get less help than their counterparts in Maine. And New Hampshire has not been able to adequately fund its schools or its public university. In any event, "local community" is only part of the story for New Hampshire, because many property tax payers are out-of-state owners of vacation homes, and many residents of the booming southern part of the state are relatively well-to-do people who obtained

college degrees elsewhere and work in the neighboring state of Massachusetts.

8. Allan Drury, "Mainers' Pay Slips, Except for the Rich," *Maine Sunday Telegram*, September 3, 2000, pp. 1A, 14A.

9. Tux Turkel, "Health Care Puts Pinch on Workers," *Maine Sunday Telegram*, September 3, 2000, pp. 1A, 14A.

10. "New Survey Dispels Myths on Citizen Engagement," News Release, Pew Partnership for Civic Change, Charlottesville, Virginia, announcing *Ready, Willing, and Able: Citizens Working for Change* (Richmond, Va.: Pew Partnership of Civic Change, 2001). For a copy of the report, see the website www.pew-partnership.org.

11. *Ready, Willing, and Able*, p. 1 (Executive Summary).

12. "New Survey," pp. 1–2.

13. "Remarks by the President in Announcement of the Faith-based Initiative," Office of the Press Secretary, the White House, January 29, 2001.

14. "Foreword by President George W. Bush," in *Rallying the Armies of Compassion* (Washington, D.C.: The White House, 2001).

15. "The Bush 'Faith-based' Initiative: Why It's Wrong" (Washington, D.C.: Americans United for Separation of Church and State, February 20, 2001). Available at the website http://www.au.org.

16. Laurie Goodstein, "States Steer Religious Charities toward Aid," *New York Times*, July 21, 2001. Available through Premium Archive at http://www. nytimes.org.

17. This possibility is discussed in "Spiritual Poverty," *New Republic* 4, no. 516 (August 6, 2001): 7.

18. Roger Finke and Rodney Stark, *The Churching of America, 1776–1990* (New Brunswick, N.J.: Rutgers University Press, 1992).

19. See the trends documented in Peter Dobkin Hall, "Vital Signs: Organizational Population Trends and Civic Engagement in New Haven, Connecticut, 1850–1998," in *Civic Engagement in*

American Democracy, edited by Theda Skocpol and Morris P. Fiorina (Washington, D.C.: Brookings Institution Press; New York: Russell Sage Foundation, 1999), pp. 211–48.

20. See the creative and rigorous "field experiment" reported in Alan S. Gerber and Donald P. Green, "The Effects of Canvassing, Telephone Calls, and Direct Mail on Voter Turnout: A Field Experiment," *American Political Science Review* 94, no. 3 (September 2000): 653–63.

21. For more details, see the AFL-CIO website at http://www.aflcio.org.

22. Harold Meyerson, "California's Progressive Mosaic," *American Prospect* 12, no. 11 (June 18, 2001): 17–23.

23. On strategies and difficulties for the reformed AFL-CIO, see John J. Sweeney, *America Needs a Raise: Fighting for Economic Security and Social Justice* (Boston: Houghton Mifflin, 1996); Richard Rothstein, "Toward a More Perfect Union: Labor's Hard Road," *American Prospect,* no. 26 (May–June 1996): 47–53; Kim Voss and Rachel Sherman, "Breaking the Iron Law of Oligarchy: Union Revitalization in the American Labor Movement," *American Journal of Sociology* 106, no. 2 (September 2000): 303–49.

24. For a good overview, see Riley E. Dunlap and Angela G. Mertig, eds., *American Environmentalism: The U.S. Environmental Movement, 1970–1990* (New York: Taylor and Francis, 1992).

25. Putnam, *Bowling Alone,* p. 162.

26. My account draws especially on Clyde Wilcox, *Onward Christian Soldiers? The Religious Right in American Politics* (Boulder, Colo.: Westview Press, 1996); Robert Wuthnow, "The Political Rebirth of American Evangelicals," in *The New Christian Right: Mobilization and Legitimation,* edited by Robert C. Liebman and Robert Wuthnow (Hawthorne, N.Y.: Aldine, 1983), pp. 167–85; and Ralph Reed, *Politically Incorrect: The Emerging Faith Factor in American Politics* (Dallas: Word Publishing, 1994).

27. Ernesto Cortes Jr., "Reweaving the Fabric: The Iron Rule and the IAF Strategy for Power and Politics," in *Interwoven Destinies: Cities and the Nation*, edited by Henry G. Cisneros (New York: Norton, 1993), pp. 691–92.

28. Excellent analyses of IAF organizing and achievements, especially in the Southwest, are to be found in Mark R. Warren, *Dry Bones Rattling: Community Building to Revitalize American Democracy* (Princeton: Princeton University Press, 2001); and Dennis Shirley, Community Organizing for Urban School Reform (Austin: University of Texas Press, 1997).

29. Warren, *Dry Bones Rattling*, pp. 35, 253. The IAF has also found a way to leverage professionalism for purposes of popular organizing. Full-time IAF organizers are reasonably well paid, with benefits sufficient to sustain adult lives. IAF organizers are experts at what they do; they have a shared ethos and are constantly learning new things. In an important sense, they have careers. In turn, IAF organizers devote themselves to training and encouraging volunteer community leaders—and then stand back a bit, to allow those leaders to define the goals of IAF campaigns. IAF organizations thus combine expertise with genuine popular involvement. New grassroots leaders are constantly mobilized, yet experienced professional organizers share their struggles and provide training in proven methods of movement building.

30. For more details, see the Stand for Children website at http://www. stand.org; and further analysis in Theda Skocpol and Jillian Dickert, "Speaking for Families and Children in a Changing Civic America," in *Who Speaks for America's Children? The Role of Child Advocates in Public Policy*, edited by Carol J. De Vita and Rachel Mosher-Williams (Washington, D.C.: Urban Institute Press, 2001).

31. For more information on civic journalism efforts, see the website of the Pew Foundation's Center for Civic Journalism: http://www.pewcenter.org/ doingcj/.

32. For an intelligent review and commentary on current strategies of campaign finance reform, see John B. Judis, "Goo-Goos versus Populists," *American Prospect*, no. 30 (January–February 1997): 12–14.

33. For an excellent account of nineteenth-century popular party politics and the elite reformist reactions against it, see Michael E. McGerr, *The Decline of Popular Politics: The American North, 1856–1900* (Oxford: Oxford University Press, 1986).

34. Paul Kleppner, *Who Voted? The Dynamics of Electoral Turnout, 1870–1980* (New York: Praeger, 1982).

35. Karen M. Paget, "Citizen Organizing: Many Movements, No Majority," *American Prospect*, no. 2 (Summer 1990): esp. 123–24.

36. This point is developed in Judis, "Goo-Goos versus Populists."

37. The commission's Final Report was made public on August 1, 2001, and is available at the website http://www.reformelections.org.

38. See especially Wendy M. Rahn, John Brehm, and Neil Carlson, "National Elections as Institutions for Generating Social Capital," in *Civic Engagement in American Democracy*, edited by Theda Skocpol and Morris P. Fiorina (Washington, D.C.: Brookings Institution Press; New York: Russell Sage Foundation, 1999), pp. 111–60.

39. Richard B. Freeman, "What, Me Vote?"(discussion paper prepared for the Russell Sage Conference on Inequality, June 2001), p. 14.

40. On the social dynamics of nineteenth-century U.S. elections, see McGerr, *Decline of Popular Politics*.

41. Marshall Ganz, "Motor Voter or Motivated Voter?" *American Prospect*, no. 28 (September–October 1996): 41–49. See also Ganz's "Voters in the Crosshairs: How Technology and the Market are Destroying Politics," *American Prospect*, no. 16 (Winter 1994): 100–109.

42. For a summary of campaign finance laws and movements in the states, see Robert Dreyfuss, "Reform beyond the Beltway: States as Laboratories of Clean Money," *American Prospect*, no. 38 (May–June 1998): 50–55.

43. On this, see Theda Skocpol, *Boomerang: Health Care Reform and the Turn against Government* (New York: Norton, 1997).

TABLES AND FIGURES

TABLES

FIGURES

INDEX